COLLECTIONS

A Harcourt Reading / Language Arts Program

*Excitement awaits you
along these pathways
to adventure!*

COLLECTIONS

A Harcourt Reading / Language Arts Program

PATHWAYS TO ADVENTURE

SENIOR AUTHORS

Roger C. Farr • Dorothy S. Strickland • Isabel L. Beck

AUTHORS

Richard F. Abrahamson • Alma Flor Ada • Bernice E. Cullinan • Margaret McKeown • Nancy Roser
Patricia Smith • Judy Wallis • Junko Yokota • Hallie Kay Yopp

SENIOR CONSULTANT

Asa G. Hilliard III

CONSULTANTS

Karen S. Kutiper • David A. Monti • Angelina Olivares

Harcourt

Orlando   Boston   Dallas   Chicago   San Diego

Visit *The Learning Site!*
www.harcourtschool.com

PATHWAYS TO ADVENTURE

Dear Reader,

Everyone loves to take part in an adventure—whether it's exploring an exciting place, playing a new instrument, or joining a team. But as you may know from reading a good book or listening to friends, learning about the experiences of others can also be a thrill.

Prepare to share adventures from all over the world—from high above Earth's atmosphere to the powerful oceans below, from Alaska's snowy wilderness to cities and schools just like yours. You will read stories developed in the minds of imaginative writers and adventures experienced by real people in real places. In **Pathways to Adventure,** you will meet brave characters, including some American heroes, who either seek a challenge or are faced with one unexpectedly. Maybe you will find that someone else's adventure is like one of your own! Come travel with us in search of excitement, surprise, and adventure.

Sincerely,

The Authors

The Authors

theme
Look Inside
Contents

THEME

TEAM WORK

A CHANGING PLANET

Contents

Theme

Express Yourself

Contents

SCHOOL RULES

FISH FOOD

CONTENTS

THEME

AMERICAN
ADVENTURE

CONTENTS

Using Reading Strategies

A strategy is a plan for doing something well.

You probably already use some strategies as you read. For example, you may **look at the title and illustrations before you begin reading** a story. You may **think about what you want to find out while reading.** Using strategies like these can help you become a better reader.

Look at the list of strategies on page 17. You will learn about and use these strategies as you read the selections in this book. As you read, look back at the list to remind yourself of the **strategies good readers use.**

- Use Prior Knowledge
- Make and Confirm Predictions
- Adjust Reading Rate
- Self-Question
- Create Mental Images
- Use Context to Confirm Meaning

- Use Text Structure and Format
- Use Graphic Aids
- Use Reference Sources
- Read Ahead
- Reread
- Summarize and Paraphrase

Here are some ways to check your own comprehension:

✔ Make a copy of this list on a piece of construction paper shaped like a bookmark.

✔ Have it handy as you read.

✔ After reading, talk with a classmate about which strategies you used and why.

THEME
Look Inside
contents

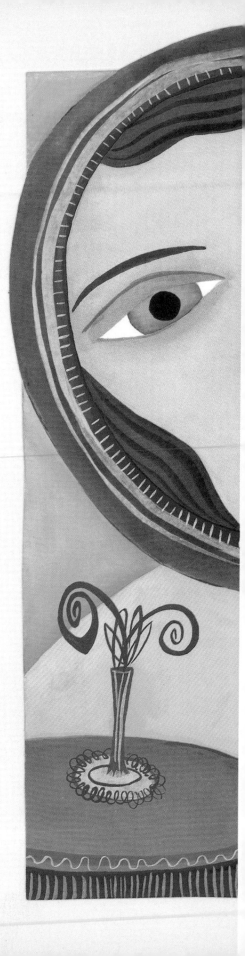

Reader's Choice

The Black Stallion

by Walter Farley

REALISTIC FICTION

Alec learns about survival and friendship on a desert island with a majestic, wild creature—a black stallion.

Award-Winning Author

READER'S CHOICE LIBRARY

Zora Hurston and the Chinaberry Tree

by William Miller

BIOGRAPHY

Inspired by her mother, a young and curious Zora discovers that her dreams have no limits.

Notable Social Studies Trade Book

READER'S CHOICE LIBRARY

The Hot and Cold Summer
by Johanna Hurwitz

REALISTIC FICTION

Best friends Rory and Derek are planning their best summer ever. Will their plans and friendship survive when a girl comes to visit for the summer?

Texas Bluebonnet Award

Kids Explore the Gifts of Children with Special Needs
by Westridge Young Writers Workshop

BIOGRAPHY

Written by kids, this book features 10 individuals with disabilities who beat the odds. Learn from people whose experiences may be different from our own.

Yang the Youngest and His Terrible Ear
by Lensey Namioka

REALISTIC FICTION

Yingtao and his friend come up with a plan to save the Yangs' musical reputation.

Award-Winning Author

21

The Hot And Cold Summer

by Johanna Hurwitz

illustrated by Greg Couch

Texas Bluebonnet Award

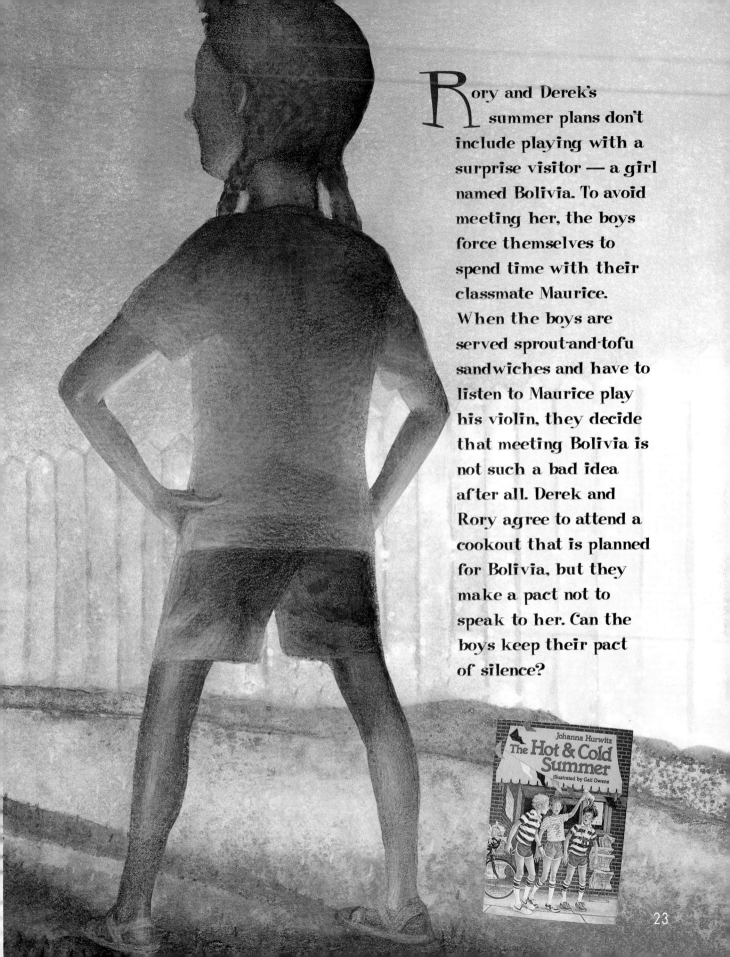

Rory and Derek's summer plans don't include playing with a surprise visitor — a girl named Bolivia. To avoid meeting her, the boys force themselves to spend time with their classmate Maurice. When the boys are served sprout-and-tofu sandwiches and have to listen to Maurice play his violin, they decide that meeting Bolivia is not such a bad idea after all. Derek and Rory agree to attend a cookout that is planned for Bolivia, but they make a pact not to speak to her. Can the boys keep their pact of silence?

Derek and Rory grinned at one another. The cake, the hamburgers, and the bottle of root beer that was waiting on the table were the least that they should get in compensation for Bolivia. The boys waited, knowing the two girls would emerge from behind the Golding's hedge at any moment.

Sure enough, the hedge parted and first Mr. and then Mrs. Golding and then a redheaded girl walked into the Dunn's yard. "This is Bolivia!" said Mrs. Golding proudly. She said it in the same way she often introduced a new type of cookie or cake, as if Bolivia was something she had created in her kitchen. Rory took a quick look and then shifted his gaze. He didn't want to appear interested. He noticed, however, that he had been right about one thing. Bolivia was several inches taller than he was.

"Hi, Bolivia. Welcome to Woodside!" said Mr. Dunn. "I'm just putting on the hamburgers. How do you like yours?"

"I like mine well done," said Bolivia.

"Fine," said Mr. Dunn. "So do Rory and Derek." He turned to the boys, who were trying to edge away from the guest of honor. Derek's mother grabbed him. "Bolivia, this is Derek. He and Rory will be your friends this summer."

Neither boy said anything.

"How's Lucette settling in?" asked Mrs. Dunn. Rory realized for the first time that Bolivia's little sister hadn't come to the barbecue.

"She's fine. At first she was very quiet, but just before we left the house she said her first word to me. She knows ten words. It's so exciting," said Mrs. Golding.

Bolivia turned to Rory and Derek. "I couldn't bring Lucette to the barbecue because the smoke might be bad for her," she explained. "Do you want to come to my aunt's house and see her?"

These were the first words Bolivia spoke directly to the boys.

Rory shook his head no. Derek also shook his head.

"Don't be shy," said Mr. Golding. "Go meet Lucette."

Rory shook his head again.

"You fellows are missing something really special," said Mrs. Dunn as she removed the plastic wrap from the salads.

Rory couldn't understand his mother. Why should he get excited over someone else's baby sister? He didn't care that Lucette had said her first word. Edna had known a lot of words by the time she was two. What was so special about Lucette?

Derek leaned toward Rory and whispered, "If we keep our mouths full of food, we can't talk."

Rory grinned. If his mother had told him once, she had told him a thousand times not to talk with food in his mouth.

"Right." He nodded.

The boys picked up paper plates. "Can we start eating?" asked Rory.

"If you're so hungry that you can't wait, go ahead," said Mrs. Dunn. Both boys piled their plates with potato salad and cole slaw.

Bolivia picked up a plate, too.

Edna pulled on Bolivia's skirt. "I made the cole slaw," she said.

"No kidding," said Bolivia.

"I made the potato salad, too," said Edna.

"The burgers are ready," called Mr. Dunn.

The three older children went to get their meat.

"You know," Bolivia said, turning to Rory and Derek, "last summer I was in Israel with my parents. They make hamburgers out of turkey there."

It was hard to imagine turkey hamburgers, although Rory thought they probably would be better than vegetable burgers with sprouts.

"Gobble, gobble," said Derek.

"What?" asked Bolivia.

"Gobble, gobble," he repeated.

Rory kicked Derek. His friend wasn't exactly speaking to Bolivia, but it was close.

Derek got the message. He stuffed his mouth with potato salad.

"Do you like my potato salad?" asked Edna.

"Rory, tell Bolivia about Woodside. This is her first visit here," Mr. Dunn called from his position at the grill.

Rory shoveled in a large forkful of potato salad and turned to his father, pointing to his mouth.

"There's a lot of things to do around here," said Mrs. Curry, since neither of the boys were speaking. "There's the town pool." She turned to Derek. "Which are the days when the public library is showing free movies for kids?" she asked.

Derek took an enormous bite out of his hamburger and shrugged his shoulders.

Rory licked some ketchup off his fingers and went back to refill his plate. Luckily he was very hungry after the lunch at Maurice's house.

"You like my cole slaw?" asked Edna.

"Where else have you traveled with your parents?" asked Mrs. Dunn.

Good, thought Rory. Let the grown-ups keep Bolivia busy talking. She sounded like a geography book, listing all the foreign countries where she'd been: Israel, Egypt, Mexico, France, Spain. . . .

After a little while, Bolivia turned to the boys again. "Would you like to come over tomorrow and play with Lucette?" she asked. "We could teach her some new words. I'll let you feed her if you like."

Girls really have no idea what boys like to do, Rory thought. What boy in his right mind would want to sit around playing nursery school with a little baby? He shook his head no.

"How about you?" asked Bolivia, turning to Derek.

"No," said Derek. Then realizing what he had done, he pushed another forkful of potato salad into his mouth.

Bolivia sat down on the ground next to Edna. She began playing "This little piggy went to market" on the little girl's bare toes. It was probably the eighty thousandth time that someone had played that baby game with Edna, but still she laughed and laughed.

Rory moved away, taking Derek with him.

"Boys, don't rush off," shouted Mrs. Curry. "We're going to cut the cake soon."

Bolivia was not going to scare them off the cake, Rory decided. Especially since it had chocolate frosting. So the boys moved back to the center of activity. Mrs. Golding was busy discussing something with the two mothers. Mr. Golding, the neighborhood authority when it came to cars, was talking to Mr. Dunn and Mr. Curry about motors.

Rory saw Bolivia go through the hedge back to the Golding's house. Maybe she had to use the bathroom, he thought. But just maybe, she was getting the message that he and Derek didn't want her around.

With Bolivia gone, at least for a few minutes, the boys could stop eating and rest. It was hard work keeping your mouth stuffed with food.

"What should we do tomorrow?" asked Derek.

"Let's go to the pool," said Rory. "Mrs. Golding never signs up for a pool card and so Bolivia won't be allowed in."

"What if it rains?" asked Derek.

Rory looked up at the sky. It was still light and there wasn't a single cloud. "It won't rain," he said. "But if it does, we'll go over to Maurice's again."

"Okay," said Derek. "But if we go, I'm taking ear plugs with me. I've heard enough of that *Carmen*."

Rory stuck his hand into his pocket and pulled out a sprout from the sandwich he had disposed of earlier in the day. "A souvenir of the first afternoon hiding from Bolivia," he said, presenting it to Derek.

"This is just the beginning of July," said Derek. "Do you realize how many more days there are till she goes home?"

"As many days as there were sprouts in that sandwich," said Rory, sighing.

"It's going to be a long, long summer," agreed Derek.

At any other time, the thought of a long, long summer would have filled the boys with delight. But now it stretched endlessly before them.

The morning after the barbecue, Derek and Rory met outside at nine-thirty. The boys wore their trunks under their clothes and each had a towel and a sandwich. Mrs. Dunn called after them, "Ask Bolivia to go with you," but Rory pretended not to hear. He had no intention of knocking on the Goldings' door. Anyway, Bolivia wouldn't have a membership card to the pool yet. And Rory didn't know if she had a bike. He didn't want to go anywhere with that girl and especially not if he had to go on foot. He looked around and was relieved that she was not in sight. He glanced up at the window of Bolivia's room and for a second, he thought he saw one of the curtains move. But then all was still again. It was probably just a little breeze.

"Let's get going," he said to Derek, who had been checking the air in his tires. "We want to make our getaway while the coast is clear."

Suddenly the boys heard a shriek.

"Help, help! Lucette has escaped!"

Derek and Rory looked at each other. What was the big fuss? Had Bolivia's little sister climbed out of her playpen or something?

Bolivia stuck her head out of the upstairs window. "Have you seen Lucette?" she called.

The boys shook their heads. How could little Lucette manage the heavy door? "She's got to be inside the house," said Derek.

"No. I saw her go out the window," Bolivia shouted.

Rory dropped his bike in surprise. How could the baby get out the window?

"Go around the back," demanded Bolivia. "I'll come and look with you. She must be in one of the trees."

Derek and Rory stood stunned. Had Bolivia lost her senses? If the baby had fallen out the window, she would be lying on the ground. It was impossible that she would land in a tree.

Mrs. Golding came running out of the house. "Should we

call the fire department?" she asked her niece.

"Call an ambulance or the police," said Rory. His heart was beating loud. He knew how he would have felt if Edna had fallen out the window.

Mr. Golding had gone out the back door. "I see her. I see her," he called from the backyard. "She's in the Dunns' mimosa tree."

Rory ran to the back of his house followed by Derek, Bolivia, and Mrs. Golding. He couldn't see any baby in the tree. "Where is she?" he shouted to Mr. Golding. He wondered if she had fallen out the window and then climbed the tree. It seemed incredible. He and Derek had been trying to climb that tree for years.

"It's all my fault." Bolivia was crying. "I opened the door so she could walk on my arm, and the next thing I knew she was flying around and around the room."

"She must be scared in a new place," said Mrs. Golding, putting her arm around her niece. "Don't cry. We'll all help catch her."

"I'll get a ladder," said Mr. Golding.

Rory watched as the old man leaned his ladder against the side of the tree.

"Hey, look at that!" shouted Derek.

Rory looked where his friend was pointing. On the very topmost branch of the mimosa tree was a large green bird with a blue-and-red head.

"It's a parrot!" he shouted. He had never seen one before except in the encyclopedia, but there was no mistaking that size or color.

"Of course it's a parrot," Bolivia shouted at him. "What did you think Lucette was? An elephant?"

It wasn't only their vow of silence that kept Rory and Derek from admitting they had thought Lucette was a baby.

While they were shouting, the bird flew from the mimosa tree to the maple.

No sooner had the ladder been put in place there than the bird flew over the hedge and into the next yard, landing in a locust tree. Mr. Golding looked red in the face from the exertion of moving the ladder back and forth.

"Let me help," called Mr. Dunn, coming from the house. Twice a week, even during the summer, he took classes in school administration so that he might someday become a principal. Now he forgot his courses as he dropped his attaché case with his papers and books and ran toward Mr. Golding.

hello there yourself!

"Hello there. Hello there," shrieked Lucette as she flew from tree to tree.

"Hello there, yourself!" Derek called back. He looked at Rory. Rory hadn't told him not to speak to a bird.

Mrs. Dunn came outside, followed by Edna. The little girl began jumping up and down. "I see her!" she shouted. "Catch her! Catch her!"

"Hello there!" Lucette called down to them.

"I'm going to call the fire department," Mr. Golding said. "They have taller ladders, and we have an awful lot of trees around here for Lucette to investigate."

"Hello there!" Edna called up to the bird.

Mrs. Dunn put her arms around Bolivia. "Don't worry. We won't let her get away." She comforted the girl as Lucette flew into the branches of one tree and then another. The swimming pool was forgotten as Rory and Derek chased in and out of the hedges, keeping their eyes on the bird.

"Could we get her down with some food?" asked Derek when he stopped to catch his breath. "What does she like to eat?"

"Fruit," said Bolivia.

Everyone rushed home except the two men with the ladder. Rory brought back some grapes. Derek had an apple. "Hello there!" shouted Edna, waving a banana for Lucette.

They made a pile of all the fruit in the Golding yard. Lucette hovered in the air above it for a moment, but she didn't land.

"What else does she like?" asked Mrs. Dunn. "This isn't working."

Mr. Dunn climbed down the ladder as the bird flew off once again. "None of my courses in running a school have prepared me for a morning like this," he said, wiping the sweat off his forehead.

In the distance they could hear approaching sirens. The fire department was on its way.

Dogleg Lane was filled with onlookers. People driving by got out of their cars to see what was happening. Neighbors came out of doors. Three large fire trucks pulled up in front of the Golding house. The firemen, wearing their helmets and tall boots, leaped off the trucks dragging ladders and long hoses with them.

"My vegetables could use a little water," said Mr. Dunn from where he was stationed.

"There's no fire," shouted Mrs. Golding. "It's a bird in the tree."

"Birds belong in trees," said one of the firemen, not yet understanding that Lucette was a pet bird who belonged in a cage.

"Hello there. Hello there!" Lucette greeted the new arrivals. She seemed to be having a great time.

Rory looked over at Bolivia. She was smiling. She looked like she was having a great time, too. For someone who had been crying a few minutes ago, she didn't seem unhappy now. Either she had wonderful faith in the Woodside Fire Department or she was not really worried about the bird.

"Music!" Bolivia remembered suddenly. "Lucette loves country music."

Derek ran into his house and came out with the little transistor radio he had gotten on his last birthday. He fiddled with the dials, looking for a station that played country music.

"That's good," shouted Bolivia. "Leave it there."

Derek stood holding his radio at full volume and looking up at Lucette.

"Hello there," shouted the bird, swooping lower.

Strains of "Country Roads" came over the radio. The neighbors that had crowded around began to sing and clap their hands in time to the music.

Mrs. Golding began introducing Bolivia to the people that she recognized. Bolivia smiled at everyone. She was really enjoying this commotion very much, Rory decided.

"Can your parrot do any tricks?" asked one of the onlookers.

"She knows ten words, and she can play dead, and she comes flying to my arm when I call her," said Bolivia proudly.

She noticed Rory standing nearby listening and added hastily, "But she won't come now. She's in a new place and she's overexcited by all the people."

The firemen got a call on their radio. There was a real fire somewhere. As quickly as they arrived, they disappeared with their sirens wailing. "We'll come back later if you still need us," one of the men called back as they departed.

Lucette seemed to be getting tired. She wasn't flying so much. She sat in the Curry's maple tree and looked around her.

"Who's my bird?" shouted Bolivia.

"Lucette. Lucette," the bird answered.

"Hey, she knows her name!" shouted Derek.

Rory was as excited by the bird as Derek. But he also had a strong suspicion that the whole morning had been planned by Bolivia. The more he thought about it, the more certain he was that she had opened the cage and the window on purpose. She had probably seen him through her window as he waited for Derek and she had decided to mess up the morning for them.

"I've got her. I've got her," shouted Mr. Dunn in triumph, as he slowly came down the ladder.

"Hello there!" Lucette greeted all the people in the yard. Everyone burst into applause and ran to get a closer look at the bird. The Goldings looked exhausted and relieved that this first emergency was over. Mr. Dunn handed Lucette over to Bolivia, looking very pleased with himself. It wasn't every morning that he climbed into trees to catch a bird.

"I feel like Tarzan," he said to Mrs. Dunn.

Derek just couldn't keep from asking Bolivia questions. "Where did you get her?" he wanted to know. "How many words can she say? Could she learn my name?" He was thrilled that Lucette was this clever bird and not the baby sister he and Rory had expected.

"You naughty girl," Bolivia scolded her pet. "I'm going to put you into your cage right now." She looked at Derek and said, "This has been a tiring morning for her. But tomorrow you can come over and help me clean her cage and feed her. Maybe I can teach her to say your name," she offered.

"Super," said Derek, not remembering until the words were out of his mouth that he had promised Rory he would never, ever speak to Bolivia.

Think About It

❶ Why might Bolivia be happy that Lucette got away?

❷ What mistaken idea did the boys have about Lucette? Why might they have made this mistake?

❸ What went wrong with Derek and Rory's plan not to speak to Bolivia, and what did they learn from what happened?

Meet the Author
Johanna Hurwitz

What influenced you to become a writer?

Books have been a part of my life as long as I can remember. My father owned a secondhand bookstore. Even though he eventually gave up the store, he never gave up the books. Every room of our house was filled with books. No wonder everyone in our family loved to read! I especially liked to read series books. That might be the reason why I've continued to write about the characters in *The Hot and Cold Summer*.

Where do you get ideas for your books?

My own children, who are now grown up, sparked many of my ideas when they reported on activities at school and with their friends. Other ideas come from students I meet on visits to schools and libraries. Anything can happen in my books because everything in them comes from real life.

Where do the characters from *The Hot and Cold Summer* come from?

I really met someone who had a daughter named Bolivia. As soon as I heard that name, I knew it was perfect and I would have to "borrow" it for a book. Derek and Rory are based on my own son and his friends, boys I see in my neighborhood. Boys that age do not want to talk to girls or fuss over babies, and they will do anything to avoid it.

Response Activities

Live and Learn

MAKE A SPEECH Imagine that when Rory goes back to school, his teacher asks him to give a short speech on the topic "Experience Is the Best Teacher." Rory decides to talk about what he learned from the experience of meeting Bolivia. Prepare the speech you think Rory might give, using an outline or notes on index cards to organize the main ideas. Then deliver the speech to your classmates.

Lucette on the Loose

CREATE A FLYER Imagine that Lucette has flown away. Create a flyer that Bolivia can post around the neighborhood to help find her missing pet. Use art materials or computer software to create a flyer that will catch people's attention. Be sure to include all the information that people will need to identify Lucette and return her to Bolivia.

Mind Your Manners

WRITE ETIQUETTE RULES When Rory and Derek
first met Bolivia, they knew they were not being polite
to her. How should you act when you are introduced
to someone? Write some rules of etiquette, or good
manners, for young people to follow when they meet
other people that are about the same age.

Hello There!

ROLE-PLAY A SCENE What might happen if a talking
parrot like Lucette flew into a window of your school?
With a small group, role-play the scene that you imagine.
You can role-play not only yourselves and the parrot but
also others who might become involved, such as your
teacher and principal. If you wish, make your scene funny.

Prefixes and Suffixes

These words are from "The Hot and Cold Summer."

| forkful | directly | refill | impossible |

A word part has been added to the beginning or end of each base word. You have seen the word parts *-ful, -ly, re-,* and *im-* before. They are called prefixes and suffixes.

- A word part added to the beginning of a base word is a **prefix**.
- A word part added to the end of a base word is a **suffix**.

The following paragraph is from the selection. The chart below identifies the prefixes and suffixes. Notice how each one adds to the meaning of the base word.

For someone who had been crying a few minutes ago, she didn't seem unhappy now. Either she had wonderful faith in the Woodside Fire Department or she was not really worried about the bird.

Prefix	Base Word	Suffix	New Word and Its Meaning
un–	happy		unhappy – not happy
	wonder	-ful	wonderful – full of wonder
	real	-ly	really – in a way that is real

Understanding how words are put together can help you determine the meaning of new words. Knowing the meaning of a prefix or suffix can often help you figure out the meaning of an unfamiliar word. Keep in mind that some words only *look* as if they have a prefix or suffix. For example, in the word *uncle,* the letters *un* are not a prefix.

Read the paragraph below. Identify the prefixes and suffixes in the underlined words. Tell what the words mean.

It seemed <u>unlikely</u> that Tori would become friends with Mario. Their interests were very <u>dissimilar</u>. But when Tori saw how much fun it could be to play with Mario's pet parrot, their differences were no longer <u>meaningful</u>.

WHAT HAVE YOU LEARNED?

1. If a friend tells you she <u>misplaced</u> her notebook, what does she mean? How does the prefix help you?

2. What is the difference between a prefix and a suffix? List as many prefixes and suffixes as you can think of.

TRY THIS • TRY THIS • TRY THIS

Write a dialogue between two friends. In your dialogue, use words with some of the prefixes and suffixes you identified in "What Have You Learned?" Underline these words.

Visit *The Learning Site!*
www.harcourtschool.com

SEES BEHIND TREES

by Michael Dorris

illustrated by Rocco Baviera

Teachers' Choice
SLJ Best Book
Booklist Editors' Choice
Notable Trade Book for
the Language Arts

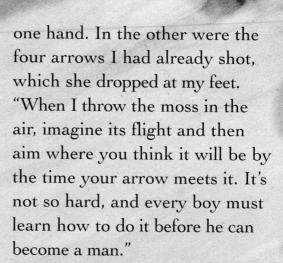

"TRY HARDER. TRACK IT with your eye before you shoot."

My mother's anxious voice snapped in my ear as loudly as the string of my bow.

"Track what?" I asked for the third time this morning. Before me all I could see was the familiar blur of green and brown that meant I was outside in the forest on a sunny day. Then, by squinting, I could sense something coming toward me, smell the familiar pemmican scent of berries mixed with dried meat, recognize the tread of moccasins I had heard a thousand times before. Gradually one blurry image began to stand out from all the others and an instant later it turned into my approaching mother. When she was close enough for me to touch, I could tell from her face and from the tenseness of her body that she was worried.

"This," she said, shaking the clump of moss that she held in one hand. In the other were the four arrows I had already shot, which she dropped at my feet. "When I throw the moss in the air, imagine its flight and then aim where you think it will be by the time your arrow meets it. It's not so hard, and every boy must learn how to do it before he can become a man."

A rumbling noise came from my stomach and my mother smiled her I've-got-an-idea smile. "Think of the moss as your breakfast," she suggested. "Imagine it is a corn cake, hot from the ashes, soooo delicious."

I could almost taste it on my tongue, feel its crunch as I bit down, smell the sweet fullness it would bring. "Couldn't I eat first, just this once?" I pleaded. "I'm sure I could find the moss in the sky if I weren't so hungry."

For a moment I thought my mother would give in, and I leaned toward her, blinking as though a steaming golden corn cake would appear in her hand to replace the straggly plant. But all that changed was my mother's expression.

"Walnut." My name in her mouth was tired, pounded into flour. "You know the rule: you must find the target before breakfast can find you."

I nodded. If that was the rule, I wouldn't eat for a long time. We had faced this matter of what I couldn't see many times before — when my mother would point to something I couldn't locate or throw a ball I couldn't catch —

but it had never before been such serious business. Now we couldn't just act as though nothing was wrong. Now we had to solve the problem. We had struggled with it every morning since, three days ago, my mother had decided it was time to teach me, her oldest child, how to use a bow and arrow. I had never once succeeded and I knew that sooner or later she would give up, make some excuse, and feed me. But it would not be soon.

"Maybe if you made your eyes smaller?" My mother encouraged me by bringing her cheeks so close to her forehead that she looked like a dried onion, and I made the mistake of laughing.

"Today . . . ," my mother said in the same voice she had used when I was younger and she told me not to play with sharp knives. She picked up an arrow from the ground and sternly held it out for me to take. She walked back toward the place where she threw the moss into the air. "Today, we will *not* surrender." Before I could object she had

49

disappeared again into that mist of color and noise that surrounded me like the roof and walls of a very small house.

"Now!"

I quickly pointed my arrow high above the place where her voice came from, and released it.

"Better," she called. "The sunlight must have confused you. Try again."

There were many *other* things I could do, I told myself when finally, with not a single victory, we came home. I could make a whistle from a stiff reed using only the sharp edge of a clamshell. I could sing a song after hearing it just one time. I could find wild strawberries, even clusters of violets, by closing my eyes and following the directions of my nose. I could hear my father's footsteps before anyone else. "He's back," I would inform my brothers and sisters, giving them a little longer to stop playing and compose themselves. So why couldn't I shoot?

"Is there some trick to it?" I asked my mother's brother, Brings the Deer, one evening as we were sitting in front of our house, watching fireflies as they flickered before our faces. He was the best archer in our whole family, so he should know.

"Practice is the only trick," my uncle said, sounding more like my father than himself. Usually, since he was younger than my mother and didn't yet have any children of his own, he was less serious.

"It's been days and days, and I'm no better."

"Maybe . . ." Brings the Deer's tone was gentler, more understanding. "Maybe your bowstring is not tight enough?" He reached over to where it rested by my leg and tested it. "No, it seems all right. Maybe you're closing your eyes at the last moment before you shoot? *I* did that myself when I first started."

I shook my head.

"Maybe . . . How many fingers am I holding up?"

I tipped my head. The dusky light was dim, but I could still see my own hands, balled into fists. "Fingers?"

"How many?"

I couldn't tell how many arms he was holding up, much less fingers. "Three?" I guessed.

"How many now?"

"Two?"

"Now?"

"Five?"

There was a silence. "Walnut, I was holding up no fingers at all."

"I knew that," I said, though it wasn't true. "I was making a joke."

But Brings the Deer didn't laugh.

The next morning when my mother woke me for shooting practice, we went to a new part of the forest. That was only the first odd thing.

"Put down your bow and sit on this rock," my mother said, patting a large flat stone at the base of a pine tree. Then, from her sack she brought out a tightly woven sash, placed it over my eyes, and tied it with a length of grapevine.

"What are you doing?" I wanted to know.

"Shhh," she said. "Describe this place to me."

"But I've never been here before and I can't see."

"Shhh," she said again. "Look with your ears."

At first, there was nothing to hear—just . . . forest. But the longer we didn't talk, the more separate parts announced themselves: the hush of a brook just behind me and, farther beyond that, the rush of a river. The buzz of a beehive on a tree not far over to my right. The beat of a hummingbird's wings as it dove in and out of a cluster of . . . what was that smell? . . . *roses* near where my mother— who, I could tell, had just oiled her hair this morning—sat.

"Don't move," I said as I heard her prepare to shift her weight. "It's only a hummingbird."

"*What's* only a . . . ? Oh," she whispered. "How beautiful. What else do you see, Walnut?"

So I told her—there were so many things that it took the whole morning to list them all. And the amazing fact was, I completely forgot to be hungry for breakfast. From that day on, instead of shooting arrows we went each dawn to a new spot and stayed until I had surprised my mother at least four times by what I could see but she could not.

At the end of the summer there was always a great feast— and that was when boys my age had to prove by their accurate shooting that they were ready to be grown up.

"I'm not going," I told Brings the Deer. We were lying on our backs on the bank of the pond at the south end of the village, waiting for fish to swim into our net. "You said I had to practice and I have not practiced. Instead I played games with my mother."

"So she's told me," he said. All around us was the noise of people working. Some were gathering hollow green and yellow gourds in huge piles that made a popping sound when they knocked together. Others were stacking firewood—I could hear them stumbling up with their arms full, dropping the load with a rolling crash, and then the even tap-tap-tap of setting the logs straight. Even Brings the Deer was replacing the old bluebird feathers on his fancy headband with new ones. From off to one side I picked up the rich hickory smell of stewing venison.

"My father will be ashamed." My best friend Frog was, I knew, even now out somewhere practicing his aim. I didn't know why he was nervous—he told me that he had been able to shoot moss out of the air on his very first try.

"Have you asked him?"

"Who, Frog?" Had even Brings the Deer heard of Frog's talent?

"Your father. Have you talked to him about this?"

"No, but . . . he's coming now."

Brings the Deer stood up and looked all around. "Where?"

"On the other side of the pond," I told him, just as my father called our names.

"Walnut? Brings the Deer? Where are you?"

"I see him now," said my uncle. "Over here," he yelled.

While we waited for my father—he walked like a beaver, his feet flat and wide apart—to make his way over to us, Brings the Deer sat next to me and shook his head. "It's amazing," he laughed, and admired the design of the new feathers. "My sister did not exaggerate."

Before I could say anything, my father burst from the rest of the colors around us and sat down on my stomach.

"Ah," he sighed, and stretched his arms. "A dry, comfortable seat at last."

"I can't breathe!" I tried to shove him off me, but he was too heavy.

"How very strange," my father said to Brings the Deer. "I thought I heard my son speak from inside my own body."

"Yes," Brings the Deer replied. "It's what a bird must feel when she sits on her nest after the chicks hatch."

"I am sinking into the mud," I muttered, and poked my father beneath his ribs with my finger.

Why was he being so playful, as if I were still a very little boy?

"What's this? What's this?" he cried, cocking his head and jumping up. "Walnut, what are you doing down there? Come home quickly. The contests are going to start early."

"Father . . . ," I began. How I hated to embarrass him.

"No time for talking. This year there is going to be an extra trial, *much* harder."

"Harder than hitting a target?" I might as well stay in the mud instead of cleaning up.

Boys my age were already waiting in the clearing where ball games were played. Each one had his bow and quiver of arrows. As we passed my friend Frog close enough for me to glance directly into his face I realized that though he was nervous and excited, he wasn't half as unhappy as I felt.

The flat afternoon sun made the colors of the earth and rocks as bright as if they were wet. There was no wind to stir the branches of the trees and give me an excuse for missing my shots. The sky was the pale, shiny blue of a trout's scale.

Brings the Deer gave my arm a squeeze and then went over to join the crowd of adults and small children watching in the shade nearby. I was sure my mother must be among them. I wondered what she was thinking. When people learned she hadn't taught me how to shoot, they might criticize her. Ay-yah-yah.

The weroance, our most important person, the expert on hunting, stood nearby. She raised her hands for quiet, and when everyone was still, she spoke in the slow, booming voice she saved for the most solemn moments. It seemed to come from deep within her body, to be blown through a horn of shell, to rattle like the skin of a hand drum.

"Sometimes," she said, "the people need someone to do the impossible. As necessary as hunting is, as necessary as growing and harvesting plants, sometimes we need even more than those tasks can provide. We need someone with the ability to see what can't be seen. And we won't have the regular contest until someone passes this new one."

There was a silence, then all the boys around me began to whisper to one another.

"What does she mean?" worried one.

"How can they expect us to do that?" another demanded. "Isn't it enough that our mothers have taught us how to shoot moss from the sky?"

"So," the weroance went on steady as the beat of a large bird's wings, "the first test will be for . . ."

I missed what she said because something fell at my feet. I looked down—it was the sash and a length of grapevine. My mother must have tossed it.

"See behind *trees*?" Frog repeated the weroance's words, and the boy next to me looked toward the forest uncertainly.

But I knew what to do. I tied the sash around my eyes and remained very still. The wind made fingers through the trees and I used them to feel my way in each direction. My mind flew the way a hawk must fly, skimming over all that was ordinary, alert for a dart of something out of place. I paid no attention to the rustle of leaves or the rain of a waterfall. Those expected sounds—those sounds I knew from all my morning games with my mother—I put to one side, and waited.

What was that? A dead branch snapped. A rock, slightly closer, tumbled down a hill. A breath was drawn in.

"Who will begin?" The weroance interrupted my ears. "You," she said.

And Frog tried, without much hope, "I see a raccoon. He is asleep in the bough of a tree."

"You," she said. Another voice, Sleeps Late, no more confident, answered. "I see a . . . spiderweb, strung on the brambles of a mulberry bush."

"Now you," she said, but this time there was no reply. "You. Walnut."

I thought so hard that my head felt tight between my ears. I was afraid to make a mistake in front of so many people, but then I pretended it was my mother asking me to listen, curious and interested as she had been every morning.

"A man is coming from the south," I said. "He is light on his feet but has a limp. He is not young, for he must breathe hard to climb. He is . . ." I stopped talking, shut my eyes even behind my blindfold, and concentrated. There was no mistaking it. "He is laughing! It is Gray Fire!"

I heard people turning to look behind me, whispering among themselves. I could almost *feel* them looking to see if I was right. That part of the forest was dense, the paths overgrown and winding.

"There!" Brings the Deer's voice was loud above the rest. "It is, it *is* Gray Fire!" The weroance's brother! He had been given his name because he was so quiet he could pass through the village like smoke.

Strong hands untied the vine that bound the sash around my eyes. My father's hands. They lingered for just an instant on my hair. I'm sure no one else but me noticed.

"This part of the contest is over," the weroance announced. "Each boy except the one who passed must now prove himself with a bow in order to earn the right to his grown-up name."

"And what of the boy who passed?" my mother called out from where she stood. "What about my Walnut?"

"When a boy passes the test he is no longer a boy," the weroance answered. "He no longer wears a boy's name."

Everyone stopped what they were doing to hear what she would say next. I turned the sash in my hand, the sash my mother had woven. It was soft to the touch, as if it had been made from silky moss.

"Sees Behind Trees," the weroance pronounced, "is now a young man."

Think About It

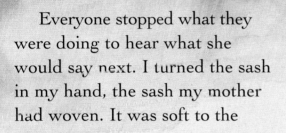

1. What important lesson do the boys learn when Walnut receives his new name?

2. What does this story say about people's different strengths?

3. Why do you think there is an extra trial at the feast this year?

About the Author
Michael Dorris

Michael Dorris was a member of the Modoc Indians on his father's side of the family. He said, "I lived on a reservation part of the time when I was a child, so I knew my Indian relatives. That part of my background was front and center." He also read a lot when he was young. He said, "The thing I like about reading is that it puts you in charge. You can stop and start, you can reread something, and you can imagine what the characters and places look like. When you read, you're a participant in the story. When you're watching television, you're not."

Sounds of Nature

Three Poems

SHAPE POEM

When Birds Remember

by Robert Froman
lettering by Ray Barber

Birds in a tight
cloud flying off
on an important
errand they had
almost forgotten about.

Sudden Silence

Birds scattered in a tree top cheeping twiting fluttering scratching fidgeting. clucking twitching twittering squeaking fluttering chirping flitting whistling rustling Pecking trilling

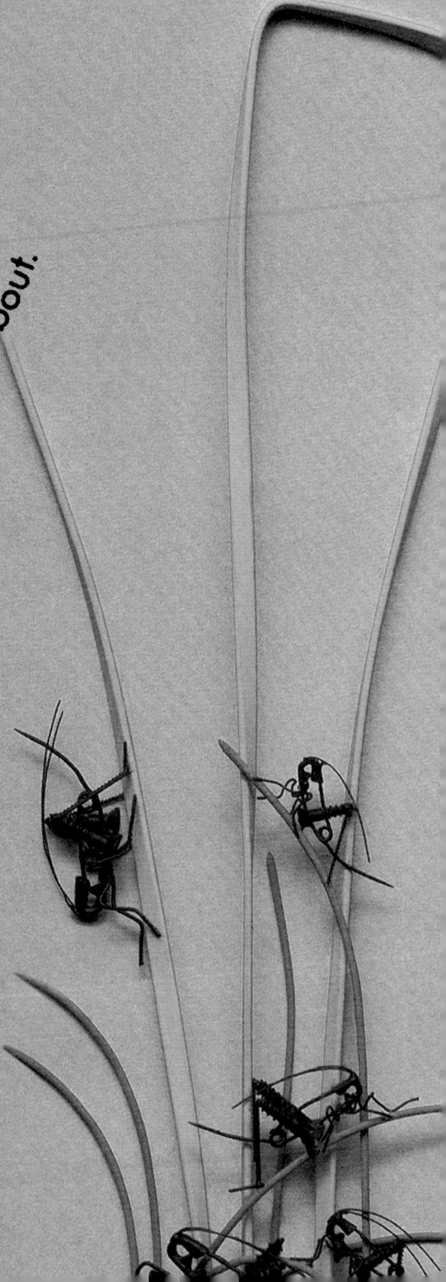

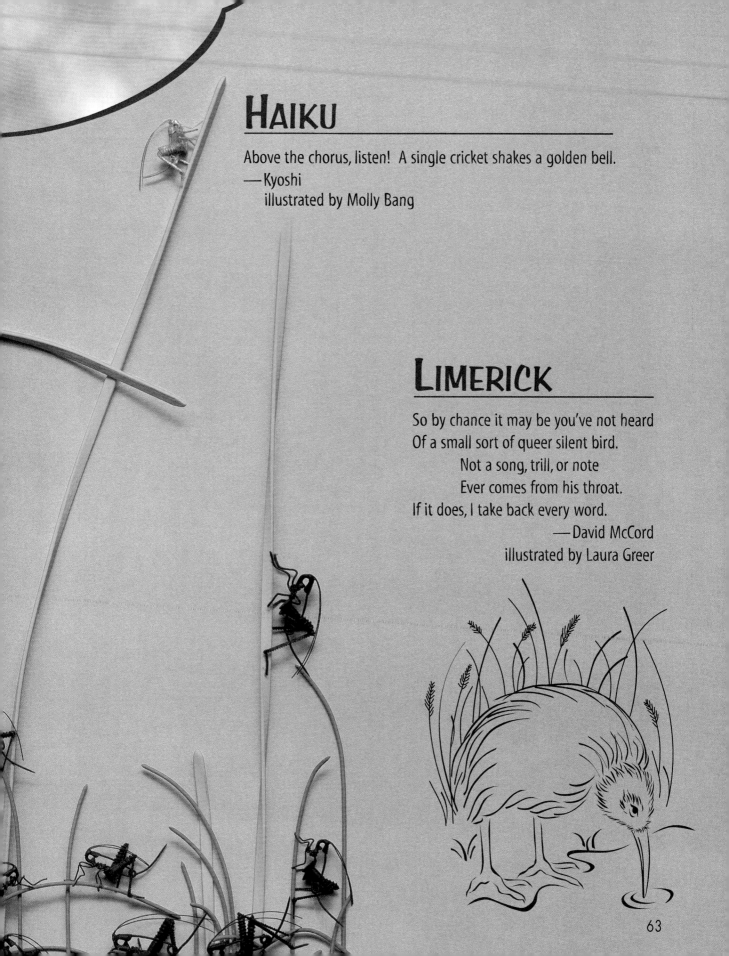

HAIKU

Above the chorus, listen! A single cricket shakes a golden bell.
—Kyoshi
    illustrated by Molly Bang

LIMERICK

So by chance it may be you've not heard
Of a small sort of queer silent bird.
    Not a song, trill, or note
    Ever comes from his throat.
If it does, I take back every word.
       —David McCord
    illustrated by Laura Greer

RESPONSE

A New Name

DESIGN A T-SHIRT Imagine that you will be given a new name that tells something special about you, such as "Sings in the Chorus." It may be based on a skill you have or on something you did. Design a T-shirt that shows your new name in pictures or symbols. Display your shirt, and see if classmates can guess your name.

A Friend in Need

ROLE-PLAY A SITUATION Working in a small group, think of situations in which it might be helpful to have a friend who could "see behind trees." Choose one situation, and plan a scene for your group to role-play for classmates. Be sure to show how this ability is helpful.

ACTIVITIES

Using Other Senses

DESIGN A PRODUCT Design a new product to help people who cannot see well. Your invention should allow people to use senses other than sight to do something they cannot see well enough to do. Write a brief description of your product, and include diagrams or sketches.

Making Connections

WRITE A REVIEW Suppose that Walnut read the three poems, "Haiku," "When Birds Remember," and "Limerick." What might he say about these poems? From his point of view, write one or more sentences about each poem, expressing his thoughts about it.

Yang the Third and Her Impossible Family

by Lensey Namioka
illustrated by Kees de Kiefte

Though they now live in Seattle, Washington, Yingmei's family still follows many Chinese customs, such as referring to the children by their birth order: Eldest Brother, Second Sister, Third Sister, and Fourth Brother.

Yingmei (Third Sister) wants to become an American more than anything else. To accomplish this —

- She changes her name to Mary.
- She keeps a list of American words and phrases.
- She accepts a kitten from Holly Hanson, the most popular girl at school, even though it is forbidden.

Yingmei tries very hard, but she can't control everything that happens. In particular, she can't prevent her family members from saying and doing things that embarrass her in front of her new friends.

Parents'
Choice

Lensey Namioka
Yang the Third
and
Her Impossible Family

The companion to
Yang the
Youngest
and
His Terrible
Ear

Illustrated by Kees de Kiefte

I tried to squeeze my left leg behind my cello case in the backseat. It was a week after Kim's birthday party, and we were on the way to a rehearsal of the All-City Orchestra. The best players from the Seattle elementary schools had been selected to form a citywide orchestra, which rehearsed once a week.

Holly and I had been chosen from our school; so had Kim. The rehearsals were held in an auditorium across town from our neighborhood, so Mrs. Hanson and Mrs. O'Meara took turns driving the three of us to the rehearsals.

It was nice of Mrs. Hanson and Mrs. O'Meara to include me. My cello was only half-size, but it still took up a lot of room, and I had a struggle fitting it in the car.

"What time is your tryout on Wednesday, Holly?" asked Mrs. Hanson, who was driving that week. "I have to make sure I can get time off to take you over."

Holly was silent for a moment. "I might have to call it off. The accompanist is sick, and I'm not sure she'll be able to play."

Mrs. Hanson turned her head sharply to look at Holly. The car swerved, and she got it back into the lane before she spoke again. "But that's awful! You've been practicing the piece for ages! And it's too late for you to prepare some unaccompanied piece! Why didn't you tell me earlier?"

"It's not the end of the world, Mom," muttered Holly.

"Can't your music teacher find another accompanist?" asked Mrs. Hanson. "There must be other pianists around!"

"It's a hard piece, that Brahms. We won't be able to get anybody ready by Wednesday."

I could see the tendons on Mrs. Hanson's neck. It occurred to me that *she* was the one who was really bothered, not Holly.

A brilliant idea suddenly hit me. "Mrs. Hanson, my mother can play the accompaniment for Holly's tryout."

We had arrived at the auditorium. Mrs. Hanson stopped the car and slowly turned to look at me. "Are you sure? She can't stop if she makes a mistake, you know. It would ruin Holly's piece."

Mother might do a lot of embarrassing things, but if there was one thing I felt confident about, it was her musical ability. "My mother has played a lot of chamber music with other people, so she never loses the beat even if she makes a mistake."

"Thank you for the offer, Mary," Mrs. Hanson said. But she still looked doubtful.

It might be mean of me, but I hoped Holly's accompanist would stay sick. This was a chance for Mother to get on Mrs. Hanson's good side for a change. Holly would be grateful to me for saving her audition.

Halfway through the rehearsal we had a break. Holly came to the cello section and made her way to my stand. "Can I talk to you for a minute, Mary?"

I could tell that she was unhappy about something. "Sure, Holly," I said. "What's wrong?"

She absently ran her finger across the horsehair of her viola bow, and some of the resin flew up in a fine powder. "It's about your mother accompanying me for the tryout," she said finally. "I don't really care about getting in to the Junior Chamber Orchestra, you know. My mom wants me to join, because it's such a select group and they have a summer camp on Orcas Island."

A summer camp where people just made music! It sounded like heaven. Playing in the All-City Orchestra was fun, but being in the Junior Chamber Orchestra would be a real privilege. I tried not to feel envious. "I'd give anything to join something like that! Is it very expensive?"

Holly nodded. "It costs a bundle, but my dad will pay for it. In fact he's one of the main supporters of the orchestra. But frankly, I'd rather have the money for something else — like raising purebred dogs."

She grimaced as she looked around the rehearsal hall. I didn't know what to say. Were we really that different? Did she really think purebred dogs are more important than music?

On the way home, Mrs. Hanson seemed more friendly. "Your mother is a professional pianist, isn't she? Maybe I *will* ask her to play for Holly's tryout if the regular accompanist can't make it, Mary."

I looked at Holly and saw that she was gently shaking her head. If I asked Mother to play the accompaniment, Holly might get mad and wouldn't let me be her friend anymore. After I had worked so hard to get this far with her!

Then I thought of Mother. I thought of how many social blunders she had been making. If she got to play in Holly's tryout, the Hansons would find out what a good pianist she was and respect her a lot more.

It was hard to decide. So I just mumbled something.

"Fine!" Mrs. Hanson said cheerfully. "I'll give your mother a call tomorrow."

It was nice that Fourth Brother cared about my feelings...

As Mrs. Hanson dropped me at our house, I ran into Mr. and Mrs. Sylvester. "We saw that kitten again, Mary," said Mr. Sylvester. "It seems to hang around a lot. I wonder if it's a stray. Maybe we can take it home."

"I don't want a cat, Benny," said Mrs. Sylvester. "Cats are stuck-up animals, and they care only about themselves. I want another dog. I want a beagle like Jenny!"

Her voice quavered a little, and I knew she still missed their dog.

"Now, now, Denny," said Mr. Sylvester. "We'll find a beagle just like Benny one of these days."

When I went in the house, Fourth Brother was making himself a peanut butter and jelly sandwich in the kitchen.

"I thought you didn't like peanut butter," I said.

"I knew you were embarrassed because I was always eating bean sprouts for lunch," he said. "So I thought I'd try to get used to peanut butter."

It was nice that Fourth Brother cared about my feelings. He took a big bite of the sandwich. "Anyway, I couldn't find anything else to eat," he mumbled.

I remembered why I wanted to talk to him. "Did you hear what the Sylvesters said? They saw Rita again!"

Fourth Brother licked the peanut butter from the roof of his mouth and swallowed. Then he said, "It's okay as long as she comes when I play the dinner signal."

"But if Mrs. Sylvester gets another dog, it might tear Rita to pieces!"

"We'll have to talk her out of it," said Fourth Brother.

That was easy enough to say. But what could we do if the Sylvesters finally found a beagle to replace Jenny?

Mother's face turned pink. I could tell she was pleased.

I had too many things to worry about. Rita kept escaping from the basement. Having Mother accompany Holly might ruin my friendship with her. And my family kept disgracing themselves in public.

Once I saw a juggling act in China. A girl balanced three plates simultaneously by spinning them at the ends of three chopsticks. I felt like that juggler. At any minute, one of the plates might fall and smash into bits.

Mrs. Hanson called Tuesday night when we were having dinner. I answered the phone. "Mary," she said, "do you still think your mother could play the accompaniment tomorrow for Holly's audition?"

I felt torn. If I said yes, I risked losing Holly's friendship. But if she didn't want to be in the orchestra, why couldn't she just play badly at the audition? Maybe she was too proud. She didn't want her mother to see that she wasn't good enough or that she wasn't trying hard.

From where I stood in the hallway, I could see into the dining room. Mother was bringing in a stir-fried dish, and after setting it down, she wiped her forehead.

"I know it's very short notice," Mrs. Hanson was saying. "Hello? Are you still there, Mary?"

I cleared my throat. "Yes, Mrs. Hanson. I'm sure my mother would be able to do it. Can you bring the music over tonight?"

Mrs. Hanson breathed a sigh of relief. "Thank you, Mary. I'll be over as soon as I can."

"Well, we're still having supper . . . ," I told her.

"Of course, of course!" she said quickly. "I'll come at eight, shall I?"

It was strange to hear Mrs. Hanson sounding so anxious to please. I told her that eight o'clock was fine, then walked slowly back to the dining room table.

The family looked at me curiously. "What was that about?" asked Father.

"Mother," I said in a rush, "Mrs. Hanson needs a pianist to play the accompaniment for Holly's tryout. It's a Brahms viola sonata. She's bringing over the music tonight at eight. Can you do it?"

Mother's face turned pink. I could tell she was pleased. "Why, yes, I think I can. Is that the one transposed from a violin sonata?"

I didn't know, but Father and Eldest Brother did. For the rest of the meal, we discussed the piece and whether Mother could play it at such short notice.

Mother wasn't the only one who looked happy. Father said it was about time people learned how good Mother was, while Eldest Brother and Second Sister both beamed and nodded agreement.

Fourth Brother was the only one who didn't look completely happy. "I hope Mrs. Hanson doesn't mention Rita," he said to me as the two of us cleared the table.

I had forgotten about Rita! Mrs. Hanson was under the impression that we had already told my family about her. I had to prevent Mrs. Hanson from saying something.

Mrs. Hanson and Holly arrived promptly at eight. Mrs. Hanson looked around at our living room. I had given up trying to neaten the room, and there were music stands all over. My cello leaned against the sofa, and next to it was an open case containing Elder Brother's violin. Heaps of sheet music were piled on the stands, on the sofa, and on the floor. To walk across the room, you had to negotiate carefully between piles.

"Goodness, you have a lot of music!" Mrs. Hanson exclaimed. "If you had the kitten in here . . ."

I knew what she was going to say next, and I had to head her off. Before I could do anything, there was a clatter behind me. Fourth Brother had acted first: He had knocked over a couple of music stands.

As I helped him set the stands up again, he whispered to me, "You'll have to think of something else to distract her."

"As I was saying—," Mrs. Hanson began again.

"Mother," I interrupted desperately, "we haven't tuned the piano for some time. Do you think that will bother Holly?"

Mother walked over to the piano and played a blurringly fast chromatic scale across the keyboard. "It should do well enough." She turned to Mrs. Hanson. "Have you got the music?"

At last that took Mrs. Hanson's mind from Rita—for the time being. She fetched the music and handed it to Mother.

Mother looked at the score. "My husband thought it might be this sonata. I've accompanied him on it—in a different key, of course." She sat down at the piano and looked at Holly. "Shall we try it?"

Holly looked uncomfortable—the first time I had ever seen her really uncomfortable. Slowly, she took out her viola and tuned it. "I'm getting stage fright," she muttered, looking around at the circle of eyes.

"Then it would be good practice for the real audition," said Mrs. Hanson with a nervous laugh.

We moved aside piles of instruments and music and found seats. Holly and Mother began.

After a few bars, I began to worry—but not about Mother. There was nothing wrong with her piano playing. She had played the piece before, after all.

The problem was Holly. She had obviously been well taught. Her bowing was correct, her fingering neat, and her pitch true. She seemed to be following the score carefully, obeying all the dynamics signs. But there was something lifeless about her playing— and that was fatal.

My family and I looked around at one another, and I saw the same conclusion in everybody's eyes. Even Fourth Brother, who can't tell "Old MacDonald Had a Farm" from "Mary Had a Little Lamb," seemed to know from the expression on Holly's face that her heart wasn't in the music.

At the end we all clapped politely, but nobody was fooled. "I told you I had stage fright," Holly said in a low voice.

Mrs. Hanson swallowed. "You'll get over it by tomorrow, darling," she said, and the forced smile on her face was painful to see. She turned to Mother. "Thank you very much, Mrs. Yang. You played beautifully."

"Oh, no, I was simply awful!" said Mother. She knew she had done well, but for a Chinese it would be very rude to agree.

"You're a marvelous pianist, really!" insisted Mrs. Hanson.

Mother again disagreed. "I'm very poor. You must not flatter me."

"No, no!" said Mrs. Hanson. "I'm not trying to flatter you."

Holly looked impatient. "Mom, we'd better go."

"Of course, darling," Mrs. Hanson said quickly. She turned to Mother. "Holly has to get a good night's rest. We don't want her to go to the audition all tired and sleepy, do we?"

"Yes!" said Mother, smiling broadly.

Mrs. Hanson blinked. "I mean, we wouldn't want Holly to fail the audition!"

"Yes, yes!" said Mother.

The rest of the Yangs agreed. "Yes," we all said earnestly.

Mrs. Hanson and Holly stared at us. I could tell that something was wrong, but I didn't know what it was. Finally Mrs. Hanson turned abruptly and walked to the front door. "Good night!" she said curtly. Opening the door, she walked out, followed by Holly.

I went after them, determined to find out what the matter was.

"Uh — did my mother say something funny again just now?" I asked when I had caught up with the Hansons.

Mrs. Hanson stopped. "Well, it just sounded awfully strange, what all of you said. I could hardly believe my ears!"

I didn't know what she was talking about. "What did we say? What sounded strange?"

"It sounded like you wanted me to fail the audition!" said Holly.

It was my turn not to believe my ears. "We said no such thing!"

"I said we wouldn't want Holly to fail the audition," Mrs. Hanson said slowly, very slowly. "Then your family said yes — every single one of you!"

"Of course we said yes!" I cried indignantly. "We agreed with you completely! We certainly don't want Holly to fail the audition!"

The three of us stood frozen and looked at one another. To a passerby, we must have looked like three store dummies.

Suddenly Mrs. Hanson began to laugh. "Yes! We have no bananas!" she sang in a high, cracked voice.

She had gone completely mad! Maybe the anxiety over Holly's audition had driven her out of her mind. I looked at Holly. But she was laughing as well. "It's an old song my grandma used to sing," she told me.

Mrs. Hanson turned to me, still laughing. "You all said yes because you agreed with me, just like in the song 'Yes! We Have No Bananas.'"

I still didn't understand. "Was that wrong?"

Holly tried to explain. "In English, you'd say, 'No, we wouldn't want Holly to fail the audition.'"

I had thought that learning English was just a matter of memorizing a lot of new words and phrases. It is much more complicated than that. Even knowing when to say yes or no is tricky!

I turned slowly away and started for home. I'd have a lot to write in my notebook tonight. Behind my back, I heard Mrs. Hanson and Holly giggling and softly singing, "Yes! We have no bananas today!"

Suddenly I felt I had to say something. I turned again and caught up with the Hansons. "Mrs. Hanson," I said, "we're new in this country, and we can't do everything right immediately. I hope you'll try to be patient."

Without waiting for her to reply, I turned to Holly. "When you picked up your viola for the first time, you probably played a few sour notes. I bet your teacher didn't break down laughing."

By now both Mrs. Hanson and Holly had sobered. "You're quite right, Mary," Mrs. Hanson said quietly. "We should have been more understanding."

I turned slowly away and started for home. I'd have a lot to write in my notebook tonight.

She looked at Holly. "You should apologize, too."

Holly murmured something. Her face didn't show much expression, so I couldn't tell how she felt.

As I walked home, I thought about how unfair I had been to my family all these months. I thought they had been impossible, because they didn't make more of an effort to learn American ways.

But I am actually one of them: In spite of my list of new words and my careful study of American ways, I still make mistakes, just like the rest of the family.

I had blamed Mother more than the rest, because she had made the most embarrassing mistakes. I should have remembered that she had to spend all her time cooking and feeding us. She didn't have time to meet a lot of Americans and learn the customs of this country.

I had been ashamed of Mother. Now I was more ashamed of myself.

Think About It

❶ Why does Mary want her mother to accompany Holly on the piano at the audition?

❷ Do you think Mary is right to tell Mrs. Hanson and Holly how their laughter makes her feel? Why or why not?

❸ Why do you think the author included the description of the juggling act that Mary saw in China?

Meet the Author
Lensey Namioka

Was your family musical like the Yangs?

I'd say so. My father has composed music, and my sister is a professor of musicology, so they had very good "ears." But not me! Once, my sister hid my violin exercise book. She confessed years later that she just couldn't take listening to me practice anymore! Still, my family was supportive of other things I did.

What were some of the other things you did?

Actually, I liked playing the piano. It was really only the violin that I disliked. I hated tuning it up! I preferred reading. I was a real bookworm. After I found the public library, it became my home away from home.

What else in the story comes from your own life?

I was born in Beijing, China, and came here with my family when I was nine years old. I didn't know English when I came here, and I had to learn it at school.

Was it hard to learn English?

It wasn't as bad as it sounds. Kids learn fast, and I had good friends.

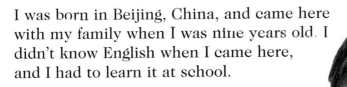

79

Response

Musical Opinions

LISTEN TO MUSIC With a small group, listen to an audiotape or a CD of orchestra music. Discuss what you like or dislike about the music, and compare it to the kinds of music you listen to most often. Construct a chart to show the musical likes and dislikes of your group.

Good Advice

WRITE AN ADVICE COLUMN Imagine that you write an advice column for a newspaper. Make up a letter that a character from this story might send you. Then write your answer to the letter. Point out what the character may be able to learn from his or her experience. If possible, use a word processing program to publish your column.

Activities

What Does It Mean?

MAKE A PHRASE BOOK You probably use slang words and phrases that don't mean what the dictionary says they mean. For example, the dictionary says *cool* means "slightly cold," but sometimes people say something is *cool* when they mean they like it. Create a phrase book to help new speakers of English understand some of these expressions. Include both the dictionary meanings and the slang meanings.

Musical Research

DRAW A DIAGRAM Choose a musical instrument mentioned in the story or another one that interests you. Use books or a computer to research how the instrument is constructed. Then make a drawing or diagram of the musical instrument, and label its parts.

Vocabulary in Context

As you read "Yang the Third and Her Impossible Family," you may have seen some words that were unfamiliar to you. If you used other parts of the story to figure out what the words meant, then you used context clues. **Context clues** are words, phrases, and pictures that surround a word and help suggest its meaning. There are different types of context clues. Some of the more common ones are shown here.

Synonym
A word that has the same meaning as another word.

Antonym
A word that means the opposite of another word.

Definition
Words that define another word.

Explanation
Words that explain the meaning of another word.

Description
Words that describe the meaning of another word.

Example
Words that describe one thing that shows what a group of words means.

Some words have more than one meaning. These are called multiple-meaning words. When you find such a word, context clues can help you figure out which meaning it has in the sentence. For example, the word *case* can mean (1) a set of events that a detective investigates, (2) a patient being cared for by a doctor, or (3) a container for keeping something in. In the following sentence, context clues show that *case* is used to describe a container for something.

After I played my cello, I put it back in its *case*.

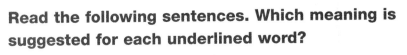

Read the following sentences. Which meaning is suggested for each underlined word?

A. The violin is played by stroking a <u>bow</u> across the strings.
 1. A knot tied with loops in it
 2. A strip of wood used for shooting arrows
 3. A rod used to play some stringed instruments

B. The violin can play notes with a high <u>pitch</u>.
 1. The highness or lowness of a sound
 2. A throw or toss
 3. The sticky sap of a pine tree

WHAT HAVE YOU LEARNED?

1. What context clues in the selection help you picture a cello?

2. Find multiple-meaning words in something you are reading on your own. List the kinds of context clues in the passage that help you figure out which meaning is suggested for each.

TRY THIS • TRY THIS • TRY THIS

Write a paragraph about an imaginary instrument. Include at least one multiple-meaning word and one word that will likely be unfamiliar to readers. Use context clues to help your readers figure out the meaning of each word.

Visit *The Learning Site!* www.harcourtschool.com

83

DEAR MRS. PARKS

A DIALOGUE WITH TODAY'S YOUTH

Teachers' Choice
Notable Social Studies
Trade Book

ROSA PARKS

WITH GREGORY J. REED

ILLUSTRATED BY LORI MCELRATH-ESLICK

osa Parks has been called the mother of the modern-day civil rights movement. In 1955 she showed courage when she insisted on her rights on a city bus in Montgomery, Alabama. Over the years, she has received many letters from students seeking advice on different issues. This selection is a collection of some of those letters and the letters Rosa Parks wrote back to the students.

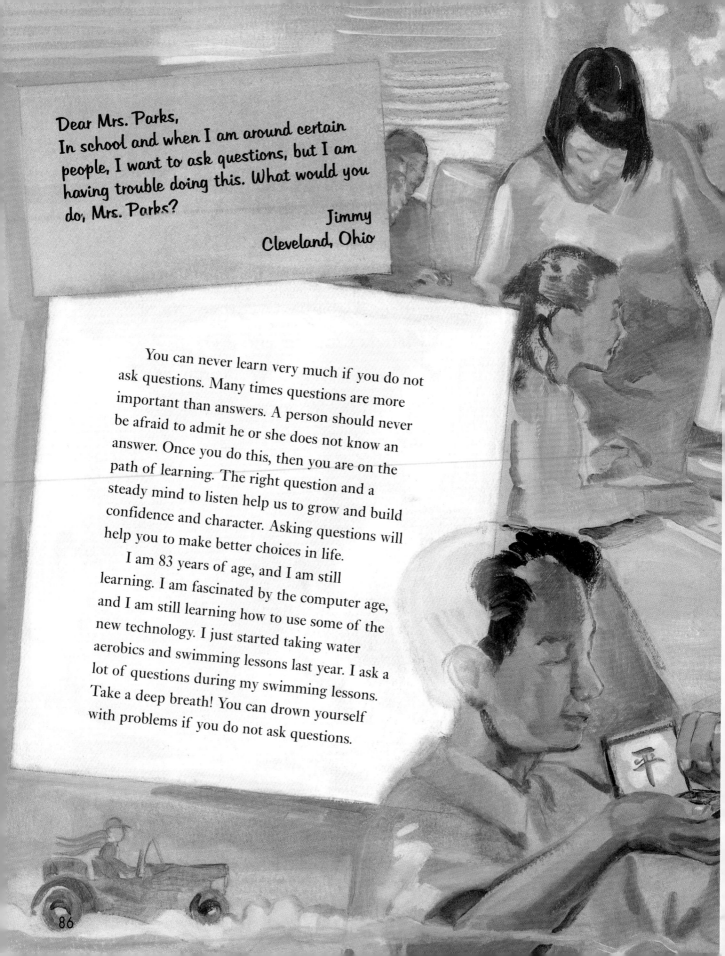

Dear Mrs. Parks,
In school and when I am around certain people, I want to ask questions, but I am having trouble doing this. What would you do, Mrs. Parks?

Jimmy
Cleveland, Ohio

You can never learn very much if you do not ask questions. Many times questions are more important than answers. A person should never be afraid to admit he or she does not know an answer. Once you do this, then you are on the path of learning. The right question and a steady mind to listen help us to grow and build confidence and character. Asking questions will help you to make better choices in life.

I am 83 years of age, and I am still learning. I am fascinated by the computer age, and I am still learning how to use some of the new technology. I just started taking water aerobics and swimming lessons last year. I ask a lot of questions during my swimming lessons. Take a deep breath! You can drown yourself with problems if you do not ask questions.

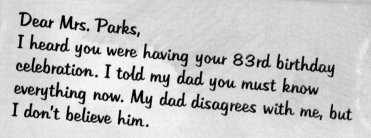

Dear Mrs. Parks,
I heard you were having your 83rd birthday celebration. I told my dad you must know everything now. My dad disagrees with me, but I don't believe him.

Richard
London, England

Your dad is right. No one knows everything. There is so much to learn and live for. There is a world of experiences awaiting us if we take the time to take part in them. Learning helps us grow and become the best person we can be. Age does not determine what we know. There are many young geniuses in life. I am still learning about life.

Today there are many changes. When I was young, cars went about 25 miles per hour. Now there are cars that can go 200 miles per hour. (I do not know why some people want to drive that fast!) Man has gone to the moon. I now keep up with much of my correspondence "on-line" on the Internet. People refer to this as "cyberspace." All this is new to me, but I am still learning.

Listen to your dad. We often act as though we know everything when we know too little. Your dad knows quite a bit. Keep an open mind. I hope your mind stays open after reading this.

Dear Mrs. Parks,
I like going to school. But I'm worrying about getting straight A's. My peers make fun of me when I get an A. I am trying to fit in.

Shata
Detroit, Michigan

I am happy to know you enjoy school. School is one of the most important developments of life that a student can experience if it is not taken for granted. Each person in life has certain gifts or talents to give back to life. I know today it is difficult at times to express your gifts because you are afraid of being ridiculed. You are not alone in your feelings. There are many other students in other cities who tell me they feel the same way. To all of you, I have one message: Work hard, do not be discouraged, and in everything you do, try to do your best. Those who make fun of you for achieving your highest potential have turned their values around backward. We are all leaders of something in life. You are a leader. Start leading, and the others will soon follow.

Dear Mrs. Parks,
I am 12 years old, and my favorite subject is math. I want to work with computers when I grow up. Did you like school when you were young?

Anthony
Las Vegas, Nevada

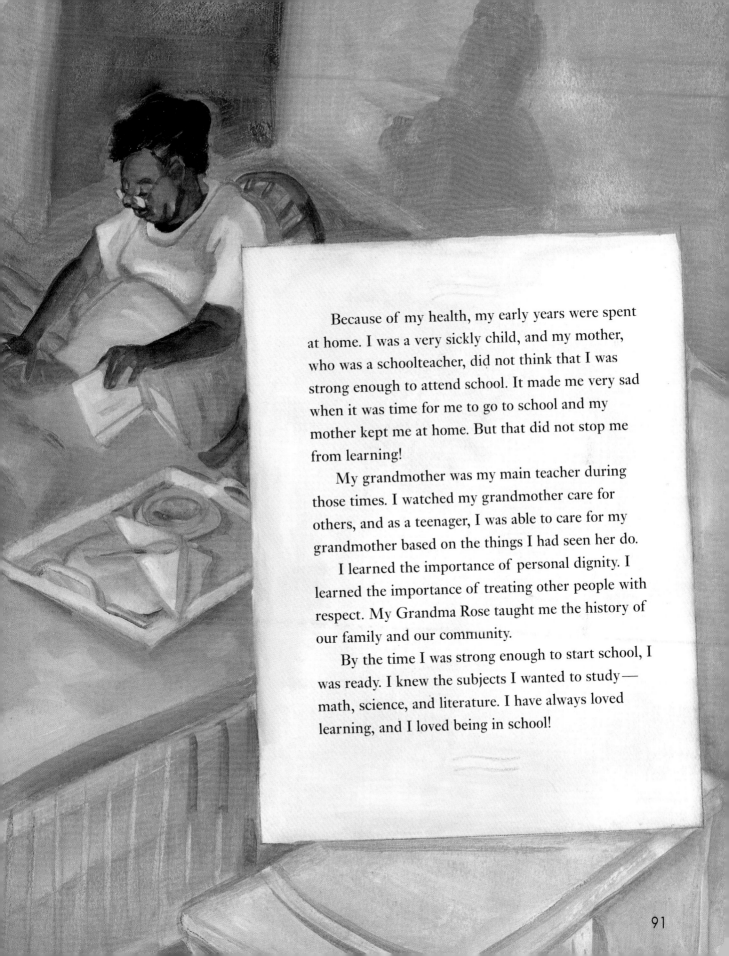

Because of my health, my early years were spent at home. I was a very sickly child, and my mother, who was a schoolteacher, did not think that I was strong enough to attend school. It made me very sad when it was time for me to go to school and my mother kept me at home. But that did not stop me from learning!

My grandmother was my main teacher during those times. I watched my grandmother care for others, and as a teenager, I was able to care for my grandmother based on the things I had seen her do.

I learned the importance of personal dignity. I learned the importance of treating other people with respect. My Grandma Rose taught me the history of our family and our community.

By the time I was strong enough to start school, I was ready. I knew the subjects I wanted to study— math, science, and literature. I have always loved learning, and I loved being in school!

Dear Mrs. Parks,
My teacher told us that you just celebrated your 83rd birthday. My great-grandmother is 85 years old. She talks about the old days all the time. Sometimes I wonder what the old days have to do with me.

Adrienne
Vienna, Virginia

When your great-grandmother talks to you about those days, you must listen, listen, listen. When she talks to you that way, she is trying to keep history alive. She seeks to inspire you by sharing stories of the past, of good times and bad times. There is no better way for us to learn from the mistakes of the past than through stories handed down from people who have lived through those times.

You will learn from listening to your great-grandmother that human nature—the way people act—does not change. The lessons that she learned when she was a child and teenager will still apply to your life today. My grandmother often spoke to me of the times when she was a little girl. As I look back, I can see that I was being informed about my ancestors and those people who paved the way for the freedoms we now have. From this I learned of their courage, faith, and sacrifices.

Listen to your great-grandmother and her stories from her past. She is preparing you to take your place in the world of tomorrow. Treasure her stories, and remember them so that you can share them with future generations.

Dear Mrs. Parks,
I am 13 years old. Did you ever think that you would live to be 83 years old? What changes have you seen in the last 50 years?

Michael
Gary, Indiana

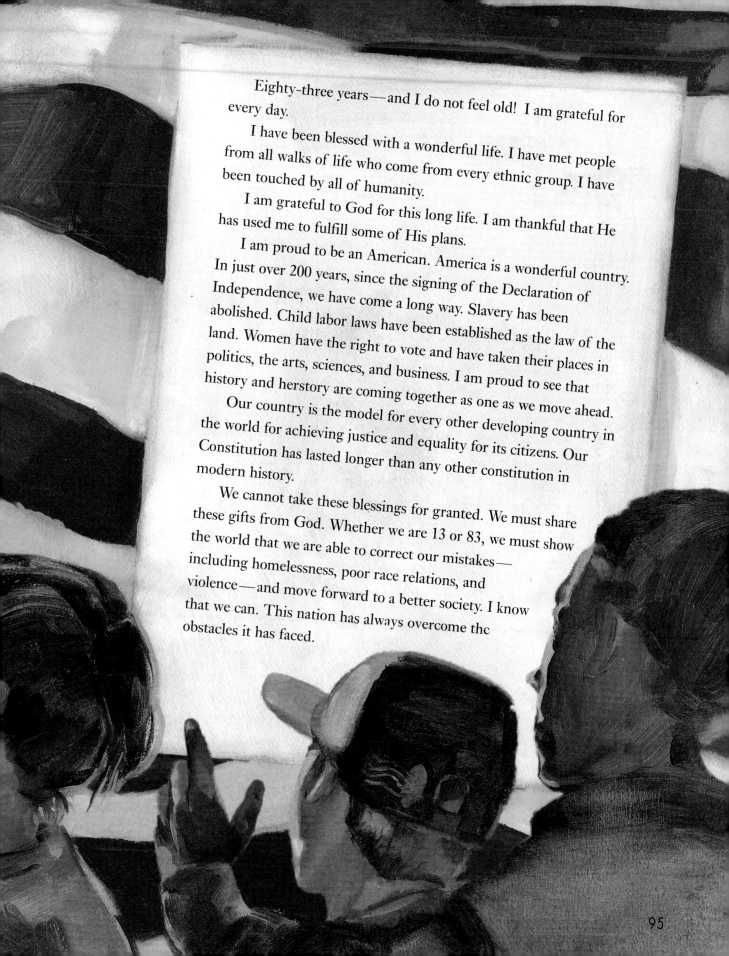

Eighty-three years—and I do not feel old! I am grateful for every day.

I have been blessed with a wonderful life. I have met people from all walks of life who come from every ethnic group. I have been touched by all of humanity.

I am grateful to God for this long life. I am thankful that He has used me to fulfill some of His plans.

I am proud to be an American. America is a wonderful country. In just over 200 years, since the signing of the Declaration of Independence, we have come a long way. Slavery has been abolished. Child labor laws have been established as the law of the land. Women have the right to vote and have taken their places in politics, the arts, sciences, and business. I am proud to see that history and herstory are coming together as one as we move ahead.

Our country is the model for every other developing country in the world for achieving justice and equality for its citizens. Our Constitution has lasted longer than any other constitution in modern history.

We cannot take these blessings for granted. We must share these gifts from God. Whether we are 13 or 83, we must show the world that we are able to correct our mistakes— including homelessness, poor race relations, and violence—and move forward to a better society. I know that we can. This nation has always overcome the obstacles it has faced.

Dear Mrs. Parks,
How can I make a difference in the world today?

Larry
St. Paul, Minnesota

By asking that question, you are making a difference. You are thinking about your place in the world and what you can do for other people.

Anyone who wants to make a difference in the world can do it. There are many ways to serve. Sometimes it can be your career choice, such as being a teacher, lawyer, minister, engineer, health care worker, or medical researcher. All of these jobs, and others, give you a chance to have a direct impact on people's lives. Other times, you can serve your community by taking part in activities during the evenings or throughout the weekend at your church or with a community group.

I always encourage those who ask how they can make a difference to consider working with young people. They have so many needs and concerns as they prepare themselves for their place in the next century. You might be the one to counsel them when they are troubled or to be a mentor to those who need someone to guide them.

All of us have talents that we can share with others. I am grateful to those who care about humanity and want to make a difference.

Think About It

❶ From what you have learned about Mrs. Parks, why do you think she took the time from her busy life to reply to these letters from young people?

❷ Which question and reply did you find most interesting? Explain your answer.

❸ Do you think this selection would have been as interesting if Mrs. Parks had written an article about her ideas and opinions without including the letters? Explain your answer.

Meet the Author
Rosa Parks

ROSA PARKS has strongly supported the peaceful pursuit of human rights, especially young people's rights, for over 40 years. She receives hundreds to thousands of letters each year. She says, "I have been truly blessed to receive so many letters from young people. I am grateful for each day God has given me to allow me to answer the letters I receive." She believes adults should set a good example for the younger generations. She says, "I am blessed to see changes in the world. But there is one thing that I hope never changes: that young people continue to seek answers to their questions. I am inspired by the energy of young minds."

AESOP'S

FABLES

RETOLD BY ANN MCGOVERN

About Aesop

Aesop was a slave who lived in Greece about 3,000 years ago. He became famous for the clever animal fables through which he showed the wise and foolish behavior of men.

Not much is really known about the life of Aesop. It is said that his wisdom so delighted one of his masters that the slave was given his freedom. It is said, too, that he became an honored guest at the courts of kings.

Aesop's fables have become a part of our daily language—a way of expressing ourselves. Haven't you heard people talk about "sour grapes" or "not counting chickens until they are hatched"?

Aesop never wrote down his stories. He told them to people, who in turn told them to others. Not until 200 years after his death did the first collection of his fables appear. Since then they have been translated into almost every language in the world. Today there are many, many versions of the tales that Aesop told in the hills of Greece so long ago.

The Crow and the Pitcher

A Crow, who was almost dying of thirst, came upon a pitcher which had once been filled with water. But to his dismay the Crow found that the water was so low he could not reach it. He tried with all his might to knock the pitcher over, but it was too heavy.

Then he saw a pile of pebbles nearby. He took one pebble in his beak and dropped it into the pitcher. The water rose a tiny bit. Then he took another pebble and dropped that in. The water rose a tiny bit more. One by one he dropped in all the pebbles. When he had dropped in a hundred pebbles, the water at last rose to the top. As the Crow drank deeply of the cool water, he said to himself, *"Where force fails, patience will often succeed."*

The Travelers and the Bear

Two men were traveling together when a Bear suddenly came out of the forest and stood in their path, growling. One of the men quickly climbed the nearest tree and concealed himself in the branches. The other man, seeing that there was no time to hide, fell flat on the ground. He pretended to be dead, for he had heard it said that a Bear will not touch a dead man.

The Bear came near, sniffed the man's head and body, and then lumbered away, back into the forest.

When the Bear was out of sight, the man in the tree slid down and said to his friend, "I saw the Bear whispering to you. What did he have to say?"

The other man replied, "The Bear told me never to travel with a friend who deserts me at the first sign of danger." He looked his companion straight in the eye. "The Bear said that, *in time of trouble, one learns who his true friends are.*"

Think About It

How are the two fables you read similar to each other?

RESPONSE ACTIVITIES

Good Advice

WRITE A LETTER Which of Rosa Parks's suggestions had special meaning for you? Write a letter to Mrs. Parks, thanking her for that piece of advice. Tell her how you plan to use her suggestion in your own life. Then share your letter with classmates.

News Radio

PRESENT A RADIO BROADCAST Imagine that Rosa Parks is a guest on a radio show, answering calls from listeners. With a small group, plan and role-play a broadcast of the show. You might play the parts of the host of the show introducing Rosa Parks to the audience, listeners calling in with their questions, and Rosa Parks answering them. Record your show, or present a live broadcast to your classmates.

Story Time

WRITE A STORY Rosa Parks reminds us that it is important to listen to stories about the past. Think about a story you have heard from an older family member or friend. Who told this story to you and why? Will you retell this same story when you are older? Write the story that you were told, or make up a story that an older person might tell about the past.

Making Connections

WRITE A FABLE Rosa Parks gives advice in her letters. Aesop's fables also give advice through their morals or lessons. Rewrite one of Rosa Parks's letters in the form of a fable. Choose animals as characters for your fable, and end with a moral.

MICK HARTE WAS HERE

by Barbara Park

illustrated by Mark Mohr

a novel by **BARBARA PARK**

MICK HARTE
WAS HERE

Mick Harte is a playful, amusing boy who likes to tease his family. But when Mick dies in a bicycle accident, his family is shattered. Every member is left to deal with the accident in his or her own way. His sister, Phoebe, must deal with her anger — toward Mick, toward other people, and toward herself.

T HREE BLOCKS FROM MY HOUSE, there used to be a
dangerous intersection. It was one of those intersections
where it was impossible for cars to pull out onto the main street
without horns honking and brakes screeching and stuff.

My father griped about it every time we drove through there.

"The city's not going to put a light in here until someone gets
hurt," he'd say. "You wait and see. It's going to take an accident
before anything gets done."

Last year there were four accidents in seven months and they
finally installed a traffic signal.

The first time we drove through it, some guy ran a red light
and Pop had to swerve out of the way to keep from hitting him.

It scared us both to death. Pop swore at the guy and then
started right in on this lecture about "how you can lead a horse
to water, but you can't make him drink."

"It's a sad lesson, Phoebe," he said. "But no matter how many
traffic lights they put in, they'll never be able to make people use
common sense and good judgment."

As he was talking, he turned around to make sure I was paying attention. While his head was turned, our car drifted into the next lane and two cars blasted their horns at us.

He made a quick recovery. It was close, though.

It was also the end of his talk on good judgment and common sense. And the lesson I ended up learning that day was that even smart guys with chemistry degrees do stupid stuff once in a while.

It's just that usually when you do stupid stuff, you luck out and get away with it. And if you luck out enough times, it's pretty easy to start believing that you're always going to luck out. *Forever*, I mean.

Like I can't even count how many soccer games I played in without shin guards before I finally got kicked in the leg and started wearing them. Over thirty, though, I bet.

And my mother had never had a major sunburn her whole entire life till she and Pop went to the beach for their anniversary last year. You can still see the blotchy places where her skin peeled from all the blisters, by the way.

And then there was Mick. Who went twelve years and five months without ever falling off his bike.

So he refused to wear a helmet.

And it's the one thing about him that I've tried to forget. And to forgive him for.

And I'm sorry, but I can't seem to do either one.

IT WAS OVER A WEEK before Mrs. Berryhill called me down to her office again. I was kind of nervous when I got her note. Even though I knew my parents had explained to her about me ditching school that day, part of me was still expecting detention.

That's why I was relieved to see another woman sitting in her office when I walked in. Mrs. Berryhill introduced us. Her name was Mrs. Somebody-or-other from the PTA.

She shook my hand and said how "sincerely sorry" she was about what happened to my brother. Then she started right in on how the PTA wanted to make sure that nothing like that ever happened again, so they were going to sponsor this big assembly on bike safety. It was already in the works, she said. There were going to be police officers, and instructional videos, and demonstrations of the latest safety gear, and yadda, yadda, yadda . . .

"We'd like to invite you to sit onstage with the other speakers," she told me. Then she took my hand again and asked if I thought maybe I could say a few words to my classmates about bike safety. Because a few words from me would have "a tremendous impact," she thought.

And through all of this, I just sort of sat there, you know? Staring at her in disbelief. Because I swear I could not figure out what planet this woman had come from.

I mean where in the world had she ever gotten the nerve to ask me something like that? Had it never even dawned on her that the timing of a bicycle-safety assembly was just a little off for me? That maybe I would have liked to see a safety assembly *before* my brother was killed?

I didn't make a scene. I just stood up and took my hand away.

"I can't," I said.

When I turned to go, Mrs. Somebody-or-other fell all over herself telling me how much she understood.

Which really killed me, by the way.

Because the woman didn't have a clue.

I DON'T KNOW when I changed my mind about speaking at the assembly.

I think it was just one of those flipflops you do sometimes. You know, like at first you have this gut reaction to something and you're positive that you're totally right. Only after a while, it creeps into your mind that the other guy may actually have a point. Then the next thing you know, his point's making more sense than your point. Which is totally annoying. But still, it happens.

It used to happen with me and Mick all the time. Like a couple of months ago, we were arguing about whether the Three Stooges were funny or not. I kept saying they were hilarious, and Mick kept saying they were just morons.

Then we started kind of wrestling around a little bit, and the next thing I know, Mick jumps up and starts slapping the top of his head with his hand and fluttering it up and down in front of my face. After that, he grabs my nose with his fist, twists it hard, and finally slaps it away with his other hand. He ended his performance with the classic Three Stooges laugh—Nyuk, nyuk, nyuk—and a quick move to boink my eyes out with his fingers.

Fortunately, I was able to block it with my hand.

Mick stopped the routine as fast as he had started it. Then, without saying a word, he stood up real dignified-like and dusted himself off.

He looked at me without the trace of a smile. "Hilarious, wasn't I?" he said dryly.

"Yes," I lied. "You were."

But deep down I had already started to feel different about the Stooges.

THERE WERE eight hundred people in the gym when I walked to the microphone that morning. I wasn't nervous, though, which really surprised me. But I swear I felt almost relaxed when I set down my bag of stuff next to the podium.

"I'm Mick Harte's sister," I said. Then I bent down and reached into my plastic bag.

"When Mick was in third grade, this is what my grandmother from Florida sent him for Christmas."

I held it up. "It's a glow-in-the-dark bow tie with pink flamingos on it."

A couple of kids chuckled a little.

"Don't worry," I said. "He never wore it. He said it made him look like a dork."

There was more laughing then. And I reached into my bag again.

"When Mick was in fourth grade, my Aunt Marge sent him this from Michigan."

I held up a hat in the shape of a trout.

"Mick said this one went beyond dork, all the way to doofus," I said.

This time everybody really cracked up. Some of the kids in the first row even stood up and started craning their necks to see what I would pull out next.

They watched as I turned the bag upside down and a cardboard box fell onto the stage.

Carefully, I set it on the podium and waited for everything to get totally quiet.

"When Mick turned ten, my parents gave him this for his birthday."

I took my time opening the lid. I mean you could really feel the anticipation and all.

But when I finally pulled Mick's gift out of the box—still brand-new—there was just this gasp.

And no one laughed at all.

No one even moved.

"This was my brother's bike helmet," I said.

My voice broke, but somehow I forced myself to finish.

"He said it made him look like a dork."

I DON'T KNOW if what I said at that assembly will make a difference. I don't know if it will help anyone use better judgment than my brother did. I hope so, though. . . . Because Mick died from a massive head injury. And yet the doctors said that just an inch of Styrofoam would have made the difference between his living and dying.

It's been a month since the accident now. Things have gotten a little better at home. Nana from Florida went back to Orlando. And my mother gets dressed in the mornings, usually. She's gone back to work, too— just two days a week, but it's a start.

We sit down to dinner every night at our new places. Eating

still isn't a big deal with us, though. Like last night we had grilled cheese sandwiches and mashed potatoes. And on Sunday all the forks were in the dishwasher so we ate potato salad with soup spoons. My mother's eased up on stuff like that. Death sort of gives you a new outlook on the importance of proper silverware.

It's called *perspective*. It means your father doesn't iron a crease in his pants every morning. And the hamburgers come in all shapes and sizes.

I've started to laugh more often. But I still feel guilty when I'm having too good a time. Which is totally ridiculous. Because if I want to feel guilty, there're lots better reasons than that. Like I'm just now starting to deal with how Mick asked me to ride his bike home that day and all.

I kept that whole memory tucked away in the back of my mind after the accident happened. But bad memories must grow in the dark, I think, because it kept on creeping into my thoughts, till it was with me almost all the time, it seemed.

113

Then last Saturday, when my father and I were riding home from a soccer game, my stomach started churning like it always does right before I'm about to blurt out an unplanned confession.

It's one of the sickest feelings there is, by the way. To realize you're about to squeal on yourself like that.

The only thing sicker is keeping it inside.

So it all came busting out. All about how Mick asked me to ride his bike that day. And how I had soccer practice so I told him I couldn't do it.

"See, Pop? Don't you get it? I could have kept the accident from ever happening. If only I had ridden his bike home, Mick would still be here right now."

I was crying a little bit now. But except for handing me the travel tissues from the dashboard, my father hardly seemed to

notice. Instead, he just kept staring out the window at the road in front of us.

Then slowly, he began shaking his head from side to side.

"I'm sorry, Pop. I'm sorry. I'm sorry," I said over and over again.

My face was buried in my hands when I finally felt him touch my shoulder.

"I'm going to make a list, Phoebe," he said. "And I want you to keep a count." His voice was real low and steady as he began.

"*If only* you had ridden Mick's bike home, Mick would still be here.

"*If only* the truck had been going a little faster or a little slower, Mick would still be here.

"*If only* his meeting had been scheduled one day earlier or one day later, Mick would still be here.

"*If only* it had been raining that day, I'd have driven him to school and Mick would still be here.

"*If only* one of his friends had kept him talking a second longer at his locker that afternoon . . .

"*If only* the house he was riding to had been in the other direction . . .

"*If only* that rock hadn't been on the sidewalk at the exact spot . . ."

He stopped then. And I was pretty sure he was finished. But all at once, he heaved this . . . awful sigh and whispered, "If only I had made him wear his helmet."

My heart broke for my father at that moment, and I reached my hand out to him.

He held on to it tight. Then he smiled the saddest smile you've ever seen.

"What number are we on, little girl?" He sounded so old.

I scooted closer to him.

"I think we're done, Pop," I said softly.

He pressed my hand to his cheek.

The two of us drove home in silence.

Think About It

1. What does Phoebe learn as a result of Mick's accident?

2. If you were a friend of Phoebe's, what might you say or do to help her get through this difficult time?

3. Why do you think this story is written as if Phoebe is telling it herself?

MEET THE AUTHOR
BARBARA PARK

Head injury is the main cause of death in fatal bicycle crashes.

Researchers tell us that if all bicyclists wore helmets, as many as one death *every day* and one head injury every *four* minutes could be prevented.*

I urge all of you who do not wear bike helmets to please reconsider your decision. Today.

Please.

It's your *life*.

*From the Division of Injury Control, National Center for Environmental Health and Injury Control, and the Division of Field Epidemiology.

This study was published in the *Journal of the American Medical Association*, December 4, 1991, Volume 266.

RESPONSE ACTIVITIES

Listen to Phoebe

WRITE A JOURNAL ENTRY Imagine that you were in the audience the day Phoebe spoke at the assembly. How might her speech have changed your feelings or opinions about bike helmets? Write an entry in your journal describing your reaction to Phoebe's speech.

Style or Safety?

HAVE A DISCUSSION Mick thought wearing a bike helmet made him look silly. Meet with a small group of classmates. Discuss whether it makes sense for young people to worry about how they look when it comes to their safety. Work together to write a brief summary of your discussion.

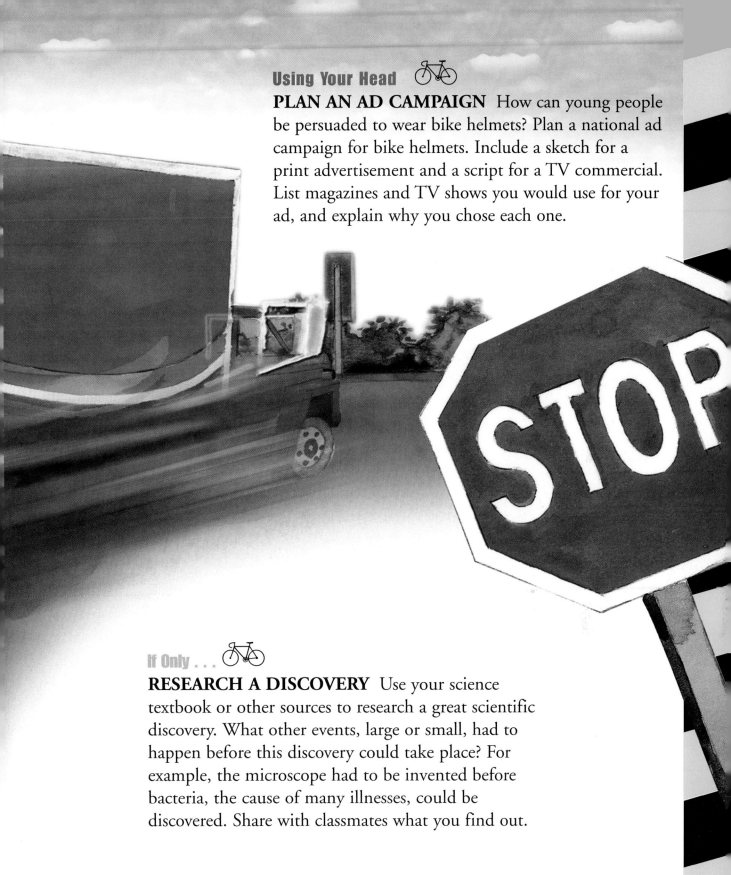

PLAN AN AD CAMPAIGN How can young people be persuaded to wear bike helmets? Plan a national ad campaign for bike helmets. Include a sketch for a print advertisement and a script for a TV commercial. List magazines and TV shows you would use for your ad, and explain why you chose each one.

If Only . . .

RESEARCH A DISCOVERY Use your science textbook or other sources to research a great scientific discovery. What other events, large or small, had to happen before this discovery could take place? For example, the microscope had to be invented before bacteria, the cause of many illnesses, could be discovered. Share with classmates what you find out.

Theme Wrap-Up

What's the Problem?

FIND THE PROBLEM Think about the main characters of the stories in this theme. Each main character faces a problem. Make a two-column chart like the one shown below. In the first column, list each main character. In the second column, write the problem he or she faces.

Character	Problem
Derek and Rory	
Walnut	
Mary	
Phoebe	

Here's the Solution!

DESCRIBE THE RESOLUTION Choose two characters from the chart, and think about the problem each one has to solve. Write a paragraph comparing and contrasting the problems these characters face and what each one learns from his or her experience. Then describe how each character changes by the end of the story.

Talk Across the Cultures

DISCUSS CULTURES The characters in this theme represent many different cultures. Work in a small group, and review the selections in this theme. Each group member should choose a quote, a sentence, or a saying from one of the selections that reflects a particular culture. Each member should then read his or her example aloud. As a group, discuss how the example reflects that culture. Discuss how the culture is similar to or different from other cultures.

TEAM WORK

CONTENTS

READER'S CHOICE

Baseball in the Barrios
by Henry Horenstein

NONFICTION

In Venezuela, where Hubaldo lives, children and adults play baseball as much as in the United States. Colorful photographs show how much Hubaldo loves the game.

Award-Winning Author
READER'S CHOICE LIBRARY

The Tarantula in My Purse and 172 Other Wild Pets
by Jean Craighead George

AUTOBIOGRAPHY

These entertaining stories about Jean Craighead George and her three kids describe what it is like to live with many different kinds of pets.

Award-Winning Author
READER'S CHOICE LIBRARY

The Landry News
by Andrew Clements

FICTION

A newspaper that begins as a hobby for fifth-grader Cara Landry suddenly becomes a lesson in learning for her entire class.

Award-Winning Author

Baseball Flyhawk
by Matt Christopher

REALISTIC FICTION

Chico Romez must prove his worth to his teammates on the Royals baseball team, but first baseman String Becker will do anything to make him feel unwelcome.

Award-Winning Author

The Million Dollar Shot
by Dan Gutman

REALISTIC FICTION

Eleven-year-old Eddie Ball wins the chance to sink a million-dollar shot at the NBA finals.

Award-Winning Author

WE'LL NEVER FORGET YOU, ROBERTO CLEMENTE

by Trudie Engel
illustrated by Gil Adams

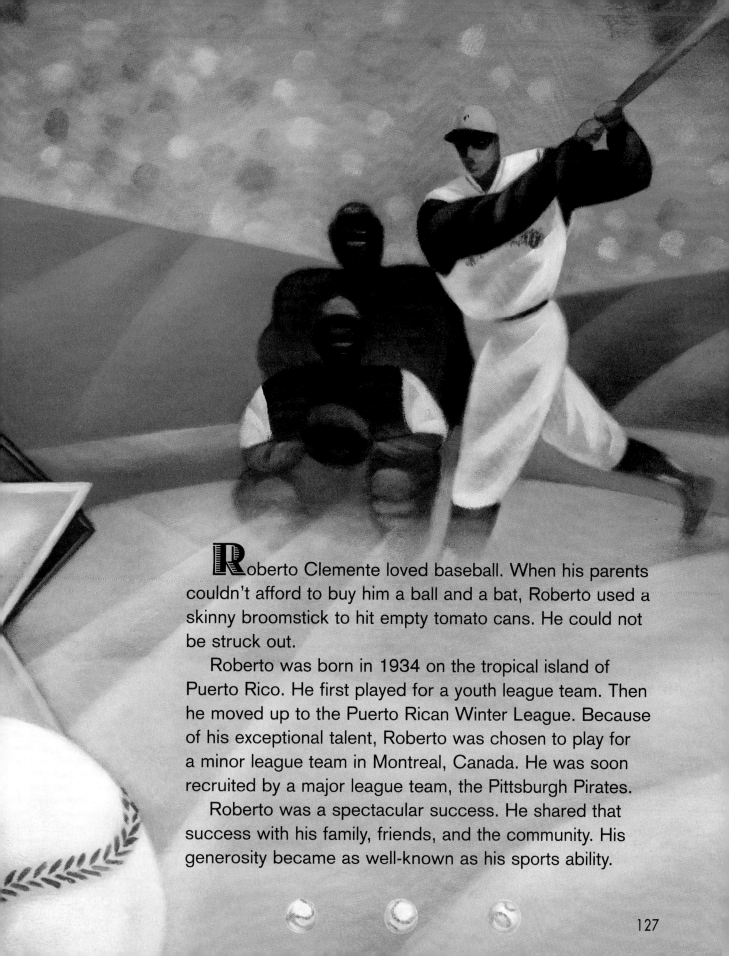

Roberto Clemente loved baseball. When his parents couldn't afford to buy him a ball and a bat, Roberto used a skinny broomstick to hit empty tomato cans. He could not be struck out.

Roberto was born in 1934 on the tropical island of Puerto Rico. He first played for a youth league team. Then he moved up to the Puerto Rican Winter League. Because of his exceptional talent, Roberto was chosen to play for a minor league team in Montreal, Canada. He was soon recruited by a major league team, the Pittsburgh Pirates.

Roberto was a spectacular success. He shared that success with his family, friends, and the community. His generosity became as well-known as his sports ability.

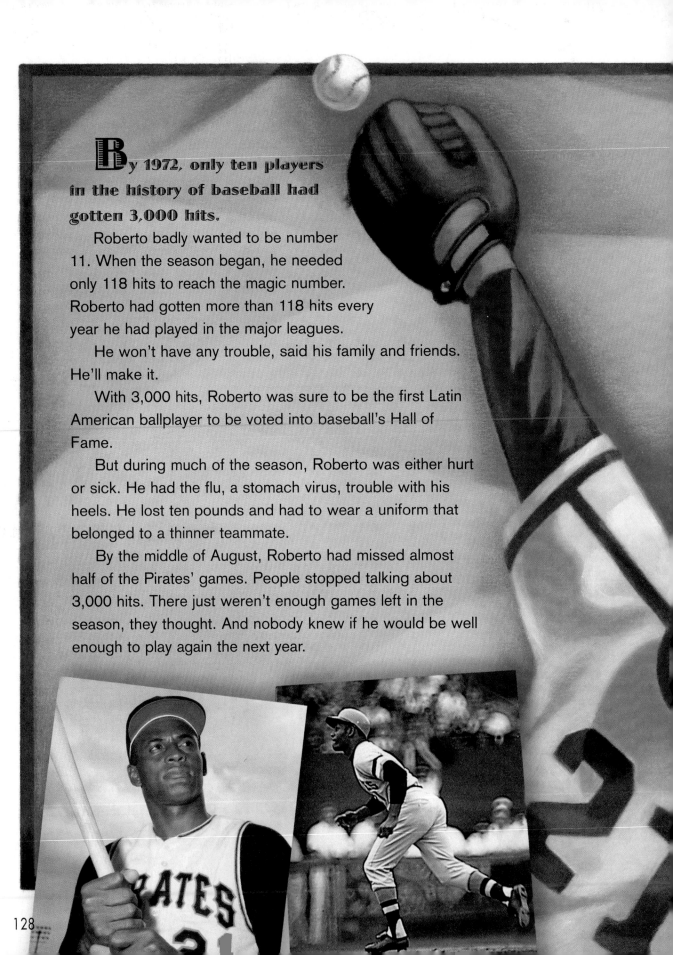

By 1972, only ten players in the history of baseball had gotten 3,000 hits.

Roberto badly wanted to be number 11. When the season began, he needed only 118 hits to reach the magic number. Roberto had gotten more than 118 hits every year he had played in the major leagues.

He won't have any trouble, said his family and friends. He'll make it.

With 3,000 hits, Roberto was sure to be the first Latin American ballplayer to be voted into baseball's Hall of Fame.

But during much of the season, Roberto was either hurt or sick. He had the flu, a stomach virus, trouble with his heels. He lost ten pounds and had to wear a uniform that belonged to a thinner teammate.

By the middle of August, Roberto had missed almost half of the Pirates' games. People stopped talking about 3,000 hits. There just weren't enough games left in the season, they thought. And nobody knew if he would be well enough to play again the next year.

With only 26 games left, Roberto still needed 25 hits to get to 3,000.

And then in September, he started to hit. Was there a chance he might get his 3,000th hit after all?

On September 28 in Philadelphia, Roberto faced Steve Carlton, the great Phillies pitcher. He hit a single to right field. It was hit number 2,999.

Right away, Roberto was taken out of the lineup. Everyone wanted him to get the 3,000th hit in Pittsburgh in front of the hometown fans.

The next night in Pittsburgh it was cold and rainy. Even so, 24,000 fans turned out to cheer Roberto on.

The Pirates were playing the New York Mets. Tom Seaver was pitching. If Seaver could win this game, it would be another twenty-game season for the Mets' ace pitcher.

The crowd cheered loudly as Roberto walked up to the plate in the first inning.

One of Seaver's fastballs whizzed over the plate. Roberto swung hard but did not get much wood on the ball. It bounced over Seaver's glove. The second baseman ran in to grab it. The ball bounced off his glove. Roberto pulled up at first base.

Was the play a hit or an error? If the scorekeeper said it was an error, Roberto would not get his 3,000th hit. It was so noisy in the stadium that only a few people heard the words, "Error, second baseman," over the loudspeaker.

All eyes turned toward the scoreboard. For what seemed like a long time, there was nothing. Then the big H for hit went up.

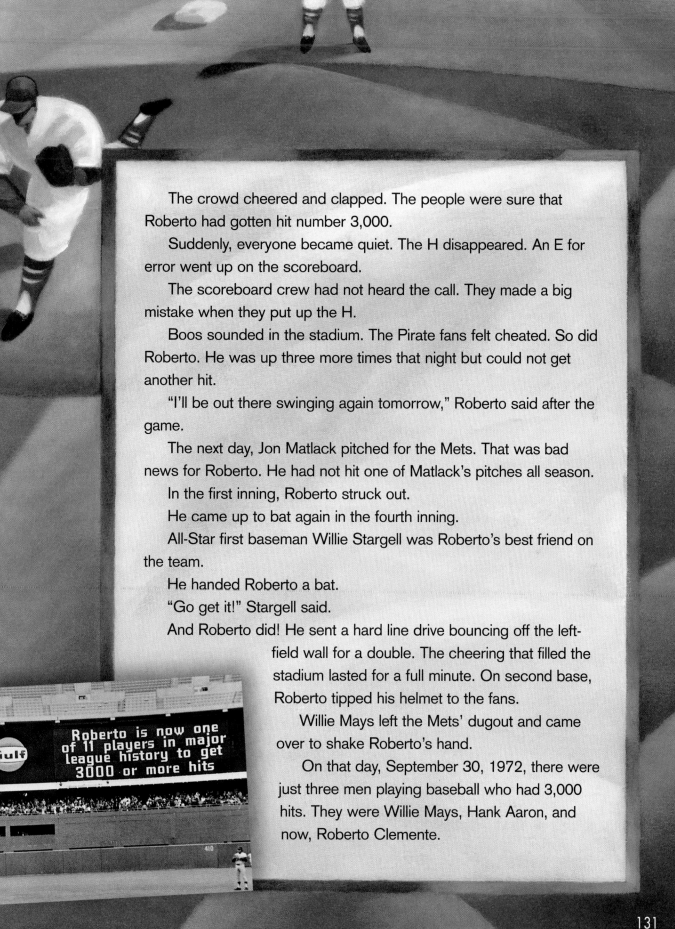

The crowd cheered and clapped. The people were sure that Roberto had gotten hit number 3,000.

Suddenly, everyone became quiet. The H disappeared. An E for error went up on the scoreboard.

The scoreboard crew had not heard the call. They made a big mistake when they put up the H.

Boos sounded in the stadium. The Pirate fans felt cheated. So did Roberto. He was up three more times that night but could not get another hit.

"I'll be out there swinging again tomorrow," Roberto said after the game.

The next day, Jon Matlack pitched for the Mets. That was bad news for Roberto. He had not hit one of Matlack's pitches all season.

In the first inning, Roberto struck out.

He came up to bat again in the fourth inning.

All-Star first baseman Willie Stargell was Roberto's best friend on the team.

He handed Roberto a bat.

"Go get it!" Stargell said.

And Roberto did! He sent a hard line drive bouncing off the left-field wall for a double. The cheering that filled the stadium lasted for a full minute. On second base, Roberto tipped his helmet to the fans.

Willie Mays left the Mets' dugout and came over to shake Roberto's hand.

On that day, September 30, 1972, there were just three men playing baseball who had 3,000 hits. They were Willie Mays, Hank Aaron, and now, Roberto Clemente.

Roberto is now one of 11 players in major league history to get 3000 or more hits

On December 23, 1972, the earth shook in
Nicaragua.

Nicaragua is a small, poor country in Central America, not far
from the island of Puerto Rico. Two days before Christmas in 1972,
a terrible thing happened there.

NICARAGUA

A giant earthquake hit the biggest city in Nicaragua.

Over 6,000 people were killed. Another 20,000 were hurt. Thousands more were left homeless. People needed food, water, and medicines.

Roberto had been in Nicaragua a month before the earthquake.

While he was there, Roberto heard about a fourteen-year-old boy who had a terrible thing happen to him. He had lost both his legs in an accident. The boy's parents had died. He needed artificial legs but had no money to pay for them.

A team in the Puerto Rican Winter League had raised part of the money the boy needed. Roberto himself gave the rest. He went to see the boy and told him he would be able to walk again. Roberto then returned to Pittsburgh.

When the earthquake hit Nicaragua, Roberto thought of his young friend. Had he lived through it? Was he all right? He had to find out.

Roberto also thought about the thousands of other people who had lost their homes and everything in them.

Caring about others who had less than he did was nothing new for Roberto. He had followed his father's teachings. He helped out other members of his family when they were in need. After his brother had died, he supported his nieces and nephews.

Roberto was kind to many people. One day during a game, the Pirates' announcer brought a deaf boy to meet Roberto. Roberto talked to the boy, using his hands and smiling.

Later, Roberto took one of his bats into the stands where the deaf boy was sitting. He gave him the bat.

On the side of the bat he wrote, "You don't have to be able to hear to play baseball and enjoy the game. Best wishes, Roberto Clemente."

So no one was surprised when Roberto started helping people in Nicaragua after the earthquake.

He went from door to door in his neighborhood in San Juan asking for money. He spoke on radio and television asking the people of Puerto Rico to give money, food, clothes, and medicines.

He helped collect the supplies that came in. And he found ships and a plane to take the food and clothing to Nicaragua.

All during the Christmas holidays in 1972, Roberto helped pack the supplies into boxes.

Two planeloads of goods had already been flown to Nicaragua. Another would go on New Year's Eve, the last day of the year 1972.

New Year's Eve is an important holiday in Puerto Rico. People come together from all over the island for family celebrations.

But Roberto decided to leave his family and fly to Nicaragua.

"I must see that the people who need the supplies really get them," he said.

And what had happened to his young friend who had lost his legs? This was his chance to find out.

The plane going to Nicaragua was a twenty-year-old propeller plane. Three weeks before, it had been in an accident. The brakes had not worked and the plane crashed into a wall. The propeller tips were badly bent.

Now, the brakes were fixed and the plane had new propellers. The plane was said to be ready to fly again.

It was supposed to take off at 4:00 P.M. in the afternoon.

But at 9:00 A.M. in the morning, the owner of the plane was still trying to find a crew to fly it to Nicaragua.

At last a pilot was found. There was a flight engineer, but he did not know much about that kind of plane.

They could not get a copilot. The owner of the plane no longer had a license to fly, but he decided to be the copilot anyway.

At 3:30 Vera, his wife, took Roberto to the airport.

The plane was not ready.

Teenage helpers were loading the plane. It was already full, but they kept putting more and more boxes in. Everyone wanted to get the last of the supplies to Nicaragua.

"Is it safe?" Vera asked.

"Look, the plane is fine," the owner said. "It will be ready soon. If it were in bad shape I wouldn't go myself." And he climbed into the cockpit.

At 5:00 P.M. Roberto got onboard. Vera waved good-bye.

It wasn't until after 9:00 P.M. that the plane rolled down the runway toward the ocean for takeoff. The San Juan Airport is just a mile from the beach.

The plane was only in the air for a few seconds before there was a loud bang. Flames shot out from one of the engines.

The people in the control tower heard the pilot say, "I'm coming back around."

Then there were two more explosions. The plane went off the radar screen in the control tower.

A man who lived in a house near the ocean heard a plane roaring overhead. He looked out the window and saw it flying so low, it almost hit the palm trees by the shore. Then he saw the plane fall into the ocean.

The man left the window to tell his son to call the police. When he came back, the plane had completely disappeared, sinking into the ocean.

It was after midnight when the phone rang at the Clementes' with the news about the plane crash. Vera rushed to the beach.

Bright orange flares lit up the night sky. Police cars parked on the beach and shone their headlights into the ocean. Coast Guard ships were in the water. Search crews looked for bodies and parts of the plane.

Nothing was found.

The next day the search went on. In the morning, the beach was full of people. Some were standing in the water. Some were holding small radios to their ears.

The search went on for weeks. Crowds were there every day.

Every afternoon, Vera Clemente came and stood in the sand and watched.

Then one day she stopped coming.

The Coast Guard picked up parts of the plane. Later, Roberto's briefcase washed up on shore.

But Roberto's body was never found.

It was hard to believe Roberto was gone. "I expected him to swim to shore someplace," one of his Pirate team-mates said.

High on the hills in Pittsburgh, there is a billboard that everyone can see from the Pirates' stadium. It is lit up brightly at night. . . .

After the plane crash, the sign said, "*Adiós, amigo.*" Good-bye, friend.

Many wonderful things were said about Roberto. That he was the best ballplayer of his time. That he was the biggest hero Puerto Rico ever had.

Roberto became the first Latin American ballplayer voted into the Baseball Hall of Fame.

But there was something else about Roberto that was even more important. "He was a *good* man," said Willie Stargell.

On opening day of 1973, the Pirates scoreboard read, "Thank you, Roberto. We will never forget THE GREAT ONE."

The city of Pittsburgh and the Pittsburgh Pirates kept their promise. They did not forget Roberto.

In July 1994, more than twenty years after the plane crash in which he lost his life, a statue of Roberto Clemente was dedicated at the Pirates' stadium in Pittsburgh.

The statue was paid for by the people of Pittsburgh and shows Roberto dropping his bat after hitting the ball. It must have been a good hit. He is just starting to run, as his eyes are fixed on the ball, far in the distance.

The statue tells us that Roberto lives on in our hearts and minds.

But he lives on in more than our memories. Roberto lives, too, in all the children that he helped.

Before he died, Roberto had plans to build a "sports city" in Puerto Rico where the poor children of the island would have a chance to learn to play different kinds of sports.

After Roberto died, Sports City was built by his family. Over the years, thousands of children have gone there.

One baseball player who got his start at Sports City is Ruben Sierra, an outfielder for the Oakland Athletics. Sierra not only made it to the major leagues, but he also played in the 1994 All-Star game.

Sierra was a poor boy from a poor village in Puerto Rico. He says he would still be there today if it hadn't been for Roberto's Sports City.

When Sierra came up to bat during the All-Star game, millions of people were watching. They saw that he wore the number 21 on his uniform.

That was Roberto's number.

Sierra says, "He was the greatest. That's why I wear his number, in honor of him."

THINK ABOUT IT

❶ Do you think Roberto Clemente achieved all he did on his own, or do you think he needed the help of others?

❷ Why do you think they called Roberto Clemente "THE GREAT ONE"?

❸ Why do you think the author used so much detail to tell about the game in which Roberto did not get a hit?

Response Activities

What Do You Know About Nicaragua?

CREATE A PAMPHLET Use an encyclopedia on-line and an atlas to research some interesting facts about Nicaragua. Create an attractive pamphlet to share the facts you learn. If you have word processing or desktop publishing software, you might use it to create your pamphlet.

Team Players

WRITE A STATEMENT Roberto Clemente's family built Sports City so that young people could learn to play sports. Many people believe that playing team sports helps young people learn to get along with each other and work together. Others disagree. What do you think? Write a statement of your opinion, and briefly explain why you believe as you do. Give examples or include research findings to support your point of view.

DESIGN A TRIBUTE The people of Pittsburgh put up a statue in memory of Roberto Clemente. Design another kind of tribute to him. For example, you might design a plaque to hang on the wall of the stadium, or a T-shirt with a special logo that represents something about Roberto Clemente's life. Display your tribute for classmates, and explain its meaning.

Role Models

DISCUSS IN A GROUP In a small group, discuss the qualities Roberto Clemente displayed that made him a good example for young people. Name some other people that you think are good role models, and tell why. Have a member of the group jot down their names and the reasons they are good role models. Then have each member tell which person would be his or her choice as a role model and why.

Draw Conclusions/ Make Generalizations

In "We'll Never Forget You, Roberto Clemente," Roberto kept trying to reach his goal of getting 3,000 hits, even though he was sick and had missed half the season. Eventually he did reach his goal.

Writers do not always state things directly. However, you can use the information an author does give you to figure things out and **draw conclusions**. From what the author tells us about Roberto's actions, plus your own knowledge and experience, you can conclude that Roberto Clemente was persistent — he did not give up easily.

Your thoughts may have taken the following path:

Facts and Details from Selection		Personal Knowledge and Experience		Conclusion
With only a few games left, Roberto started to hit.	**+**	I know that people try hard to accomplish their goals.	**=**	Roberto was persistent, and he did not give up easily.

As you read a story, you may begin to notice similarities or patterns in the characters or events. After a while, you begin to use these patterns or similarities to **make generalizations**.

For example, whenever Roberto got a hit, the crowd cheered. You could make the generalization from this that crowds cheer when their favorite player does well.

Read the paragraph at the left below. What conclusions can you draw? What generalizations can you make?

As Claudia strode to the plate, Ruben smiled broadly at the man sitting next to him and said, "That's my kid sister!" Claudia choked up on the bat. Squinting, she kept her eyes on the pitcher's right arm. As the ball sailed over home plate, she swung hard. Ruben stood up and cheered. "Way to go, Claudia. You're the best!"

WHAT HAVE YOU LEARNED?

1. As you read the selection, what conclusion did you draw about the plane's safety? What details in the story led you to that conclusion?

2. Sometimes we draw conclusions before we have all the facts. What conclusions have you drawn and then changed when you got new information?

Visit *The Learning Site!*
www.harcourtschool.com

TRY THIS • TRY THIS • TRY THIS

Think of three people you know. What conclusions have you drawn about these people based on their actions? Make a chart like the one below. Fill it in with things each person has done or said and the conclusions you have drawn about that person.

Person	Words and Actions	Conclusions

THE BOONSVILLE BOMBERS

by Alison Cragin Herzig

illustrated by
Bob Commander

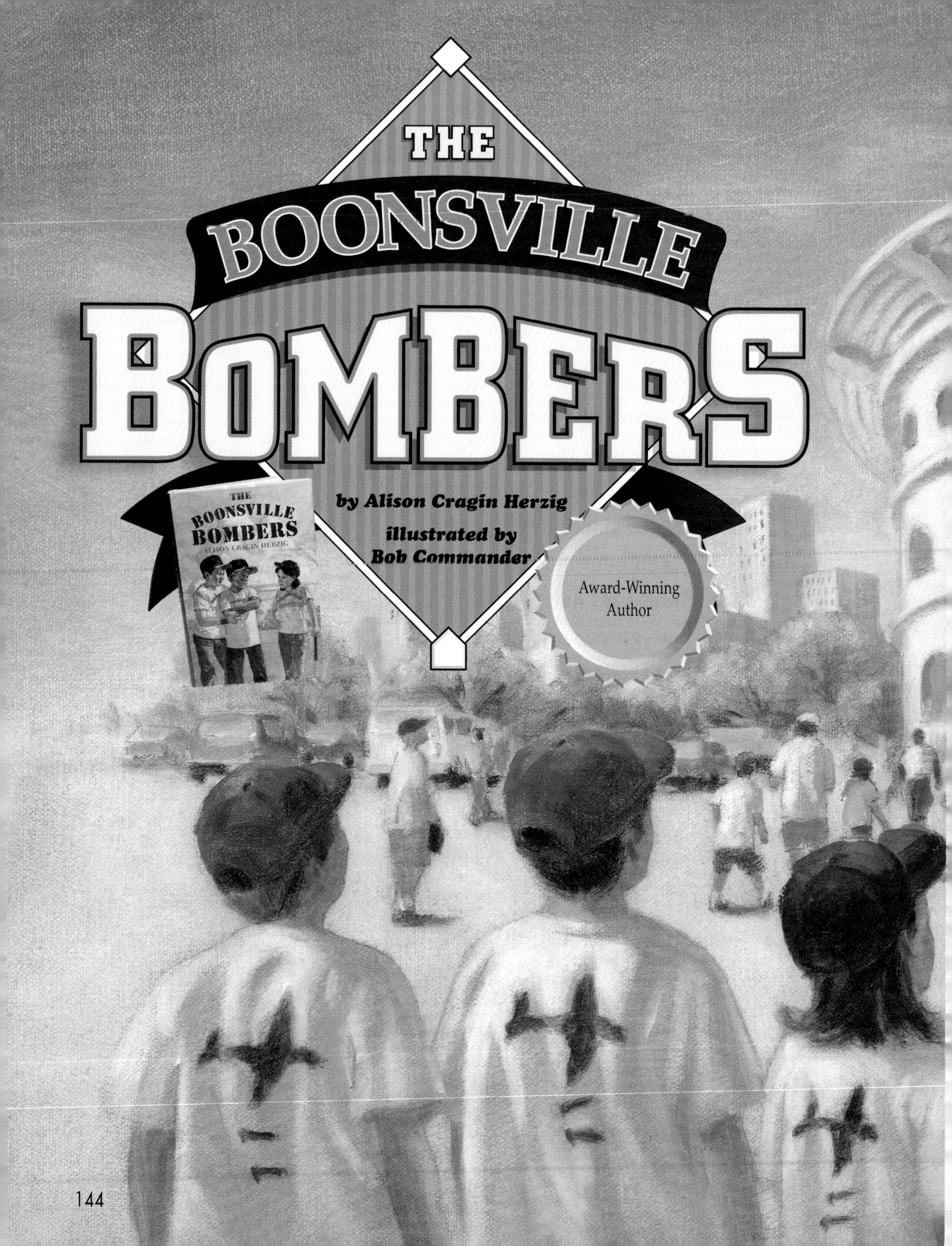

THE
BOONSVILLE
BOMBERS
ALISON CRAGIN HERZIG

Award-Winning
Author

Emma Lee Benson longs to play baseball. She especially wants to play for her brother Michael's team, the Boonsville Bombers. Unfortunately for Emma, the Bombers don't want girls on their team. When Emma, Michael, and his friend Joe go to a major-league baseball game, Emma finally gets her chance to prove she can be a valuable member of the team.

In the Pioneers' half of the eighth inning, Owen Zabriskie came up again. There were runners on first and second and two men out. A great long-drawn-out "*Oh*" filled the stadium. The fans held up an enormous hand-lettered sign in the left field bleachers. 3 OH OH OH OH-WEN! it read.

Emma leaned forward in her seat. Late afternoon shadows covered home plate, but the grass of the outfield was still green in the sun.

The pitcher reared back and threw. Owen swung.

Emma heard the sharp crack of the bat and a huge roar from the crowd. And then the ball came sailing straight toward her just the way it had when she was playing the outfield for the Bombers.

All around her, people were leaping to their feet and reaching up. Then Emma saw the ball begin to curve to the left. There was no way she could make another shoestring catch. She reached out anyway, but the ball hit the steps behind Joe, bounced once, and rolled out of sight.

Emma scrambled after it.

The fat man was trying to squeeze down onto his knees, too. Emma felt someone step on her leg. A hand grabbed at her arm. And then she saw it, under the seat in front of her. It was lying right next to an empty Cracker Jacks box, like a big white prize.

When Emma crawled out from underneath the seat, the stadium was in an uproar. Real fireworks exploded above the scoreboard and all the Pioneer players waited to mob Owen Zabriskie at home plate. The crowd was on its feet, shouting and clapping and whistling, except the fans around Emma. They were still searching for the ball.

"Mikey," Emma said.

"I almost had it!" Joe shrieked at Michael. "Did you see? It bounced right over my head!"

"Michael," Emma said, louder.

"But where did it go?" Michael asked. "Who got it?"

"I did," Emma said.

"Well, I'll be darned." The fat man hoisted himself back into his seat.

"You did?" Michael said. "You sure?"

Emma uncurled her fingers. The ball lay in the cup of her hands.

"Emma has it, Joe! Look!"

"Did you hear that, folks?" the fat man bellowed. "This lucky little lady caught the ball!"

A sea of faces turned toward Emma.

"Let me see it," Joe said.

Emma held it out. There was a dark spot, like a bruise, on the white leather.

"Gosh," Michael said. "That must be where he hit it."

"I want to hold it," Joe said. "Just for a minute."

147

"No," Emma said.

"Hey, we're on television!" The fat man waved his arms at the scoreboard. Emma looked up. She saw a picture of the crowd on the giant screen and then the picture zoomed in closer and she saw herself in her red baseball cap and her Bombers T-shirt. Michael and Joe and the fat man were in the picture, too, right next to her.

The picture faded and there was a new picture of Owen Zabriskie in the dugout giving everyone high fives.

"I don't believe it," Michael said. "Did you really catch it, Emma?"

Emma shook her head. People were still staring at her.

"I deflected it," Joe said. "I felt it touch my fingers."

"Heads up," said the fat man. "Here come the security guards."

Two men in brown pants and white shirts charged up the concrete steps. They both wore police-type badges and one of them carried a walkie-talkie.

"Which one of you kids caught the ball?" asked the guard with the walkie-talkie.

"I touched it," Joe said.

Another roar filled the stadium. Owen Zabriskie had come out of the dugout to tip his hat to the crowd.

"My sister did," Michael said.

"Good for you, missy. But we'll have to take it back now. We'll trade you this brand-new one instead."

Emma closed her fingers around the ball and hugged it against her
stomach.

"Come on, kid. It's a real important ball. Zabriskie needs it for his
trophy room."

"No," Emma said. "It's mine."

"Give it back," Joe whispered. "You want to get us in trouble?"

"But I found it," Emma said.

"Okay, missy." The guard reached into his other pocket. "We'll give you
two balls for it. Two for one. That's some deal, right?"

"No," Emma said in a low voice.

"What do you say, kid?" asked the guard.

"She said no," Michael told him.

"You want to get us sent to prison?" Joe hissed.

"You her father?" the guard asked the fat man.

"My father's in the parking lot," Michael said. "He's going to be waiting
for us at Gate 13."

The people around them began to murmur and shift in their seats. The guard unhooked his walkie-talkie. Emma heard the crackle of static. "We found the kid," the guard said into the mouthpiece. "But she won't give it up. Ask the boss what he wants us to do."

Emma pulled the brim of her baseball cap over her eyes. She tried not to listen to the squawks coming out of the black box.

"Yes, sir. Right away, sir," the guard said into the walkie-talkie. Then he turned to Emma. "Okay, miss. Let's go."

"But the game's not over." Emma clutched the ball tighter. She wished her father was there instead of Joe or the fat man.

"It's over for you," the guard said.

"I'm going with her," Michael said.

"Where are you taking us?" Joe asked.

"Why don't you leave the little girl alone," said the fat man.

"This way," the guard said to Emma. Michael crowded into the aisle next to her. The other guard closed in behind Joe. They all went down the concrete steps.

"Way to go, kid!" someone yelled at Emma.

"Hang in there," yelled someone else.

"Keep moving," ordered the guard.

At the entrance to the tunnel, Emma heard another roar from the crowd. She looked back. The teams were changing sides. She caught a last glimpse of the Pioneers running out onto the bright green field.

"I told you she'd get us in trouble," Joe said. "Now what are we going to do?" Emma looked around the small, cluttered office. Papers covered the big desk and all the pictures on the wall hung crooked. She guessed that they were somewhere in the basement of the stadium.

"Dad will come and find us," Michael said.

"Why didn't you just give them their dumb ball?" Joe glowered at Emma.

"It isn't theirs anymore," Emma said. "It was in the stands." She rubbed her fingers along the seams of the baseball and stared at the pictures. Most of them were of past Pioneers' teams with the dates of the years printed underneath.

"Maybe we could make a run for it," Michael said.

"How stupid can you get," Joe said. "The guards are right outside."

Emma could see them through the window in the door.

"Well, anyway, the game's got to be over soon," Michael said. "Then they'll have to let us go."

"I'm not spending the night here, that's for sure," Joe said.

"Stuff it," Michael said. "Someone's coming."

Emma heard a murmur of voices and the clatter of baseball cleats on the floor. There was a burst of laughter and shouting right outside the door. "Okay, you guys, later," a voice said. "I've got to take care of this first."

Michael moved closer to Emma.

Then the door opened. Owen Zabriskie came into the room.

"Oh, brother," Michael gasped. "It's him!"

He looked gigantic to Emma. From the stands he had seemed normal-sized because the field was so huge, but now he looked even bigger than on television. His cap was pushed back on his head and there was a towel draped around his neck.

"Keep everyone out of here for a few minutes, will you?" Owen Zabriskie said to the guards and closed the door.

Emma stared up at him. She could hear Michael breathing. Owen Zabriskie studied them for a moment. "So who am I dealing with here?" he asked finally.

"I guess me," Emma said. Her voice sounded funny.

"I've got to sit down," Owen Zabriskie said. "My knees aren't as good as they used to be."

"Here," Joe said. "Use my chair."

Owen Zabriskie sat down with a sigh. One leg of his white pants was stained with dirt from his slide into home plate.

"That was a great home run, Mr. Zabriskie," Michael said. "The greatest."

"I got lucky," Owen said. "He threw me a hanging fastball right on the outside corner." He wiped his face with the towel and looked at Emma. "You must have made some catch."

"I didn't catch it," Emma said. "I fielded it."

"Oh, so you're a ball player, too," Owen said. He stared at her T-shirt. "A Boonsville Bomber? I used to play Little League. Is that the name of your team?"

"It's not Little League," Emma said. "It's my brother Michael and Joe and Spike and Ben and Weasel. I play the outfield sometimes with Weasel."

"Weasel?" Owen Zabriskie grinned at her. When he smiled, he looked like the picture on his rookie card, except for the missing mustache. "Weasel?" he repeated, and then he began to laugh. "Tell me about you and Weasel."

So Emma told him about the Boonsville Bombers. "There are only four gloves, so Weasel doesn't get one," she explained.

"That's rough," Owen said.

"I don't have one, either, but I made a shoestring catch," Emma told him. "And Joe has the only bat."

"Who's Joe?"

"That's Joe," Emma pointed. "And that's my brother, Michael. He's a really good first baseman."

"Nice to meet you," Owen said. He turned back to Emma. "So you all take turns with the bat?"

"Sort of," Emma said.

Someone knocked on the door. Owen sighed. "That's the press. Tell them to hold their horses," he said to Michael. "Tell them I'm busy."

"Yes, sir." Michael went to the door and opened it a crack. "Mr. Zabriskie says he's busy. He wants you to hold your horses," he shouted and slammed the door again.

"I guess we'd better get down to business," Owen said to Emma. "What's your name, anyway? I don't think we've been properly introduced."

"Emma Lee Benson."

"Well, Emma Lee Benson, could I have a look at that ball you fielded?"

Emma went and stood beside his chair. "You can see the mark where you hit it," she said.

Owen nodded. Up close he looked a little tired. "I've still got the ball from my first major-league hit," he said, "and this is just about as important to me as that one. So, Emma Lee, do you think you and I could make a trade?"

"Okay," Emma said.

"I'll give you a whole box of new balls for it," Owen said.

Emma didn't answer. She was wondering how many balls were in a box.

"And an extra bat for the Boonsville Bombers," Owen said. "And a glove for you."

Emma didn't know what to say. A glove! A real major-league glove was better than any glove she'd ever seen at the mall.

"You drive a hard bargain," Owen said. "What if I add a glove for Weasel? I don't want to forget Weasel."

"For Weasel, too?" Emma said.

Owen looked up at Joe. "Go tell them I need a dozen balls and a bat and a couple of gloves. And tell them to make those gloves size small."

Joe went to the door. Michael nudged Emma's shoulder. "My card," he whispered.

"Oh," Emma said. "There's something else."

Owen smiled. "I figured I wasn't out of the woods yet."

"It's my brother. He has your rookie card and he wants you to sign it."

"That's an easy one," Owen said. "Get me a pen off the desk."

"Gee, thanks, Mr. Zabriskie," Michael said.

Joe came back. He was loaded with equipment.

"Anything else?" asked Owen.

"Well," Emma said. "There's my aunt Esther. She lives in New York City, but she still roots for the Pioneers. She said to say hello."

"You say hello back from me," Owen said. "And you can give her this." He pulled off his cap. "That's all I've got, except for my shoes. So, Emma Lee, do we have a deal?"

Someone pounded on the door. Mr. Benson's worried face peered through the glass.

"Yes," Emma said. "It's a deal." And she dropped Owen Zabriskie's 3,000th-hit ball into his outstretched hand.

Think About It

1. What event in the story do you think is the most important? Why?

2. If you were choosing sides for a game and everyone's baseball ability was about equal, would you choose Emma to be on your team? Why or why not?

3. When the security guards try to take the ball back from Emma she refuses. Do you agree with her reaction? Explain your answer.

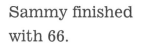

Pressure Cooker

Mark got off to a hot start by tying the record for homers in the first half of a season (37). Sammy challenged Mark by setting the one-month record for homers (20) in June 1998. He had 33 by the All-Star Break, on July 6.

Mark was favored to break Roger's record. A lot of pressure was on him. An army of reporters asked him day after day: "Can you break the record?" Mark kept saying he didn't want to talk about it until he had reached 50 homers.

Sammy, meanwhile, was smiling and having fun.

Two Amigos

Mark and Sammy became good friends as the season went along. Mark broke the record on September 8 against the Cubs. Afterward, he and Sammy hugged on the field.

Each slugger had 66 homers by September 25. Then Mark belted 4 in his last two games of the season to set the record of 70.

Sammy finished with 66.

"I can't believe I hit 70," said Mark. "It's amazing."

It was amazing for baseball fans, too, Mark! That goes for you too, Sammy!

Boom! Mark ties the record with homer number 61.

159

RESPONSE Activities

ON THE PHONE

ROLE-PLAY A PHONE CALL Work with a partner to role-play a phone call between Emma and Owen Zabriskie that takes place a week or so later. Plan what these characters might say and how they might express themselves, based on what you learned about them in the story.

BASEBALL FACTS

RESEARCH STATISTICS In the story, Owen Zabriskie got his 3,000th hit. Find some interesting baseball facts from the present or the past. You might check newspapers, almanacs, sports books, or on-line sources. Create a chart or poster, or think of another interesting way to display the facts you find.

THE DAY I CAUGHT THE BALL

WRITE A VARIATION Suppose it had been you, and not Emma, who caught the ball that day. How would you have handled the situation? What do you think the outcome might have been? Write your own version of the event, with you as the main character.

MAKING CONNECTIONS

WRITE AN ARTICLE Imagine you are a newspaper reporter watching Owen Zabriskie make his 3,000th hit, or Mark McGwire or Sammy Sosa set new home-run records. Write an article describing the event. Explain to your readers what the baseball player accomplished, as well as the fans' reactions. Remember to give your article a catchy title.

IDITAROD

BY TED WOOD

In 1925, the people of Nome, Alaska, desperately needed help. In response, people from Anchorage set out with sled-dog teams on the Iditarod Trail to deliver life-saving medicine. Today, in honor of those brave teams, two races take place along the trail: the famous Iditarod Trail Sled-Dog Race and, for young competitors, the Jr. Iditarod. This selection describes the experiences of Dusty Whittemore as he competes in the Jr. Iditarod.

Dusty and His Sled Dogs

DREAM

IDITAROD DREAM

Dusty and His Sled Dogs Compete in Alaska's Jr.

TED WOOD

Teachers'
Choice

Compete in Alaska's Jr. Iditarod

The day is clear and cold. Mount McKinley, the highest peak in North America, stands like a giant before the truck. The trip south to race headquarters in Wasilla takes four hours.

Dusty's thoughts return to last year's Jr. Iditarod, his first. He remembers the thirty-below-zero temperatures and how his glasses were so coated with ice he couldn't see the trail. And how on the return — when perhaps he'd been headed for victory — he got lost, wandering for four hours before he found the right trail. He finished fourth. But this year his glasses are gone, replaced with contact lenses, and his dog team is the best he's ever had. He can only hope the huskies take him down the right trail.

That evening they reach Iditarod headquarters, where all the racers are gathered for the pre-race meeting. He sees familiar faces from last year — Andy Willis, the favorite to win this year, and Noah Burmeister, who came all the way from Nome. One at a time the fifteen racers pick numbers from a hat to set their starting positions in tomorrow's race. (There is no number 1 position competing in the race; instead the slot is reserved to honor a dedicated supporter of that year's Jr. Iditarod race.) The racers start two minutes apart. Dusty

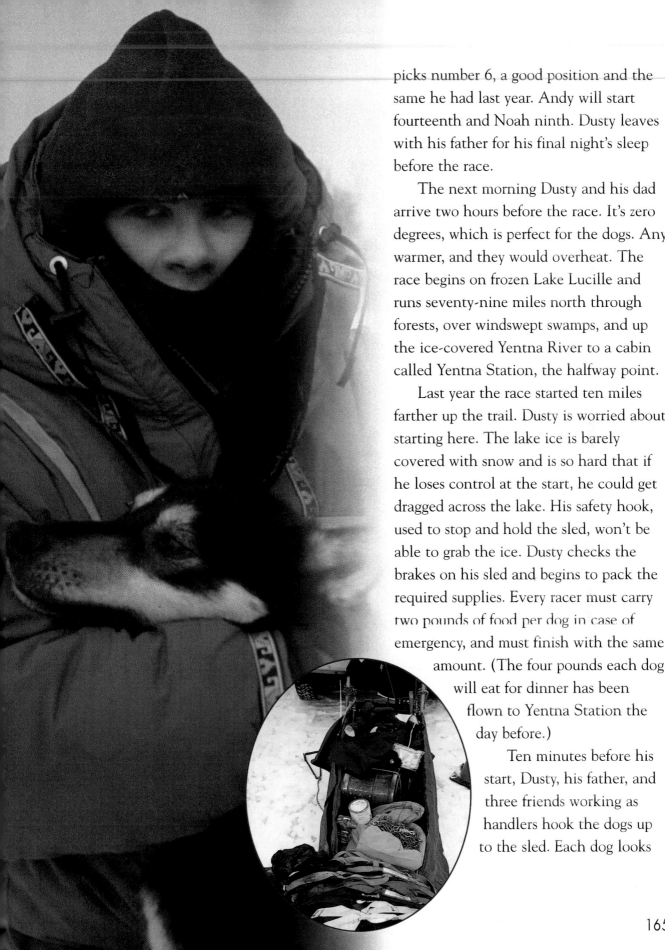

picks number 6, a good position and the same he had last year. Andy will start fourteenth and Noah ninth. Dusty leaves with his father for his final night's sleep before the race.

The next morning Dusty and his dad arrive two hours before the race. It's zero degrees, which is perfect for the dogs. Any warmer, and they would overheat. The race begins on frozen Lake Lucille and runs seventy-nine miles north through forests, over windswept swamps, and up the ice-covered Yentna River to a cabin called Yentna Station, the halfway point.

Last year the race started ten miles farther up the trail. Dusty is worried about starting here. The lake ice is barely covered with snow and is so hard that if he loses control at the start, he could get dragged across the lake. His safety hook, used to stop and hold the sled, won't be able to grab the ice. Dusty checks the brakes on his sled and begins to pack the required supplies. Every racer must carry two pounds of food per dog in case of emergency, and must finish with the same amount. (The four pounds each dog will eat for dinner has been flown to Yentna Station the day before.)

Ten minutes before his start, Dusty, his father, and three friends working as handlers hook the dogs up to the sled. Each dog looks

small but is tremendously powerful.
Dusty has to walk each dog from the
truck, lifting its front legs off the snow.
With all four legs down, a sled dog
would pull Dusty off his feet. Even
hooked up, the dogs are so excited
by the other teams it takes every
hand to hold them in place.

Dusty's team moves to the
starting line, straining against
the handlers. His mother rides
the sled with him, stepping on
the brakes to help control the sled.
She's nervous, remembering how Dusty
got lost last time. But she's also very
proud, and she kisses him good-bye
before hopping off the sled.

The dogs are pulling so hard now
that five people can barely hold them
back. Then the announcer yells, "Go!"

The handlers step away and Dusty flies from the start.

They cross the lake safely, following the red plastic cones marking the route. But as they enter the woods Dusty is on edge. He's never done this part of the trail, and it's crowded with obstacles. Snowmobiles roar along the same trail, and within ten miles he has to cross four roads. Sometimes the roads are so slick the dogs fall, or they get confused by the cars and spectators. Dusty knows he just needs to survive this part until he hits the main Iditarod trail.

At the first road, the team roars over the pavement and around a sharp turn coming off the road. But they're going too fast, and the sled skids sideways, crashing into a tree. Dusty stops dead and can't believe he didn't break the sled. *I'm out of control,* he says to himself. *I'd better slow the team down.*

Back on the trail, he uses his track brake to slow the dogs. He gets them into a strong, steady pace and is able to pass two racers only five miles from the start. He crosses the next road and quickly overtakes another racer. Right before the final road crossing, ten miles out, Dusty passes the last racer. He knows he's in the lead now, that his team is running well,

but he can't think about that. He just wants to get through this part and onto the main Iditarod trail, which he knows from last year's race.

Finally, eleven miles out, Dusty hits the familiar trail leading into the thick Alaskan forest. The team is running perfectly now, strong and fast, as they head into the hilly section of the race. Dusty is in a rhythm, too. He runs beside the sled up hills to lighten the load for his team. Around tight corners he jumps from left runner to right runner, digging in the edges to steer the sled through the curves.

The trail is only a few feet wide in the woods, and coming around a blind corner the dogs run smack into two snowmobiles stopped in the path. Unable to pass, the dogs spin and run in circles, tangling their lines before Dusty can get to them. It takes him five minutes to straighten them out and get under way. As he goes around the next curve and down a hill, he spots another snowmobile roaring full speed toward him. The machine almost hits Annie and QT in the lead, but it flies off the trail to avoid the collision. The two lead dogs stop dead, but the others can't. They pile into each other, making a huge tangle of dogs and line.

Dusty can't believe it. Two tangles in less than five minutes. He frantically unknots his team, sure that another racer will catch up to him because of the delays. A tangle is a musher's second-worst nightmare. The dogs can injure their feet in the lines, or strangle when they wrap around each other.

Finally under way, Dusty and the dogs are on edge and can't settle into a pace. *Please don't see another snowmobile*, he says to himself. Then he spots moose tracks on the trail, and his fears mushroom. Running into a moose is a musher's worst nightmare. Because dogs look like wolves to a moose, a moose may attack a team and can kill several dogs before a musher can frighten it off. There's no going around a moose. If Dusty sees one, all he can do is wait for it to move and hope it doesn't charge.

But the team carries him safely out of the forest and onto a wide, open meadow. Dusty passes a small wooden sign that says "Nome 1,049 miles" and knows from the year before that he can relax for a while through these barren flats. The flats lead to frozen Flathorn Lake, three and a half hours from the start. Here, on the edge of the lake, Dusty takes his first break. He tosses all the dogs fish snacks, big chunks of frozen salmon that will keep their energy up. He says hi to each as well, checking their feet for injuries. QT and Blacky have splits in the webs between

their toes, so Dusty puts booties on their feet to protect them as they run.

He takes only five minutes, still expecting to see another racer coming close behind. Trails cross in every direction at the lake, and it's here that Dusty got lost last year. Today, he chooses the right path and speeds out onto the huge snowy lake. It's like running on an ocean of white; Dusty feels relaxed and at home. Out on the lake he suddenly realizes how big his lead is. He can see five miles behind him and there's not one racer in sight. He can't believe it. *Where are Andy and Noah?* he asks himself.

From the lake Dusty turns on to the Susitna River. It looks like a winding snow highway disappearing into the wilderness. Here, he stops at the one checkpoint in the race, and while an official examines his sled and required cargo, Dusty checks the dogs. He decides to take Annie off the lead. She's been looking back while running and seems nervous. She must not have recovered from the encounter with the snowmobile, Dusty thinks.

Dusty moves young Jazz to lead with QT. But Jazz proves too inexperienced, and three miles from the checkpoint Dusty switches Jazz for Bettie. Now the team is running well again, and they move quickly, silently, up a tributary of the Susitna called the Yentna River. There's no need to yell orders here. They know the way to Yentna Station, but Dusty still calls their names to keep them happy.

Just after five P.M. — seven hours after he started — Dusty arrives at Yentna Station, the halfway point and overnight stop. The station is a little log house that can only be reached by plane, snowmobile, or dog sled. Visitors can stay in the house, but racers can't. By the rules, they have to stay with the dogs.

Dusty feels great. He knows he's had a fast race — but, more important, the dogs look fresh and are still eager to run. He smiles to himself, knowing that his training has paid off.

But there's no time to relax. He has hours of dog chores to do. Each racer gets

one bale of straw for bedding; after Dusty ties the sled off to a small tree, he spreads the straw around the dogs. It will protect them from the cold snow as they sleep.

Next, he fires up his stove to melt snow for water. While it heats, he fills a cooler with twenty pounds of hamburger and dry food. He pours the heated water into the cooler, letting the frozen meat soak up the warm liquid. Twenty hungry eyes watch as Dusty finally dishes up the warm meal.

After dinner, Dusty checks the dogs' feet for web cracks, putting on ointment where needed. Then he hears other dogs and looks up. He'd forgotten about the other racers. It's Noah, the second racer to arrive at Yentna — thirty-eight minutes behind Dusty. Andy arrives next, eight minutes after Noah. Over the next four hours the remaining racers straggle in. Everyone is required to stay at Yentna ten hours. Dusty arrived so early that his departure time is three-thirty the next morning. He decides not to sleep and helps the other racers build a big fire in the snow. They all help each other; that's the rule of the wilderness.

Before his three-thirty start, Dusty melts more water for the dogs, feeds everyone, packs his sled, and finally makes sure his headlamp batteries work for the trip back.

It's snowing lightly as he leaves Yentna, and there's no moon. The only light comes from Dusty's headlamp. The dogs are excited to run, but Dusty doesn't like the night. He can't see the trail markers or nearby moose. The dogs are his only eyes, so he chooses Bettie and QT to lead him out. They did the trail once, Dusty figures, so they can do it again.

Once again the dogs are gobbling up the miles. They run the Yentna River and Flathorn Lake in the dark; at first light, Dusty stops at the Nome sign. As he gives the dogs fish snacks, he finally lets himself believe that if nothing bad happens he can expect to win. Dusty and his team move through the hills easily and take all four road crossings smoothly.

Finally, the lake appears, like a welcome mat, and Dusty begins to smile as he heads for the finish. He's running so fast that the spectators and most of the racers' families haven't arrived yet. But he spots his mother and father cheering him on, and when he crosses the finish line his mother showers him with hugs and kisses. His father's proud smile is so big it almost looks frozen with happiness.

TV and radio announcers swarm Dusty. "How does it feel to win, Dusty?" they ask.

"I would have had a big smile even if I'd come in last," he says. "But it feels great to win."

Because he ran so fast, rumors are flying that Dusty has mistreated his dogs, pushing them too hard. But now, looking at them, everyone knows this isn't true. The dogs are still strong, barking, jumping, and eager to run farther. Dusty has treated them just right. He knows they are his trusted partners — and they're champions.

Think About It

❶ How does the Jr. Iditarod protect the racers and the dog teams?

❷ Would you enjoy training for and competing in the Jr. Iditarod? Why or why not?

❸ What does the author do to make the selection about Dusty and the Jr. Iditarod interesting?

TED WOOD

Ted Wood, also known as Edward John Wood, sometimes writes under the name Jack Barnao. In addition to being the author of science fiction, two mystery series, television scripts, a play, and many novels, he is also a photographer. His photos of Dusty and his sled dogs are featured in *Iditarod Dream* as well as many magazines.

RESPONSE

Teaming Up

MAKE A LIST

In the Iditarod, people and animals work together as a team. List other situations in which humans and animals work as partners. If you wish, use on-line encyclopedias or other research tools in your school library to add examples to your list.

Steps Toward a Goal

CREATE A CHART

To win the Iditarod, Dusty had to plan carefully and work hard. Do you have a goal that you hope to achieve? For example, you might want to make the basketball team, learn how to play the guitar, or get better grades in math. Create a chart showing the steps you plan to follow to reach your goal. Use a statement of your goal as the title of the chart.

ACTIVITIES

Iditarod Expressions

CREATE A DANCE

Work with a group to create a dance based on the Iditarod. You might want to show some of the things that happened in the story. For example, you might use pantomime to express the confusion of the dogs when they met the snowmobiles. You might use movement to show how the team ran in a strong, fast rhythm along the trail. Perform your dance for your class.

If Dogs Could Talk

WRITE A DIALOGUE

Suppose the sled dogs could talk among themselves. What might they have said to each other when they heard the rumors that Dusty had mistreated them? Write their imaginary conversation in the form of a dialogue.

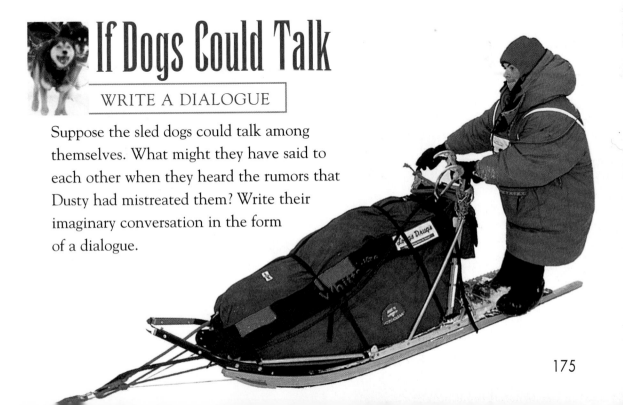

Sequence

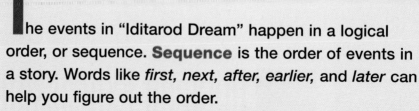

The events in "Iditarod Dream" happen in a logical order, or sequence. **Sequence** is the order of events in a story. Words like *first, next, after, earlier,* and *later* can help you figure out the order.

A diagram can show the sequence of events. In the diagram, one event leads to another event and so on. Look below and notice how one event leads to another.

Dog sled comes around a blind corner.

Dogs run into two snowmobiles.

Dogs run in circles, tangling their lines.

Dusty straightens the lines.

Another snowmobile appears on the road.

Front dogs stop in their tracks.

Other dogs pile into them.

Notice the sequence of events in this passage from "Iditarod Dream." Use a diagram like the one shown to identify the sequence of events.

Dusty's thoughts return to last year's Jr. Iditarod, his first. He remembers the 30°-below-zero temperatures and how his glasses were so coated with ice he couldn't see the trail. And how on the return — when perhaps he'd been headed for victory — he got lost, wandering for four hours before he found the right trail. He finished fourth.

Event

Event

Event

Event

Event

WHAT HAVE YOU LEARNED?

1. Suppose the author had written about the events in "Iditarod Dream" out of sequence. Explain why this would be confusing.

2. Think of something you have learned to do. What sequence of events led to your success?

TRY THIS • TRY THIS • TRY THIS

Unexpected events sometimes result in disasters in stories. Think of a book or movie in which things did not go as planned. What sequence of events resulted in the disaster? Use a diagram like the one above to show the sequence.

Visit *The Learning Site!*
www.harcourtschool.com

Woodsong

BY GARY PAULSEN

ILLUSTRATED BY LEE CHRISTIANSEN

ALA Notable Book
Teachers' Choice
SLJ Best Book

Author Gary Paulsen once
lived deep in the Minnesota
wilderness in the company of forty-
one sled dogs. He observed these
beautiful animals closely, made
connections with many of them, and
learned powerful lessons about
toughness, trust, and teamwork.

It is always possible to learn from dogs and in fact the longer I'm with them the more I understand how little I know. But there was one dog who taught me the most. Just one dog.

Storm.

First dog.

He has already been spoken of once here when he taught me about heart and the will to pull. But there was more to him, so much more that he in truth could take a whole book.

Joy, loyalty, toughness, peacefulness—all of these were part of Storm. Lessons about life and, finally, lessons about death came from him.

He had a bear's ears. He was brindle colored and built like a truck, and his ears were rounded when we got him so that they looked like bear cub ears. They gave him a comical look when he was young that somehow hung onto him even when he grew old. He had a sense of humor to match his ears, and when he grew truly old he somehow resembled George Burns.

At peak, he was a mighty dog. He pulled like a machine. Until we retired him and used him only for training puppies, until we let him loose to enjoy his age, he pulled, his back over in the power curve so that nothing could stop the sled.

In his fourth or fifth year as a puller he started doing tricks. First he would play jokes on the dog pulling next to him. On long runs he would become bored and when we least expected it he would reach across the gangline and snort wind into the ear of the dog next to him. I ran him with many different dogs and he did it to all of them—chuckling when the dog jumped and shook his or her head—but I never saw a single dog get mad at him for it. Oh, there was once a dog named Fonzie who nearly took his head off, but Fonzie wasn't really mad at him so much as surprised. Fonzie once nailed me through the wrist for waking him up too suddenly when he was sleeping. I'd reached down and touched him before whispering his name.

Small jokes. Gentle jokes, Storm played. He took to hiding things from me. At first I couldn't understand where things were going. I would put a bootie down while working on a dog and it would disappear. I lost a small ladle I used for watering each dog, a cloth glove liner I took off while working on a dog's feet, a roll of tape, and finally, a hat.

He was so clever.

When I lost the hat it was a hot day and I had taken the hat off while I worked on a dog's harness. The dog was just ahead of Storm and when I kneeled to work on the harness—he'd chewed almost through the side of it while running—I put the hat down on the snow near Storm.

Or thought I had. When I had changed the dog's harness I turned and the hat was gone. I looked around, moved the dogs, looked under them, then shrugged. At first I was sure I'd put the hat down, then, when I couldn't find it, I became less sure and at last I thought perhaps I had left it at home or dropped it somewhere on the run.

Storm sat quietly, looking ahead down the trail, not showing anything at all.

I went back to the sled, reached down to disengage the hook and when I did, the dogs exploded forward. I was not quite on the sled when they took off so I was knocked slightly off balance. I leaned over to the right to regain myself, and when I did I accidentally dragged the hook through the snow.

And pulled up my hat.

It had been buried off to the side of the trail in the snow, buried neatly with the snow smoothed over the top so that it was completely hidden. Had the snowhook not scraped down four or five inches I never would have found it.

I stopped the sled and set the hook once more. While knocking the snow out of the hat and putting it back on my head I studied where it had happened.

Right next to Storm.

He had taken the hat, quickly dug a hole, buried the hat and smoothed the snow over it, then gone back to sitting, staring ahead, looking completely innocent.

When I stopped the sled and picked up the hat he looked back, saw me put the hat on my head, and—I swear—smiled. Then he shook his head once and went back to work, pulling.

Along with the jokes, Storm had scale eyes. He watched as the sled was loaded, carefully calculated the weight of each item, and let his disapproval be known if it went too far.

One winter a friend gave us a parlor stove with nickel trim. It was not an enormous stove, but it had some weight to it and some bulk. This friend lived twelve miles away—twelve miles over two fair hills followed by about eight miles on an old, abandoned railroad grade. We needed the stove badly (our old barrel stove had started to burn through) so I took off with the team to pick it up. I left early in the morning because I wanted to get back that same day. It had snowed four or five inches, so the dogs would have to break trail. By the time we had done the hills and the railroad grade, pushing in new snow all the time, they were ready for a rest. I ran them the last two miles to where the stove was and unhooked their tugs so they could rest while I had coffee.

We stopped for an hour at least, the dogs sleeping quietly. When it was time to go my friend and I carried the stove outside and put it in the sled. The dogs didn't move.

Except for Storm.

He raised his head, opened one eye, did a perfect double take—both eyes opening wide—and sat up. He had been facing the front. Now he turned around to face the sled—so he was facing away from the direction we had to travel when we left—and watched us load the sled.

It took some time as the stove barely fit on the sled and had to be jiggled and shuffled around to get it down between the side rails.

Through it all Storm sat and watched us, his face a study in interest. He did not get up, but sat on his back end and when I was done and ready to go I hooked all the dogs back in harness—which involved hooking the tugs to the rear ties on their harnesses. The dogs knew this meant we were going to head home so they got up and started slamming against the tugs, trying to get the sled to move.

All of them, that is, but Storm.

Storm sat backward, the tug hooked up but hanging down. The other dogs were screaming to run, but Storm sat and stared at the stove.

Not at me, not at the sled, but at the stove itself. Then he raised his lips, bared his teeth, and growled at the stove.

When he was finished growling he snorted twice, stood, turned away from the stove, and started to pull. But each time we stopped at the tops of the hills to let the dogs catch their breath after pulling the sled and stove up the steep incline, Storm turned and growled at the stove.

The enemy.

The weight on the sled.

I do not know how many miles Storm and I ran together. Eight, ten, perhaps twelve thousand miles. He was one of the first dogs and taught me the most and as we worked together he came to know me better than perhaps even my own family. He could look once at my shoulders and tell how I was feeling, tell how far we were to run, how fast we had to run—knew it all.

When I started to run long, moved from running a work team, a trapline team, to training for the Iditarod, Storm took it in stride, changed the pace down to the long trot, matched what was needed, and settled in for the long haul.

He did get bored, however, and one day while we were running a long run he started doing a thing that would stay with him—with us—until the end. We had gone forty or fifty miles on a calm, even day with no bad wind. The temperature was a perfect ten below zero. The sun was bright, everything was moving well, and the dogs had settled into the rhythm that could take them a hundred or a thousand miles.

And Storm got bored.

At a curve in the trail a small branch came out over the path we were running and as Storm passed beneath the limb he jumped up and grabbed it, broke a short piece off—about a foot long—and kept it in his mouth.

All day.

And into the night. He ran, carrying the stick like a toy, and when we stopped to feed or rest he would put the stick down, eat, then pick it up again. He would put the stick down carefully in front of him, or across his paws, and sleep, and when he awakened he would pick up the stick and it soon became a thing between us, the stick.

He would show it to me, making a contact, a connection between us, each time we stopped. I would pet him on top of the head and take the stick from him—he would emit a low, gentle growl when I took the stick. I'd "examine" it closely, nod and seem to approve of it, and hand it back to him.

Each day we ran he would pick a different stick. And each time I would have to approve of it, and after a time, after weeks and months, I realized that he was using the sticks as a way to communicate with me, to tell me that everything was all right, that I was doing the right thing.

Once when I pushed them too hard during a pre-Iditarod race—when I thought it was important to compete and win (a feeling that didn't last long)—I walked up to Storm and as I came close to him he pointedly dropped the stick. I picked it up and held it out but he wouldn't take it. He turned his face away. I put the stick against his lips and tried to make him take it, but he let it fall to the ground. When I realized what he was doing, I stopped and fed and rested the team, sat on the sled and thought about what I was doing wrong. After four hours or so of sitting—watching other teams pass me—I fed them another snack, got ready to go, and was gratified to see Storm pick up the stick. From that time forward I looked for the stick always, knew when I saw it out to the sides of his head that I was doing the right thing. And it was always there.

Through storms and cold weather, on the long runs, the long, long runs where there isn't an end to it, where only the sled and the winter around the sled and the wind are there, Storm had the stick to tell me it was right, all things were right.

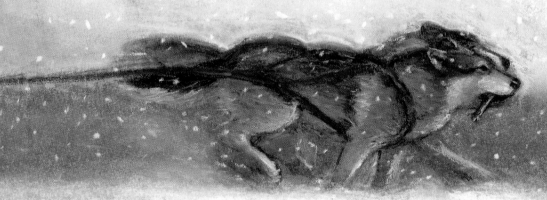

Think About It

❶ In what ways did Storm communicate with the author? How did this communication help them work together?

❷ Would you like to have a dog like Storm for a pet? Why or why not?

❸ What does the author do to give you a clear and vivid mental picture of Storm?

MEET THE AUTHOR
Gary Paulsen

Gary Paulsen was not a strong reader as a child. Then one event changed his life forever. He says, "One day as I was walking past the public library in twenty-below temperatures . . . I went in to get warm and, to my absolute astonishment, the librarian asked me if I wanted a library card. . . . When she handed me the card, she handed me the world."

Gary Paulsen is now a successful author of adult westerns, fiction, nonfiction, short stories, plays, and children's literature. He says, "I knew . . . that whether I was successful or not, whether it *worked* or not, I would write until I died. I had absolutely no choice." He has written nearly one hundred books and almost two hundred articles and short stories for adults and young people. He says, "I have become what I hoped for . . . and sometimes prayed for, and never, not in a million years, thought I would become—a successful author."

Response Activities

Personal Opinion

HAVE A DISCUSSION

How intelligent are dogs? How much do they really understand?
Do they experience the same feelings as humans? In a small group,
discuss reasons people might agree or disagree with the author of
"Woodsong." Then pass around a sheet of paper so that each
group member can briefly record his or her opinion and tell
whether it has changed as a result of your discussion.

Storm's Song

WRITE SONG LYRICS

What kind of music would you choose for a
song about running sled dogs? Would the
music be slow or fast, happy or sad? Choose
a piece of music that you think expresses
something about this activity. Create your
own song about running sled dogs by
writing words to go with the music.

Picture This
DRAW A BIG PICTURE

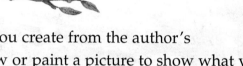

What mental picture did you create from the author's description of Storm? Draw or paint a picture to show what you imagine Storm looks like. Show Storm doing something in the picture that you think is characteristic of him.

Human Humor
WRITE AN ANECDOTE

The narrator tells about Storm's sense of humor. A good sense of humor often helps when people are working together. Think of a time in your own life when someone's sense of humor helped make a job easier or more fun. Write a short story about what happened, and share it with classmates.

Island of Blue Dolp

by Scott O'Dell

illustrated by Rich Nelson

Newbery Medal
ALA Notable Book
Lewis Carrol
Shelf Award

the hins

Karana lives peacefully with her people on an island off California's coast. When her father, the chief, trusts a group of strangers and allows them to hunt on the island, the peace is shattered. The hunters turn their weapons on Karana's people, killing many, including her father, and leaving them with no way to defend themselves.

The new chief decides to lead his people away to a new island — to what he hopes will be a safer home.

We took nothing with us when we thought we would have to flee, so there was much excitement as we packed our baskets. Nanko strode up and down outside the houses, urging us to hurry.

"The wind grows strong," he shouted. "The ship will leave you."

I filled two baskets with the things I wished to take. Three fine needles of whalebone, an awl for making holes, a good stone knife for scraping hides, two cooking pots, and a small box made from a shell with many earrings in it.

Ulape had two boxes of earrings, for she was vainer than I, and when she put them into her baskets, she drew a thin mark with blue clay across her nose and cheekbones. The mark meant that she was unmarried.

"The ship leaves," shouted Nanko.

"If it goes," Ulape shouted back, "it will come again after the storm."

My sister was in love with Nanko, but she laughed at him.

"Other men will come to the island," she said. "They will be far more handsome and brave than those who leave."

"You are all women of such ugliness that they will be afraid and soon go away."

The wind blew in fierce gusts as we left the village, stinging our faces with sand. Ramo hopped along far in front with one of our baskets, but before long he ran back to say that he had forgotten his fishing spear. Nanko was standing on the cliff motioning us to hurry, so I refused to let him go back for it.

The ship was anchored outside the cove and Nanko said that it could not come closer to the shore because of the high waves. They were beating against the rocks with the sound of thunder. The shore as far as I could see was rimmed with foam.

Two boats were pulled up on the beach. Beside them stood four white men and as we came down the trail, one of the men beckoned us to walk faster. He spoke to us in a language which we could not understand.

The men of our tribe, except Nanko and Chief Matasaip, were already on the ship. My brother Ramo was there too, Nanko said. He had run on ahead after I had told him that he could not go back to the village for his spear. Nanko said that he had jumped into the first boat that left the cove.

Matasaip divided the women into two groups. The boats were pushed into the water, and while they bobbed about we scrambled into them as best we could.

The cove was partly sheltered from the wind, but as soon as we went through the passage between the rocks and into the sea, great waves struck us. There was much confusion. Spray flew, the white men shouted at each other. The boat pitched so wildly that in one breath you could see the ship and in the next breath it had gone. Yet we came to it at last and somehow were able to climb onto the deck.

The ship was large, many times the size of our biggest canoes. It had two tall masts and between them stood a young man with blue eyes and a black beard. He was the chieftain of the white men, for he began to shout orders which they quickly obeyed.

Sails rose on the tall masts and two of the men began to pull on the rope that held the anchor.

I called to my brother, knowing that he was very curious and therefore would be in the way of the men who were working. The wind drowned my voice and he did not answer. The deck was so crowded that it was hard to move, but I went from one end of it to the other, calling his name. Still there was no answer. No one had seen him.

At last I found Nanko.

I was overcome with fear. "Where is my brother?" I cried.

He repeated what he had told me on the beach, but as he spoke Ulape who stood beside him pointed toward the island. I looked out across the deck and the sea. There, running along the cliff, the fishing spear held over his head, was Ramo.

The sails had filled and the ship was now moving slowly away. Everyone was looking toward the cliff, even the white men. I ran to one of them and pointed, but he shook his head and turned from me. The ship began to move faster. Against my will, I screamed.

Chief Matasaip grasped my arm.

"We cannot wait for Ramo," he said. "If we do, the ship will be driven on the rocks."

"We must!" I shouted. "We must!"

"The ship will come back for him on another day," Matasaip said. "He will be safe. There is food for him to eat and water to drink and places to sleep."

"No," I cried.

Matasaip's face was like stone. He was not listening. I cried out once more, but my voice was lost in the howling wind. People gathered around me, saying again what Matasaip had said, yet I was not comforted by their words.

Ramo had disappeared from the cliff and I knew that he was now running along the trail that led to the beach.

The ship began to circle the kelp bed and I thought surely that it was going to return to the shore. I held my breath, waiting. Then slowly its direction changed. It pointed toward the east. At that moment I walked across the deck and, though many hands tried to hold me back, flung myself into the sea.

A wave passed over my head and I went down and down until I thought I would never behold the day again. The ship was far away when I rose. Only the sails showed through the spray. I was still clutching the basket that held all of my things, but it was very heavy and I realized that I could not swim with it in my arms. Letting it sink, I started off toward the shore.

I could barely see the two rocks that guarded the entrance to Coral Cove, but I was not fearful. Many times I had swum farther than this, although not in a storm.

I kept thinking over and over as I swam how I would punish Ramo when I reached the shore, yet when I felt the sand under my feet and saw him standing at the edge of the waves, holding his fishing spear and looking so forlorn, I forgot all those things I planned to do. Instead I fell to my knees and put my arms around him.

The ship had disappeared.

"When will it come back?" Ramo asked. There were tears in his eyes.

"Soon," I said.

The only thing that made me angry was that my beautiful skirt of yucca fibers, which I had worked on so long and carefully, was ruined.

The wind blew strong as we climbed the trail, covering the mesa with sand that sifted around our legs and shut out the sky. Since it was not possible to find our way back, we took shelter among some rocks. We stayed there until night fell. Then the wind lessened and the moon came out and by its light we reached the village.

As we neared the huts I heard a strange sound like that of running feet. I thought that it was a sound made by the wind, but when we came closer I saw dozens of wild dogs scurrying around through the huts. They ran from us, snarling as they went.

The pack must have slunk into the village soon after we left, for it had gorged itself upon the abalone we had not taken. It had gone everywhere searching out food, and Ramo and I had to look hard to find enough for our supper. While we ate beside a small fire I could hear the dogs on the hill not far away, and through the night their howls came to me on the wind. But when the sun rose and I went out of the hut, the pack trotted off toward its lair which was at the north side of the island, in a large cave.

That day we spent gathering food. The wind blew and the waves crashed against the shore so that we could not go out on the rocks. I gathered gull eggs on the cliff and Ramo speared a string of small fish in one of the tide pools. He brought them home, walking proudly with the string over his back. He felt that in this way he had made up for the trouble he had caused.

With the seeds I had gathered in a ravine, we had a plentiful meal, although I had to cook it on a flat rock. My bowls were at the bottom of the sea.

The wild dogs came again that night. Drawn by the scent of fish, they sat on the hill, barking and growling at each other. I could see the light from the fire shining in their eyes. At dawn they left.

The ocean was calm on this day and we were able to hunt abalone among the rocks. From seaweed we wove a rough basket which we filled before the sun was overhead. On the way home, carrying the abalone between us, Ramo and I stopped on the cliff. The air was clear and we could look far out to sea in the direction the ship had gone.

"Will it come back today?" Ramo asked.

"It may," I answered him, though I did not think so. "More likely it will come after many suns, for the country where it has gone is far off."

Ramo looked up at me. His black eyes shone.

"I do not care if the ship never comes," he said.

"Why do you say this?" I asked him.

Ramo thought, making a hole in the earth with the point of his spear.

"Why?" I asked again.

"Because I like it here with you," he said. "It is more fun than when the others were here. Tomorrow I am going to where the canoes are hidden and bring one back to Coral Cove. We will use it to fish in and to go looking around the island."

Think About It

1 What problem does the narrator face, and how does she solve it?

2 If you had been a passenger on the ship would you have been in favor of waiting for Ramo? Why or why not?

3 Why do you think the author included the description of the wild dogs?

About the Author

Scott O'Dell

Scott O'Dell lived in many places when he was growing up. One strange and wonderful place was Rattlesnake Island, across the bay from Los Angeles, California. His family lived there in a house on stilts.

In 1960, when O'Dell began to write *Island of the Blue Dolphins*, he remembered those early years on Rattlesnake Island. He and other boys used logs as canoes and paddled with their hands around the bay, exploring the surrounding islands.

Years later, O'Dell and his wife rented a house on the island. Karana, the main character of the story, is based on a Mexican girl named Carolina, whose father took care of that house.

Fond memories of Rattlesnake Island and of Carolina were part of what inspired O'Dell to write *Island of the Blue Dolphins*. O'Dell hoped that his book would communicate a simple message: "Forgive your enemies and have respect for life — all life."

Souvenir

by Eve Merriam
illustrated by Kurt Nagahori

I bring back a shell so I can always hear
the music of the ocean when I hold it to my ear:

then I feel again the grains of sand
trickle sun-warm through my hand

the sea gulls dip and swoop and cry
as they dive for fish then climb the sky

the sailboats race with wings spread wide
as the wind spins them round and they glide ride glide

my lips taste a crust of salty foam
and sandpipers skitter and crabs scuttle home

where I build a castle of Yesterday
that the high tide washes away away

while I keep the shell so I can always hear
the music of the ocean when I hold it to my ear.

Response

Dinner for Two

DRAW A PICTURE

Karana and her brother spend the day gathering food. Imagine that you and a friend are stranded on an island and must work together to find food and prepare your own meals. Draw a picture of the island. Add labels to show where you find foods and what you find in each place. Then create a day's menu based on the foods you find.

In a Basket

MAKE A LIST

Imagine that you must leave your home quickly and can take with you only as much as will fit in two baskets. What will you pack in the baskets? List the items, and add a brief note explaining why you are choosing each one. Keep in mind that you will have to carry the baskets yourself.

Activities

Making Connections

DESCRIBE A BEACH SETTING

Notice how the story *Island of the Blue Dolphins* and the poem "Souvenir" contain descriptions of a beach setting. What words and descriptions are similar? Identify the differences also. Now describe another beach setting in your own words. Describe it in a short poem or short paragraph.

To Stay or Not to Stay

WRITE A NEW ENDING

The narrator of the story swims back to the island to stay with her brother. What might have happened if she had stayed on the ship? With a partner or in a small group, write a new story ending in which Karana stays on the ship and Ramo is all by himself on the island. Describe what happens to each of them.

THEME WRAP-UP

Color Your Words

LOCATE COLORFUL LANGUAGE
Choose three of the selections from
this theme. Find as many colorful
phrases in each selection as you can.
Make a chart like the one below,
showing the selection, the phrase,
and what the phrase means. Then,
write three colorful phrases of your
own. Trade papers with a classmate
to "translate" each other's phrases.

SELECTION	PHRASE	MEANING
"Roberto Clemente"	"did not get much wood on the ball"	"did not hit the ball very well"

Where Are You?

WRITE ABOUT SETTING Think
about the settings in which the
selections take place. Write a
paragraph that compares two
of the settings. What is the
same about them? How are
they different? Then show the
similarities and
differences
in a Venn
diagram.

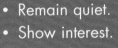

Both

Enter Stage Right

PRESENT A SCENE Work in pairs
or small groups to present a dramatic
reading of one of the selections in
the theme.

Speakers:
- Choose a scene from the selection
  that you want to present.
- Identify the purpose of the scene.
  For example, is it meant to be
  scary, funny, or sad? Keep this
  purpose in mind as you read.
- Picture the scene in your mind
  as you read. Use movement and
  expression to help your listeners
  picture the scene in their minds.
- Practice until you can perform it
  without having to look at the book
  all the time.
- Vary your voice from almost a
  whisper to a shout and from fast to
  slow, depending on the scene you
  are performing. Use your voice to
  help your listeners understand the
  scene's purpose.

Listeners:
- Focus on the speaker(s).
- Remain quiet.
- Show interest.

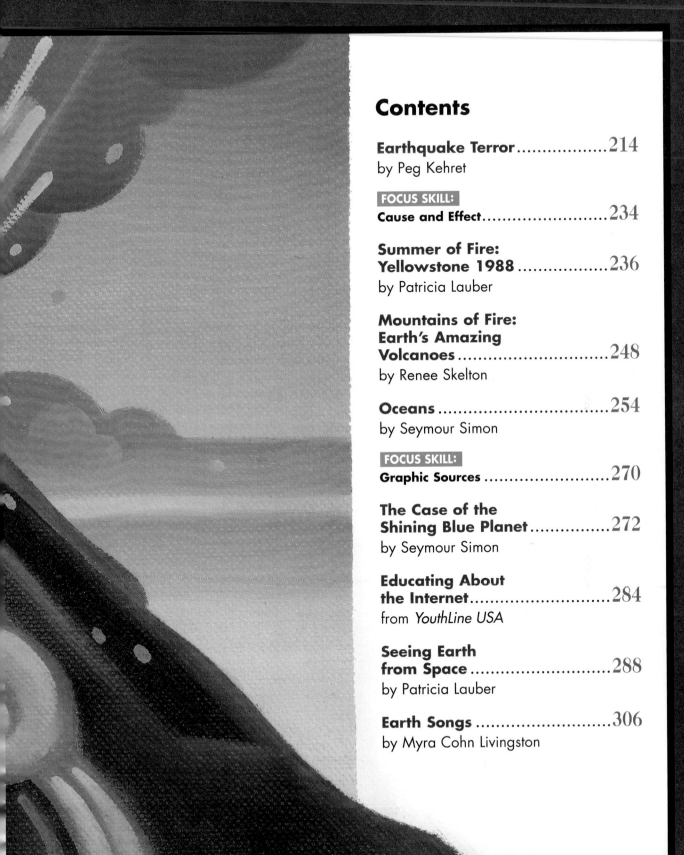

Contents

READERS CHOICE

Volcanoes
by Seymour Simon

NONFICTION

Learn some exciting and explosive facts about volcanoes and how they are necessary as well as destructive to our planet.

Outstanding Science Trade Book

READER'S CHOICE LIBRARY

Earthquake Terror
by Peg Kehret

FICTION

Jonathan and his little sister experience a violent earthquake and become stranded on an island.

Children's Choice

READER'S CHOICE LIBRARY

Birdie's Lighthouse
by Deborah Hopkinson

FICTION

When her father becomes ill, young Birdie must act as
the lighthouse keeper and keep the harbor safe.

Award-Winning Author

Snow and Ice
by Philip Steele

NONFICTION

Learn how snow and ice form and how
they affect our lives.

To Space and Back
by Sally Ride with Susan Okie

NONFICTION

Join astronaut Sally Ride as she shares
the excitement of space travel, and find
out how it really feels to be weightless.

SLJ Best Book

QUAKE TERROR

EARTHQUAKE
TERROR

Children's
Choice

PEG KEHRET

by Peg Kehret
illustrated by Mike Steirnagle

Ever since Jonathan's little sister Abby had an accident, hiking the trails on Magpie Island has become a slow march for the Palmer family. The accident left Abby's legs partially paralyzed, so she must use a walker wherever she goes.

After hiking far away from their campsite, Jonathan's mother has an accident of her own and breaks her ankle. Mr. Palmer must quickly carry her back to the car and take her to a hospital. The family's only choice is to briefly leave Jonathan, Abby, and their dog, Moose, on the deserted island.

"I wonder if Mommy and Daddy are in the car yet," Abby said.

"Probably. I'll bet they're driving out of camp right now. Maybe they're already going across the bridge."

In his mind, Jonathan could see his father unhitching the small camping trailer. He pictured the car going along the narrow, winding road that meandered from the campground through the woods. He saw the high bridge that crossed the river, connecting the island campground to the mainland.

He imagined his father driving across the bridge, faster than usual, with Mom lying down in the back seat. Or maybe she wouldn't lie down. Maybe, even with a broken ankle, she would wear her seat belt. She always did, and she insisted that Jonathan and Abby wear theirs.

Moose cocked his head, as if listening to something. Then he ran toward the trail, sniffing the ground.

"Moose," Jonathan called. "Come back."

Moose paused, looked at Jonathan, and barked. "Come!"

Moose returned but he continued to smell the ground and pace back and forth.

"Moose wants Mommy," Abby said.

217

Moose suddenly stood still, his legs stiff and his tail up. He barked again.

"Silly old dog," Abby said.

He knows something is wrong, Jonathan thought. Dogs sense things. He knows I'm worried about Mom. Jonathan patted Moose's head. "It's all right, Moose. Good dog."

Moose barked again.

"I'm hot," Abby said. "It's too hot to eat."

"Let's start back. It'll be cooler in the shade and we can finish our lunch in the camper."

Maybe he could relax in the camper. Here he felt jumpy. He didn't like being totally out of communication with the rest of the world. Whenever he stayed alone at home, or took care of Abby, there was always a telephone at his fingertips or a neighbor just down the street. If he had a problem, he could call his parents or Mrs. Smith next door or even nine-one-one.

Here he was isolated. I wouldn't do well as a forest ranger, Jonathan thought. How do they stand being alone in the woods all the time?

He rewrapped the uneaten food, buckled the backpack over his shoulders, and put the leash on Moose. The goofy way Moose was acting, he might bolt down the trail and not come back.

Jonathan helped Abby stand up and placed her walker in position. Slowly, they began the journey across the sand and into the woods, to follow the trail through the trees.

Jonathan wished he had worn a watch. It seemed as if his parents had been gone long enough to get partway to town, but it was hard to be sure. Time had a way of evaporating instantly when he was engrossed in an interesting project, such as cataloging his baseball cards, or reading a good mystery. But time dragged unbearably when he was in the dentist's office or waiting for a ride. It was hard to estimate how much time had passed since his parents waved good-bye and walked away. Forty minutes? An hour?

Abby walked in front of him. That way he could see her and know if she needed help, and it kept him from going too fast. When he was in the lead, he usually got too far ahead, even when he tried to walk slowly.

While they walked, Jonathan planned what he would do when they got back to the camper. As soon as he got Abby settled on her bed, he would turn on the radio and listen to the ball game. That would give him something to think about. The San Francisco Giants were his favorite baseball team and he hoped they would win the World Series.

Jonathan noticed again how quiet it was. No magpies cawed; no leaves rustled overhead. The air was stifling, with no hint of breeze.

Moose barked. Jonathan jumped at the sudden noise. It was Moose's warning bark, the one he used when a stranger knocked on the door. He stood beside Jonathan and barked again. The dog's eyes had a frantic look. He was shaking, the way he always did during a thunderstorm.

"What's wrong, boy?" Jonathan asked. He reached out to pet Moose but the dog tugged toward Abby and barked at her.

"Hush, Moose," Abby said.

Jonathan looked in all directions. He saw nothing unusual. There were still no people and no animals that would startle Moose and set him off. Jonathan listened hard, wondering if Moose had heard something that Jonathan couldn't hear.

Abby stopped walking. "What was that?" she said.

"What was what?"

Jonathan listened. He heard a deep rumbling sound in the distance. Thunder? He looked up. The sky was bright and cloudless. The noise came closer; it was too sharp to be

thunder. It was more like several rifles being fired at the same time.

Hunters! he thought. There are hunters in the woods and they heard us move and they've mistaken us for deer or pheasant. Moose must have seen them or heard them or possibly smelled them.

"Don't shoot!" he cried.

As he yelled, Jonathan felt a jolt. He stumbled forward, thrusting an arm out to brace himself against a tree. Another loud noise exploded as Jonathan lurched sideways.

He dropped the leash.

Abby screamed.

A bomb? Jonathan thought. Who would bomb a deserted campground?

The noise continued, and the earth moved beneath his feet. As he felt himself lifted, he knew that the sound was not hunters with guns. It was not a bomb, either.

Earthquake! The word flashed across his brain as if he had seen it blazing on a neon sign.

He felt as if he were on a surfboard, catching a giant wave, rising, cresting, and sliding back down again. Except he was standing on dry land.

"Jonathan!" Abby's scream was lost in the thunderous noise. He saw her fall, her walker flying off to one side as she went down. Jonathan lunged forward, arms outstretched, trying to catch Abby before she hit the ground. He couldn't get there fast enough.

The ground dropped away beneath his feet as if a trapdoor had opened. His legs buckled and he sank to his knees. He reached for a tree trunk, to steady himself, but before his hand touched it, the tree moved.

Jonathan's stomach rose into his throat, the way it sometimes did on a fast elevator.

Ever since first grade, when the Palmers moved to California, Jonathan had practiced earthquake drills in school each year. He knew that most earthquakes occur along the shores of the Pacific Ocean. He knew that the San Andreas fault runs north and south for hundreds of miles in California, making that land particularly susceptible to earthquakes. He knew that if an earthquake hit while he was in school, he was supposed to crawl under his desk or under a table because injury was most likely to be caused by the roof caving in on him.

That was school. This was Magpie Island. How should he protect himself in the woods? Where could he hide?

He struggled to his feet again. Ahead of him, Abby lay whimpering on the ground. Moose stood beside her, his head low.

"Put your hands over your head," Jonathan called.

The ground shook again, and Jonathan struggled to remain on his feet.

"I'm coming," he shouted. "Stay where you are. I'm coming!"

But he did not go to her. He couldn't.

He staggered sideways, unable to keep his balance. He felt as if he were riding a roller coaster standing up, except the ground rocked back and forth at the same time that it rolled up and down.

A clump of small birch trees swayed like dancers and then fell.

The rumbling noise continued, surrounding him, coming from every direction at once. It was like standing in the center of a huge orchestra, with kettle drums pounding on all sides.

Abby's screams and Moose's barking blended with the noise.

Although there was no roof to cave in on him, Jonathan put his arms over his head as he fell. The school's earthquake drills had taught him to protect his head and he did it the only way he could.

Earthquake.

He had never felt an earthquake before and he had always wondered how it would feel. He had questioned his teacher that first year. "How will I know it's an earthquake?" he asked.

"If it's a big one," the teacher said, "you'll know."

His teacher had been right. Jonathan knew. He knew with a certainty that made the hair rise on the back of his neck. He was in the middle of an earthquake now. A big one.

The ground heaved, pitching Jonathan into the air.

Jonathan hit the ground hard, jarring every bone in his body. Immediately, the earth below him moved, tossing him into the air again.

As he dropped back down, he saw the trunk of a giant redwood tree tremble. The huge tree swayed back and forth for a few moments and then tilted toward Jonathan.

Frantically, he crawled to his left, rushing to get out of the tree's path.

The roots ripped loose slowly, as if not wanting to relinquish their century-long hold on the dirt.

As Jonathan scrambled across the unsteady ground, he clenched his teeth, bracing himself for the impact.

The tree fell. Air whizzed across Jonathan as the tree trunk dropped past, and branches brushed his shoulder, scratching his arms. The redwood crashed beside him, missing him by only a few feet. It thudded down, landing at an angle on another fallen tree. Dirt and dry leaves whooshed into the air, and then settled slowly back down.

The earth shuddered, but Jonathan didn't know if it was from the impact of the tree or another jolt from the earthquake.

With his heart in his throat, Jonathan crept away from the redwood tree, toward Abby. Beneath him, the ground swelled and retreated, like ocean waves. Twice he sprawled facedown in the dirt, unable to keep his balance. The second time, he lay still, with his eyes closed. How much longer

would this go on? Maybe he should just lie there and wait until the earthquake was over.

"Mommy!" Abby's shrill cry rose above the thundering noise. Jonathan struggled toward her again, his heart racing. When he finally reached her, he lay beside her and wrapped his arms around her. She clung to him, sobbing.

"We'll be okay," he said. "It's only an earthquake."

Only an earthquake. He remembered magazine pictures of terrible devastation from earthquakes: homes toppled, highways buckled, cars tossed upside down, and people crushed in debris. Only an earthquake.

"We have to get under shelter," he said. "Try to crawl with me." Keeping one arm around Abby's waist, he got to his hands and knees and began crawling forward on the undulating ground.

"I can't!" Abby cried. "I'm scared. The ground is moving."

227

Jonathan tightened his grip, dragging her across the ground. A small tree crashed beside them. Dust rose, filling their noses.

"I want Mommy!" Abby shrieked.

He pulled her to the trunk of the huge redwood tree that had uprooted.

"Get under the tree," he said, as he pushed her into the angle of space that was created because the center of the redwood's trunk rested on the other tree.

When Abby was completely under the tree, Jonathan lay on his stomach beside her, with his right arm tucked beneath his stomach and his left arm thrown across Abby. He pulled himself in as close as he could so that both he and Abby were wedged in the space under the big tree.

"What's happening?" Abby sobbed. Her fingernails dug into Jonathan's bare arm.

"It's an earthquake."

"I want to go home." Abby tried to push Jonathan away.

"Lie still," Jonathan said. "The tree will protect us."

The dry forest floor scratched his cheek as he inhaled the pungent scent of dead leaves. He felt dwarfed by the enormous redwood and tried not to imagine what would have happened if it had landed on him.

"Moose!" he called. "Come, Moose."

Beneath him, the ground trembled again. Jonathan tightened his grip on Abby and pushed his face close to hers. A sharp *crack* rang out beside them as another tree hit the ground. Jonathan turned his head enough to peer out; he saw the redwood branches quivering from the impact.

What if the earthquake caused the redwood to move again? What if it slipped off the tree it rested on and crushed them beneath it? Anxiety tied a tight knot in Jonathan's stomach.

The earth shuddered once more. Abby buried her face in Jonathan's shoulder. His shirt grew wet from her tears. The jolt did not seem as severe this time, but Jonathan thought that might be because he was lying down.

Moose, panting with fear, huddled beside Jonathan, pawing at Jonathan's shoulder. Relieved that the dog had not been injured, Jonathan put his right arm around Moose and held him close.

As suddenly as it had begun, the upheaval stopped. Jonathan was unsure how long it had lasted. Five minutes? Ten? While it was happening, time seemed suspended and Jonathan had thought the shaking might go on for days.

The woods were quiet.

He lay motionless, one arm around Abby and the other around Moose, waiting to see if it was really over. The air was completely still. After the roar of the earthquake, the silence seemed both comforting and ominous.

Earlier, even though there were no other people in the area, he'd heard the magpies cawing, and a squirrel had complained when Jonathan tossed a rock.

Now he heard nothing. No birds. No squirrels. Not even wind in the leaves.

Think About It

❶ How does Jonathan show courage in this story?

❷ How might knowing scientific facts about earthquakes help you get through an experience like Jonathan's?

❸ How does the author create a feeling of fear?

Peg Kehret (pronounced "carrot") has been writing since childhood. She says, "I have always loved to write. When I was small, my grandfather used to pay me three cents apiece to write stories for him." At the age of nine, she wrote, published, sold, and distributed her own newspaper about dogs. During her teen years, she wanted to be either a writer or a veterinarian.

Today she says, "I'm glad I chose writing. . . . When I write, it is easy for me to slip back into my imagination and become twelve years old again."

RESPONSE ACTIVITIES

WHAT AN EXPERIENCE!

WRITE A POEM Imagine how it feels to experience an earthquake, as Jonathan did. How does the earth feel beneath you? What are your thoughts and feelings? Use specific, vivid words to write a descriptive poem about experiencing an earthquake.

EARTHQUAKE ART

CREATE AN ARTWORK Think of a way you can use art materials to represent an earthquake and the changes it can cause in the earth. For example, you might create a painting, a collage, a sculpture, or some other form of artwork.

A GOOD FRIEND?

WRITE A PARAGRAPH Does Jonathan seem like someone you would like to have for a friend? What does the story tell you about the kind of person he is? Write a paragraph explaining why you would or would not like to meet Jonathan and get to know him better.

WHAT HAPPENED NEXT?

EXTEND THE STORY With a small group, discuss what might happen when Jonathan and Abby's parents return. What might Jonathan and Abby tell their parents about the earthquake? How might their parents react? Plan and present a skit to share your group's ideas.

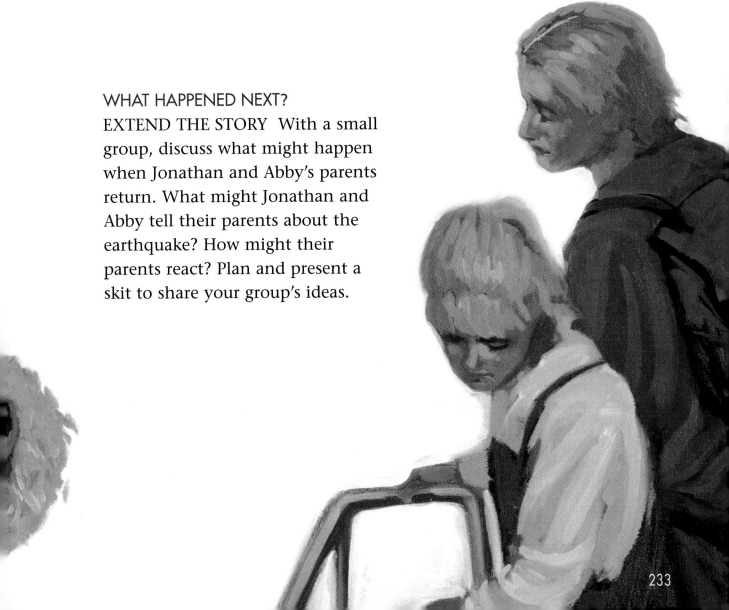

At the beginning of "Earthquake Terror," Moose, the dog, acts strangely. Later in the story the earthquake begins. It's possible that Moose acted strangely because he sensed the danger. This is a **cause-and-effect** relationship.

A **cause** is the reason something happens. An **effect** is what happens.

Cause
Earth moves violently.

Effect
Abby falls.

An effect may have many causes, and a cause may have many effects.

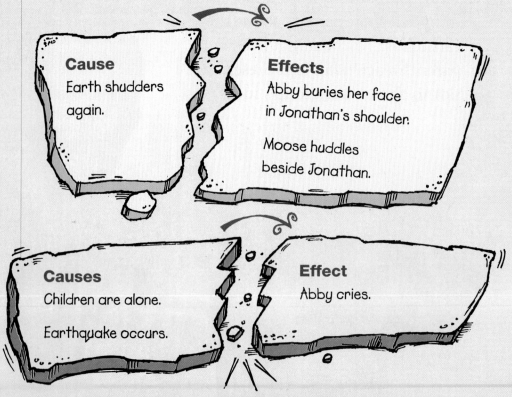

Cause
Earth shudders again.

Effects
Abby buries her face in Jonathan's shoulder.

Moose huddles beside Jonathan.

Causes
Children are alone.

Earthquake occurs.

Effect
Abby cries.

Identifying causes and effects in a selection can help you understand what happens and why.

Read the passage below. List the causes and effects in a chart like this one.

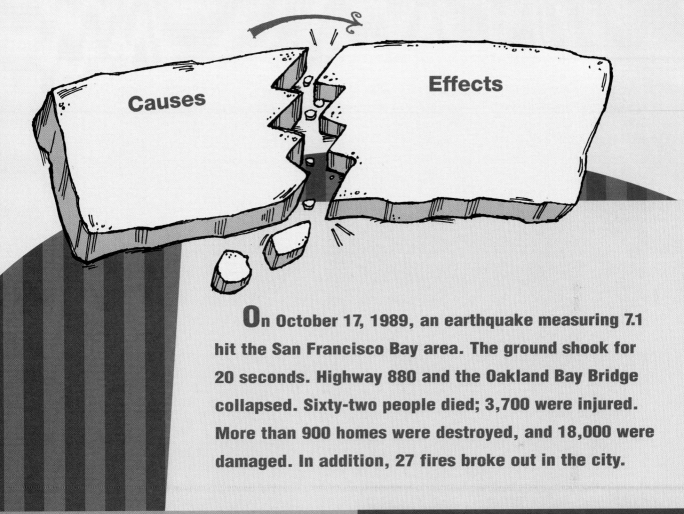

Causes

Effects

On October 17, 1989, an earthquake measuring 7.1 hit the San Francisco Bay area. The ground shook for 20 seconds. Highway 880 and the Oakland Bay Bridge collapsed. Sixty-two people died; 3,700 were injured. More than 900 homes were destroyed, and 18,000 were damaged. In addition, 27 fires broke out in the city.

WHAT HAVE YOU LEARNED?

1. In the story "Earthquake Terror," what caused Jonathan and Abby to crawl under the leaning redwood tree?

2. Sometimes nature acts with enormous strength. Think of a natural event you've experienced. What effects did it cause?

TRY THIS • TRY THIS • TRY THIS

Find and read an interesting article in your local newspaper about something that happened in your community. Create a diagram that shows the causes and effects of the events described in the article.

Visit *The Learning Site!*
www.harcourtschool.com

YELLOWSTONE 1988
SUMMER OF FIRE
BY PATRICIA LAUBER

ALA Notable Book

Teachers' Choice

Outstanding
Science
Trade Book

SUMMER of FIRE

PATRICIA LAUBER

In the summer drought of 1988
lightning strikes started wildfires
across the northern Rockies.

The summer of 1988 was hot and dry in much of the United States. Above plains and prairies, the sun blazed out of an ever blue sky, baking fields and withering crops. Ponds and streams dried up. Rivers shrank. In places the very earth cracked open as underground water supplies dwindled away.

Farther west, forests were tinder dry. Sometimes skies grew dark with storm clouds. Thunder growled and lightning crackled, but little rain fell. Lightning strikes started forest fires that raged across the Rockies and other ranges with the roar of jumbo jets on takeoff. Night skies turned red and yellow where flames soared 300 feet into the air. Smoke, carried on the winds, darkened skies as far away as Spokane and Minneapolis– St. Paul. Airline passengers, flying high above the fires, could smell the smoke. Before the rains and snows of autumn came, 2,600,000 acres had burned in the West and Alaska, an area twice the size of Delaware.

In Yellowstone the fire season started on May 24, when lightning struck a tree in the northeastern part of the park. The fire stayed small. Rain fell later in the day and put it out. That was what usually happened. In Yellowstone, winters are long and cold, summers short and often rainy. Many people thought you couldn't set fire to the forest if you tried.

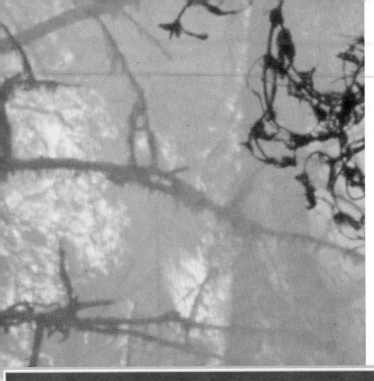

On June 23 lightning started a fire near Shoshone Lake in the southern part of the park. On June 25 another bolt of lightning started a fire in the northwest. These fires did not go out, and no one tried to put them out. Park policy was to let wildfires burn unless they threatened lives or property. Also, there seemed no reason to worry about the fires. Although winters in the 1980s had been dry, with little snow, summers had been unusually wet. The summer of 1988 was expected to be wet too.

But in 1988 the rains of summer did not come. The Shoshone and other fires blazed and spread. By mid-July, 8,600 acres had burned. Park officials decided that all fires should be put out, no matter whether they were wildfires or caused by human carelessness.

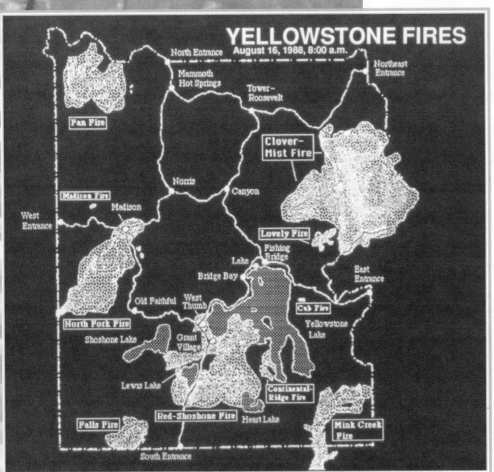

YELLOWSTONE FIRES
August 16, 1988, 8:00 a.m.

North Entrance
Mammoth Hot Springs
Tower-Roosevelt
Northeast Entrance
Fan Fire
Clover-Mist Fire
Norris
Canyon
Madison Fire
Madison
West Entrance
Lovely Fire
Fishing Bridge
Lake
Bridge Bay
East Entrance
Old Faithful
West Thumb
Cub Fire
North Fork Fire
Shoshone Lake
Grant Village
Yellowstone Lake
Lewis Lake
Continental-Ridge Fire
Falls Fire
Red-Shoshone Fire
Heart Lake
Mink Creek Fire
South Entrance

Flames raced through the forests when rain failed to come.

Fire fighters arrived by the hundreds to attack fires from the ground. Helicopters and airplanes attacked from above. But new fires started in the park. In 1988 Yellowstone had more than 50 lightning strikes, twice the normal number. Fires in neighboring national forests swept into the park. Old fires burned on. And still the rains did not come.

Cold fronts passed through, bringing winds of hurricane force with gusts of 60 to 80 miles an hour. Winds whipped and spread the fires and fed them oxygen, which fires must have to keep burning. Big fires met, merged, and became even bigger fires. In forests flames galloped through the tops, or crowns, of trees, through the canopy. Snags—dead trees that are still standing—burned like Roman candles. Boulders exploded in the heat. Sheets of flame leaped forward. Gigantic clouds of smoke ringed the horizon, looking like thunderheads, only bigger. There were days when the sun was no brighter than a full moon.

Fire fighters could put out small blazes . . . but they were helpless in the face of the big ones.

Fires jumped rivers, roads, canyons, parking lots. Glowing embers, some the size of a man's fist, shot a mile or more ahead, starting new fires. Flames were roaring through the park at a rate of four or five miles a day. One fire ran 14 miles in only four hours. On August 20, a day known as Black Saturday, more than 150,000 acres burned inside the park and in neighboring forests. The 2,000 fire fighters could no more put out these fires than they could have stopped a hurricane. But what they could do was defend the park communities—the information centers and the buildings where people slept, ate, and shopped.

By September 6 fire fighters were moving in to defend the area around the park's most famous geyser, Old Faithful. The geyser itself could not be harmed by fire, but the buildings around it could. One of them, the Old Faithful Inn, was the world's largest log building. Now one of the eight major fires in the park was bearing down on it.

Called the North Fork fire, it had started in the Targhee National Forest on July 22, when a careless woodcutter threw away a lighted cigarette. Driven by shifting winds, the fire raced into Yellowstone, turned back into Targhee, neared the town of West Yellowstone,

Flames rocketed into the crowns of trees.

then veered back into the park. There it jumped roads and rivers, snarling its way through the crossroads at Madison on August 15. By the afternoon of September 7 it was approaching Old Faithful. Long before they could see the flames, fire fighters heard the fire's deep rumble and saw a churning wall of dark smoke towering skyward.

Planes dropped chemicals to damp down fires. On the ground weary fire fighters were wetting down buildings.

The fire came on, a mass of red flames whipped by winds gusting up to 50 miles an hour. Sparks and embers were everywhere, flying over the inn, parking lots, and geyser, and setting fire to the woods beyond. At the last moment the wind shifted and the fire turned to the northeast, away from Old Faithful.

Saturday, September 10, began as another bad day. One arm of the North Fork fire was threatening park headquarters at Mammoth Hot Springs, and another arm was a quarter of a mile from Tower Junction. The forecast was for winds of up to 60 miles an hour. But the sky was thick with clouds, and the temperature was falling.

By early afternoon, September 10 had turned into a day of hope. Rain was drenching the area around Old Faithful. The next morning snow blew along the streets of West Yellowstone. It sifted through blackened forests and dusted herds of bison and elk. Scattered islands of fire would burn until November blanketed them in snow. But the worst was over.

At long last the summer of fire had ended. During it, eight major fires and many smaller ones had burned in Yellowstone. To people who had watched the fires on television news, it seemed the park must lie in ruins. But this was not so. The geysers, steam vents, and hot springs were unharmed. Park communities had been saved. Nearly two thirds of the park had not even been touched by fire.

Long hours of hard work tired the women and men who fought the fires.

It was true that many once-green areas were now black and gray. Yet it was also true that they were not ruined. Instead, they were beginning again, starting over, as they had many times in the past. Fire has always been part of the Yellowstone region. Wildfire has shaped the landscape and renewed it. Yellowstone needs fire, just as it needs sun and rain, and its plants have developed ways of surviving fire.

Pockets of flames and embers continued to burn after the worst was over.

Finally the snows of November put an end to the fires.

Think About It

❶ How was the summer of 1988 different from other summers at Yellowstone?

❷ What did you learn in this selection about forest fires in Yellowstone?

❸ How do the author's descriptions help you understand what happened?

MEET THE AUTHOR

PATRICIA LAUBER

How did you gather information to write a book like
Summer of Fire?

When I am thinking about writing a book,
I start by reading everything I can find on
the subject. Then, if possible, I like to go
and see the place for myself. That was
why I visited Yellowstone National Park
the summer after the big fires.

**What did you discover on your visit to
the park?**

The fire wasn't the disaster it seemed on television.
Yellowstone has long, cold winters and short summers.
In these conditions, decay takes place slowly and dead
matter piles up. A forest fire is nature's housekeeper. It
releases nutrients locked up in dead matter and makes them
available again to plants.

Even though I knew how nature worked, I was surprised
to see how quickly life had returned to the burned areas.
Wildflowers were in bloom. Meadows were green. New trees
and shrubs were sprouting. Scientists were busy studying how
some forms of life helped out others. Yellowstone Park was a
showcase of how nature takes care of itself.

MOUNTAINS OF FIRE

Text by Renee Skelton

Earth's Amazing Volcanoes

FOR 600 YEARS IT LAY QUIET, like a sleeping dragon. Then in June 1991, Mount Pinatubo in the Philippines awoke with a violent eruption. The volcano shot a plume of ash and gas more than 20 miles high and sent rocks tumbling down its sides at 100 miles an hour. Farms and villages were buried. Thousands of people fled for their lives. About 800 died. In cities miles from the volcano, ash fell like dirty snow (bottom right). Volcanic gas reacted with atmospheric gas, blocking enough sunlight to cool Earth's surface.

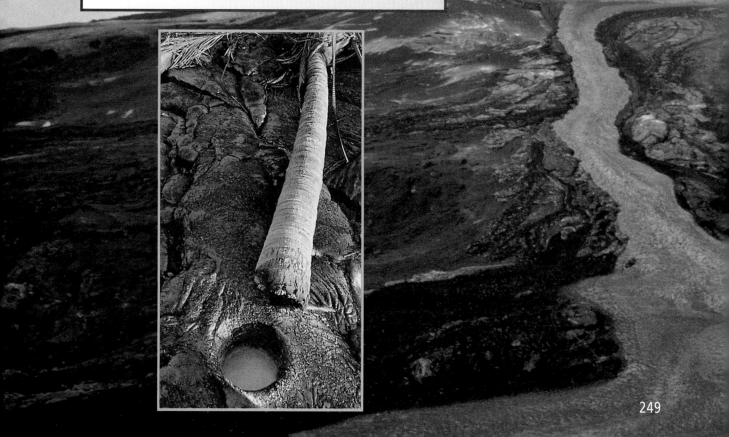

Now, nearly seven years later, much of the land around Pinatubo lies buried under 30 feet of volcanic debris. Each rainy season washes even more cement-like sludge down the volcano's slope, covering more land. The volcano has destroyed the homes of more than 100,000 people.

The world has hundreds of "sleeping dragons" like Pinatubo that may someday awake. Where are they? Can we predict when they will erupt? Read on to learn the burning truth about volcanoes.

KILAUEA: Destroyer, Creator
Hawaiian volcanoes such as Kilauea (kee-lau-WAY-uh) shoot fountains of hot lava (right), but generally do not explode violently like Pinatubo. Still, their rivers of lava burn anything in their path—from trees (below) to houses. Kilauea has erupted continually for 15 years. Its lava destroys but also creates. Flowing into the sea, it forms new land along the coast. Volcanoes started building the Hawaiian islands millions of years ago.

THE BIRTHPLACE of volcanoes lies far beneath the earth's surface. There, incredible heat melts rock. This melted rock is called magma. The magma rises through cracks in the solid rock above it. Gases dissolved in the magma begin to form bubbles and build pressure. When the pressure is great enough, the magma bursts through the earth's surface as lava. The result: a volcanic eruption.

Sometimes volcanoes erupt explosively, spewing hot ash, gas, and chunks of rock. In other eruptions, lava oozes out of the volcano's vent, or opening, and flows down its side.

"Once we know how a [particular] volcano works, we can better predict when something will happen," says Dr. Bill Rose, of Michigan Technological University, in Houghton. He's a volcanologist, a scientist who studies volcanoes.

Volcanologists use several tools for predicting eruptions. Tiltmeters measure changes in the volcano's shape. Seismographs record earthquakes caused as magma moves inside the volcano. Spectrometers detect gases released before eruptions. And photographs taken by satellites reveal clues about volcanic activity.

After identifying a volcano likely to erupt dangerously, volcanologists monitor it with instruments and watch for signals of an explosion. Volcanologists predicted the eruption of Mount Pinatubo and raised the alarm. "We were able to warn people and save lives," Rose says.

1. Thin, fluid magma oozes from cracks but does not explode.

2. Slightly thicker magma traps gases. Pressure builds until ash and rock explode through the volcano's opening. Debris builds a volcanic cone.

3. Thicker, more pasty magma forms a plug dome in the volcano's opening. When the dome bursts, it releases hot ash and rocks that rush down the volcano's slopes.

4. In the thickest magmas, large amounts of gas build pressure. When the gas breaks through the surface, it shoots ash and rocks miles high.

ERUPTIONS—Volcanoes erupt in one of four ways.

PARADISE LOST, An Island Blows Its Top

During nearly 400 eruption-free years, the volcanic island of Montserrat in the Caribbean Sea was a quiet paradise. But its Soufriere Hills volcano (top right) began erupting violently in 1995. Then, in June 1997, the eruptions turned deadly. The eruptions sent fiery ash, gases, and rocks racing down the volcano's slopes toward farms and towns. The eruptions destroyed Plymouth, the capital. They also set trees on fire and spread a thick blanket of ash over the southern two-thirds of the Island.

ALL IS LOST

The Montserrat volcano destroyed a way of life. Warnings came in time for most of the people living close to the volcano to escape. The majority of Montserrat's 11,900 residents have moved off the island (right) and many may never return home.

THE RING OF FIRE

Earth's crust is formed by moving slabs of rock called plates. Most volcanoes occur where two plates collide and one is forced under the other. Earth's heat melts the lower edge of the sinking plate. Melted rock rises to the surface and escapes through volcanoes. Most active volcanoes are around the edges of the Pacific (below), where continental and ocean plates meet.

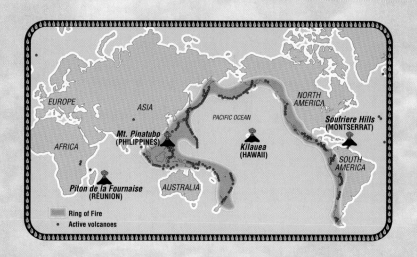

EUROPE
ASIA
AFRICA
PACIFIC OCEAN
NORTH AMERICA
Soufriere Hills (MONTSERRAT)
Mt. Pinatubo (PHILIPPINES)
Kilauea (HAWAII)
SOUTH AMERICA
Piton de la Fournaise (RÉUNION)
AUSTRALIA

▬ Ring of Fire
• Active volcanoes

Think About It

From what you have learned about volcanoes, do you think they are helpful, harmful, or both? Explain your answer.

RESPONSE

To Burn or Not to Burn

WRITE AN EDITORIAL The selection says that it is park policy to let wildfires burn unless they threaten lives or property. Write an editorial stating whether you agree or disagree with this policy. Give your reasons. Use one or more facts from the selection to support your point of view.

Fire Music

DESCRIBE MUSIC Imagine that you are creating a piece of music called "Summer of Fire: Yellowstone 1988." What instruments do you hear? What sounds do they make? What rhythms do you feel? Write a description of the music you hear in your mind.

ACTIVITIES

Making Connections

PERFORM A SKIT With a small group, plan and rehearse a skit about a U.S. Senate committee meeting. Some group members will be senators; some will be scientists. The senators must decide whether to spend more tax money to study environmental changes caused by forest fires and volcanoes. The scientists have been invited to tell the senators why these studies are important. Present the skit to classmates.

Talking to Firefighters

CONDUCT AN INTERVIEW What challenges do firefighters face in your own community? What kind of training have they had? Make a list of questions that you would like to ask a firefighter. Then arrange to talk to one. You may want to ask permission to record the interview on tape. Present what you learn to classmates.

OCEANS

SEYMOUR SIMON

Award-Winning
Author

by
Seymour
Simon

OCE

ANS

Earth is different from any
other planet or moon in the Solar System: It is the only one with
liquid water on its surface. In fact, more than 70 percent of the
earth's surface is covered by oceans. Although we speak of the
Atlantic and Pacific as separate oceans, the world is really covered
by a single body of water in which the continents are islands.

If you visit the shore, you'll soon notice the daily rise and fall of the water, which we call tides. Tides are caused by the gravitational pull of the moon and the sun. Even though the moon is much smaller than the sun, the moon is so much closer to the earth that its pull is much stronger. As the earth rotates, the ocean waters nearest the moon are pulled outward in a traveling bulge called high tide. There is also a traveling tidal bulge on the side of the earth opposite the moon. Here, the moon's pull on the waters is less, so there is a second high tide. Because of the double tidal bulges, most places on the coast have two high and two low tides every twenty-four hours and fifty minutes.

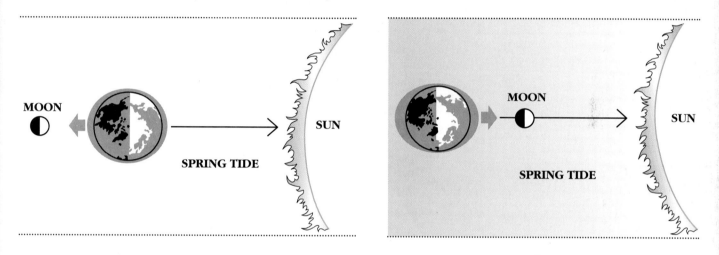

Twice a month, when the sun and the moon are lined up with the earth, their gravitational pulls combine and produce the biggest tides, called spring tides. The sun and moon also pull at right angles to each other twice a month. Then we get the smallest tides, called neap tides.

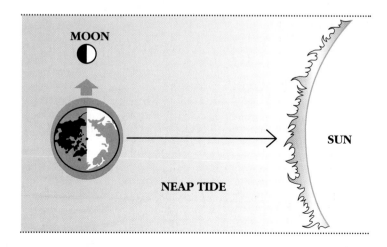

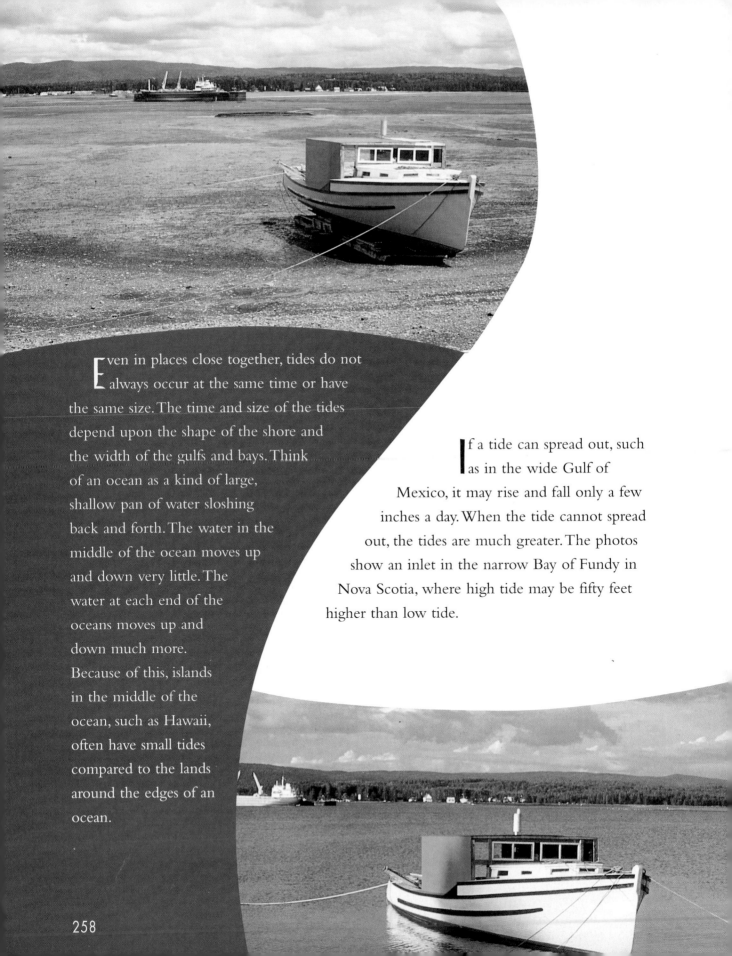

Even in places close together, tides do not always occur at the same time or have the same size. The time and size of the tides depend upon the shape of the shore and the width of the gulfs and bays. Think of an ocean as a kind of large, shallow pan of water sloshing back and forth. The water in the middle of the ocean moves up and down very little. The water at each end of the oceans moves up and down much more. Because of this, islands in the middle of the ocean, such as Hawaii, often have small tides compared to the lands around the edges of an ocean.

If a tide can spread out, such as in the wide Gulf of Mexico, it may rise and fall only a few inches a day. When the tide cannot spread out, the tides are much greater. The photos show an inlet in the narrow Bay of Fundy in Nova Scotia, where high tide may be fifty feet higher than low tide.

The waves commonly called tidal waves really have no connection with the daily tides. The name scientists use for this kind of wave is tsunami, pronounced SUE-nami, a Japanese word for sea wave. A tsunami is generated by a violent undersea earthquake or volcanic explosion. The shock forms a wave that can move across an ocean at five hundred miles per hour, as fast as a jet plane. In the open ocean, a tsunami is only two or three feet high and hardly noticeable; but when it approaches a shore, a tsunami may build up to a huge size and hit with the force of a runaway train.

These three photos show the arrival of a tsunami on the shores of the island of Oahu, Hawaii. The tsunami was generated by an earthquake 2,500 miles away in the Aleutian Islands, Alaska. This tsunami resulted in over fifty deaths and much property damage.

When the wind blows across the surface of ocean waters, little ripples form. As the wind continues to blow, the ripples grow into waves. The size of a wave depends upon the speed of the wind, how long it blows, and the fetch. The fetch is the distance over which the wave travels. The faster the wind, the longer it blows, and the greater the fetch, the bigger the waves.

In the open ocean, where the wind is blowing and making waves, the waves are all different sizes and shapes and go in different directions. As the waves move away from where they began, some travel faster than others and they form groups of about the same wavelength. The waves are now long and smooth and are called a swell.

aves moving across the ocean carry the energy of the wind, but the ocean water does not move along with the wave. As the wave passes, the particles of water move up and down and around in a little circle. If you watch a stick floating on water as waves pass by, you'll see that it bobs up and down but stays in just about the same place. Only the energy of the waves moves forward.

The high spot of a wave is called a crest and the low spot is called a trough. The distance between two crests (or two troughs) is called the wavelength. The height of a wave is the distance from crest to trough.

Storm-driven waves in the ocean can build up to great heights. The largest wave on record was 112 feet high, the height of a ten-story building. Oceangoing ships can ride over most waves. Small ships can ride up one side of a wave and down the other. Large ships can usually ride through waves without too much difficulty. During a hurricane or severe storm, however, a huge wave can dump hundreds of tons of water onto a ship in a few seconds, smashing it apart and sending it to the bottom.

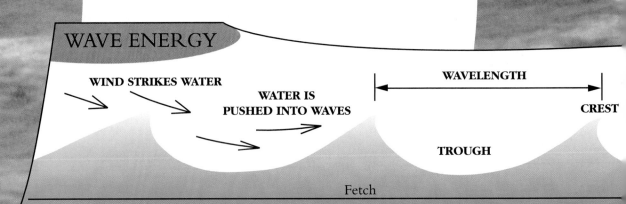

WAVE ENERGY

WIND STRIKES WATER

WATER IS
PUSHED INTO WAVES

WAVELENGTH

CREST

TROUGH

Fetch

CRESTS RUSH FORWARD AS BREAKERS

**BASE OF WAVES STRIKES
OCEAN FLOOR AND SLOWS DOWN**

When an ocean wave reaches the shallow water of shore, it begins to travel more slowly and its shape begins to change. Some people say that "the wave begins to feel the bottom." Waves begin to pile up and grow higher as those in the back come in faster than those in the front are moving.

As the waves slow down, the crest of the wave tries to continue at the same speed, until finally it topples over into the trough of the wave in front and becomes a breaker.

When waves break on the shore, the surf begins. Sometimes surf can break just a few yards from shore. However, if the shore is shallow, surf can form hundreds of yards out to sea. The waves on shallow beaches, such as this one in Hawaii, spill over slowly as they roll up the shore.

Even rocky coastlines are worn away by the power of the surf. The softer kinds of rock are worn away first, leaving rocky spires or platforms of harder rock. These, too, will eventually be worn down by the pounding of the waves. In other places, the incoming surf carries sand particles from one spot to another, slowly building up beaches and dunes. Every moment of every day, the sea is at work reshaping the land.

Think About It

1 Why is it important for us to learn about the oceans?

2 Would you like to read other selections by this author? Why or why not?

3 How does the author help you understand the scientific facts in the selection?

Seymour Simon

I taught science for twenty-three years, and often I couldn't find the right book on a topic I wanted to teach. So I began to write my own books. I try to write the way I talk when I'm teaching and actually talking to students. I want to explain *why* and *how* something happens, not just *what* happens.

If you take a walk and *really* look, listen, and feel the world around you, it can be a strange experience. You begin to observe things you never paid much attention to. You begin to wonder about things that you've seen thousands of times—clouds, trees, rocks, machines. You ask questions: Does that dark cloud mean that it is going to rain? Why do some leaves turn red in the fall, while others turn yellow? What kind of rock has glittery little specks in it? How is an airplane able to fly? These kinds of questions, and the questions my students asked me, prompted me to write science books. My books are full of questions.

Response Activities

Near or Far

DISCUSS IN A GROUP

How far is your city or town from the ocean? Work with a small group to estimate the distance. You might use a map or an atlas to help you. Then discuss the advantages and disadvantages of living as near to the sea or as far away from it as you do. Create a list of the advantages and disadvantages as your group talks about them.

Science and Art

CREATE A PICTURE

Artists who draw or paint nature scenes often use scientific facts to help them create a realistic or accurate picture. Draw or paint an ocean or seacoast scene — a seascape. Use information from the article to make your picture lifelike. Write one or more sentences telling how the information in the article helped you create your picture.

Ocean Moves

CREATE DANCE STEPS

Invent a new dance step based on something you read in the selection. For example, you might call your step "the ripple," "the breaker," "the tsunami," or another name that relates to the oceans. Compare the step you invent with those of classmates. Try combining your ideas to create more complicated steps.

Picture Power

PRESENT A TALK

Imagine that you are a guide at a photo exhibit. Choose a photograph from "Oceans" that you find especially dramatic or powerful. Prepare a brief talk about it to present to your classmates, the viewers of the exhibit. Explain how looking at this photograph can help the viewer understand more about the oceans.

Graphic Sources

The selection "Oceans" includes several diagrams. These **graphic sources** help readers "see" and understand information in the selection. Maps, diagrams, schedules, graphs, charts, and tables are all types of graphic sources.

Take a look at the diagram below from "Oceans." The diagram helps you see information described in the selection. Notice how the artist has combined words and pictures by labeling parts of the diagram.

WAVE ENERGY

Wind strikes water

Water is pushed into wave

WAVELENGTH

CREST

TROUGH

FETCH

Crests rush forward as breakers

Base of waves strikes ocean floor and slows down

Graphics are helpful because sometimes we cannot imagine something until we see it. Graphics help make things clearer.

Read the following passage from "Oceans." Draw a diagram that shows the earth as it is described in the passage. Be sure to include labels in your diagram.

In fact, more than 70 percent of the earth's surface is covered by oceans. Although we speak of the Atlantic and Pacific as separate oceans, the world is really covered by a single body of water, and the continents are essentially islands.

WHAT HAVE YOU LEARNED?

1. Think of something you'd like to tell others about the oceans of the world or about the weather. What kind of graphic might help you communicate clearly — a map, a diagram, a graph, a chart, or a table? What information would you include in your graphic?

2. Look through your other textbooks, the newspaper, or a book from your library. How do the graphics help you understand the text?

TRY THIS • TRY THIS • TRY THIS

Using only a diagram, show how to do a simple task, such as making a sandwich or folding a paper airplane. Then you and a partner can trade diagrams and put words to each other's graphics.

Visit *The Learning Site!*
www.harcourtschool.com

THE **CASE** OF THE **SHINING** BLUE PLANET

by **Seymour Simon**
illustrations by **Leo Espinosa**

"I think this is my breakthrough science discovery, Einstein," Stanley Roberts said. The teenage science buff impatiently pushed back his long black hair, which was forever falling over his eyes. "I know this is the New Year's weekend, but I'm glad you came over to my laboratory. Now take a look at my computer. I just found this incredible website. You won't believe the opportunities to make science explorations that I found on the Internet."

"You mean like the backward space alien," Einstein said innocently. He liked the older boy but enjoyed kidding him. "Or the photograph of the biggest animal ever seen? You thought those people were going to send you a dinosaur photograph taken by a time machine. And when you paid them twenty-five dollars, they sent you a photo of a blue whale, which really is the biggest animal that ever lived."

"Never mind about that," said Stanley impatiently. "Those are small failures in the life of a scientist. This will be a great success. I'm sure of it!"

Einstein walked slowly through Stanley's "laboratory." The attic room was overflowing with electronic gear, computers, a humanoid figure that looked like a half-finished robot, plastic containers, rocks and minerals, and all kinds of test tubes and beakers. It was even more cluttered than the last time Einstein was there.

"Stanley," Einstein said, "I think you should remember that if at first you don't succeed, try reading the directions."

"Is that so, Einstein?" Stanley said. "Then just tell me what you think about this. Look at the photograph on the computer monitor."

Einstein looked at the screen. It showed a picture of a beautiful blue-and-white globe. Einstein knew that it was a photo of Earth taken from space. He knew that the blue and white were caused by Earth's atmosphere, its clouds, and its oceans. Underneath the photo was a caption that said the picture had been taken recently from a space satellite by astronauts as their spacecraft orbited Earth.

"This website is all about sending up a space satellite for communications and research," said Stanley. "The person in charge of the project was a cosmonaut from the former Soviet Union. His name is Dr. Kronkheit. He told me that he and several other cosmonauts had never been publicized because they had been doing spy research."

"I thought spies buy their equipment at a snoopermarket," said Einstein. "What does Dr. Kronkheit want you to do?"

Stanley disregarded Einstein's joke. "Dr. K. wants me to send him fifty dollars. That money enrolls me in the satellite program and allows me to perform one experiment in space. For every additional fifty dollars, I can perform one more experiment. Would you like to join, too?"

"It sounds very strange to me," said Einstein. "Sending up a space satellite costs a lot of money."

"That's what I thought, too," replied Stanley. "But Dr. K. sent me a lot of detailed pages of mathematical formulas that explain how he can send up a satellite for a lot less

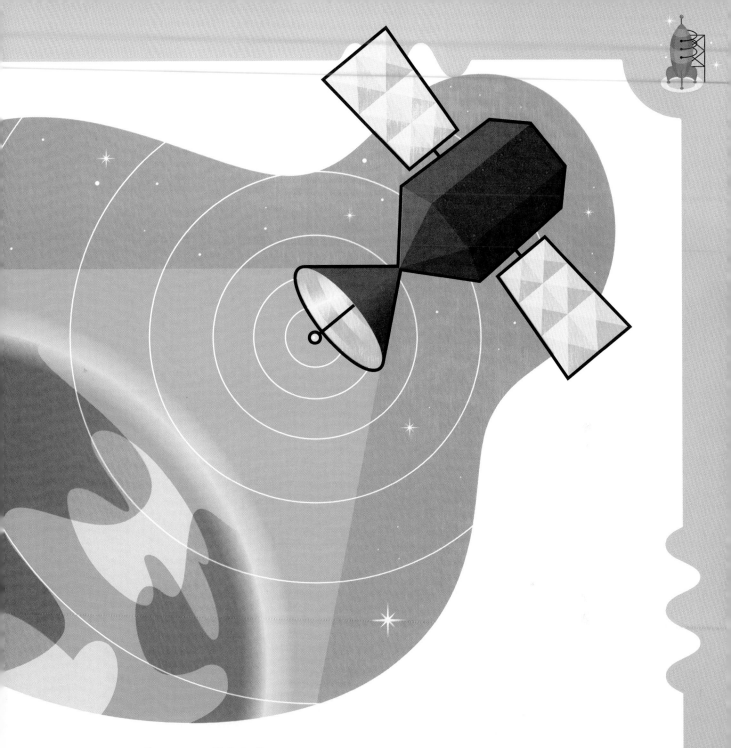

money than you think."

"Do you understand the formulas?" asked Einstein.

"No," admitted Stanley. "But just read Dr. K.'s description of blasting off from Earth. Here it is on his website. Let me go to that link."

Stanley used his computer mouse to move a pointer over a blue line at the bottom of the page that read: *Click here for a description of Kronkheit's first space launch.* Stanley clicked twice with the button on his mouse, and a page of text appeared on the screen. "Read this," Stanley said.

Einstein looked at the screen and began to read:

Starting in the 1950s, experimental rocket planes have taken photographs of Earth from the edge of space. But the most spectacular photographs of our shining blue-and-white planet have been taken by the spaceships that the Soviet Union and the United States sent into space from the 1960s until the present day.

No one who has ever been in a spaceship will ever be able to forget the thrill of first seeing our planet from space. I'll never forget my first liftoff in a rocket ship in the early 1960s. It was a winter day, with blue skies and white clouds. When the rocket ship blasted off, we passed quickly through the clouds and could see their tops below us. The altimeter read one hundred miles, and we were going up fast. All around us the blue sky spread out as far as you could see. Above us, the moon and the stars twinkled in the blue. It was the most beautiful sight I have ever seen.

Einstein pushed back his glasses, which were slipping off the end of his nose. "I don't think the so-called Dr. Kronkheit has ever been a cosmonaut," he said. "And I wouldn't send him any money if I were you, Stanley," he added.

Can you solve the mystery: What made Einstein realize that Dr. Kronkheit was a phony cosmonaut?

"Why?" asked Stanley. "The Earth does look blue and white from space."

"Our planet does look like a blue globe from space," Einstein agreed. "But it's surrounded by darkness. The blue sky, the white clouds, and most of the other colors we see in the sky come from light being reflected in different directions when the light collides with air and water molecules. But as you go higher than twelve miles above the surface, the sky begins turning dark around you, because there are fewer molecules of air and water."

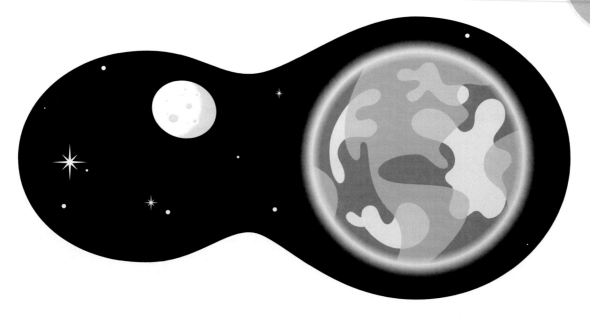

"But the Earth still looks blue and white from space," said Stanley.

"Yes," said Einstein. "If you look down from a spaceship, the planet still looks blue and white. But darkness is all around you, and the moon and the stars are set against a black sky, not a blue one."

"Oh," said Stanley dejectedly. "I guess I shouldn't listen to so-called experts without making sure of their facts."

Think About It

❶ Why is Stanley lucky that Einstein has a good understanding of science?

❷ When do you think this story was written, and how can you tell?

❸ Would you have enjoyed reading this story more or less if the author hadn't challenged you to solve the mystery?

INTE

Vol. 1 Number 1   from *YouthLine USA*

A Worldwide Network

Do you ever use a computer to send e-mail or to "surf" the World Wide Web? If so, you are using the Internet, a worldwide network of computers that communicate with each other. Millions of Internet users around the world can find information, shop, play games, and send messages, using only a phone line, a modem, and a computer.

In the 1960s, the United States government needed a secure method for communicating with the military during war. Knowing that this new method should not rely on a central computer, the designers created a network that would work even if one of the computers in the network failed. Today this network, now known as the Internet, has become a technology with more uses than anyone ever imagined.

About the RNET

First Edition

For Your Information:

The Internet is a wonderful tool for learning new things. But you can't assume that everything on the Internet is meant for kids. Movies and television shows have ratings that tell whether the content is appropriate for kids or not. Web sites don't have any rating system, so you have to judge for yourself. Of course, if you aren't sure, you should always check with your parents or with a teacher.

> **"You can't assume that everything on the Internet is meant for kids."**

Here are a few important rules to remember when you are online:

- Remember that no matter how many times you write to someone, either in a chat room or by e-mail, the person is still a stranger. While most strangers are nice, there are those few who are not. So, you have to be careful . . . always.
- Never give out your phone number or address to anyone.
- Never arrange to meet with somebody in person.
- If you are at all uncomfortable—about what someone is saying, or about something you are reading or seeing on a Web site — shut off your computer. Get your parents to look at the site and explain it to you.

THINK ABOUT IT

Why is it important to know the safety rules when you use the Internet?

285

RESPONSE ACTIVITIES

FACTS THAT MATTER

MAKE A CHART In this story Einstein Anderson's knowledge of science comes in handy. List some facts you have recently learned in science. Then create a chart that lists each fact along with a real situation in which it might prove useful.

FALSE ADVERTISING

CREATE A SIGN How would you warn people about advertisements like the one Stanley saw on the Internet? With a partner, create a sign to post in your school's library or computer center to help students avoid Stanley's mistake.

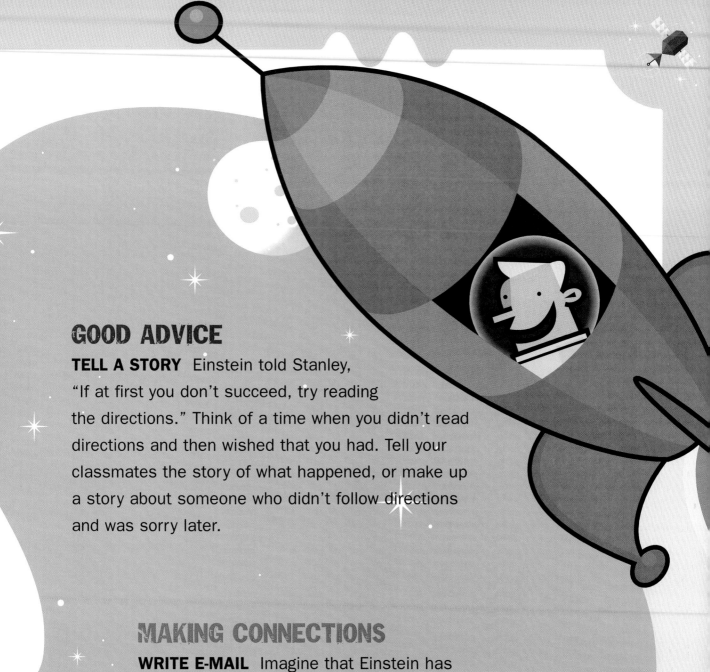

GOOD ADVICE

TELL A STORY Einstein told Stanley, "If at first you don't succeed, try reading the directions." Think of a time when you didn't read directions and then wished that you had. Tell your classmates the story of what happened, or make up a story about someone who didn't follow directions and was sorry later.

MAKING CONNECTIONS

WRITE E-MAIL Imagine that Einstein has read "Educating About the Internet" and wants to tell Stanley about the article. On the computer or on paper, write Einstein's message to Stanley.

SEEING
EARTH

FROM SPACE

SEEING EARTH FROM SPACE

BY PATRICIA LAUBER

ALA Notable Book
Children's Choice
SLJ Best Book

BY PATRICIA LAUBER

PLANET EARTH

On their way to the moon, Apollo 8 astronauts looked back and saw a bright blue globe, partly masked by white clouds and set against the black of space. At that moment they became the first people ever to see Earth as a planet. Their photographs and others show us Earth

as we can never see it for ourselves. They also show us something we know but find hard to believe: We are all flying through space. Our spaceship is the Earth, whirling around the sun at 67,000 miles an hour.

Other new views come from photographs taken by astronauts orbiting a few hundred miles above Earth's surface. These astronauts are too close to see the full face of the Earth. But they see large pieces of it at one time, something we cannot do. Trying to see the Earth from its surface is like looking at a large painting while standing up against it. We see only details. To see the picture, we must back off.

Astronauts in orbit have backed off from Earth. They see the full length of rivers, the folds of mountains, the birth of hurricanes, the straight lines of roads and bridges that mark the cities of the world. Their photographs give us a space tour of our home planet.

Still different pictures of Earth come from satellites carrying sensors, radar, and other instruments. They show us things that the human eye cannot see for itself.

Together, all these views of Earth teach us much about our planet, whether by showing us the unseen or by taking us sight-seeing with the astronauts.

Astronauts sometimes look down at giant storms,
such as the eye of Typhoon Pat over the Pacific.

They also see signs of human activities that worry them. This golden haze over the Indian Ocean near Madagascar is not natural but man-made, a sign of air pollution. The sun is glinting off smoke particles in the air.

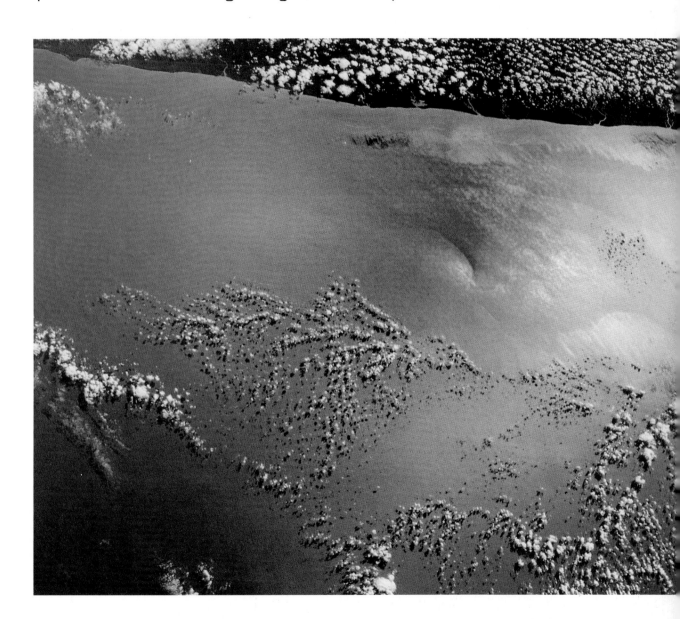

Islands glide by, tiny outposts in the seas that cover two-thirds of Earth. Most of them grew from undersea volcanoes. Eruptions built mountains so high that they broke through the surface of the sea and became islands.

Once an island is born, life arrives. Seeds and plants wash up on its shores. Insects and seeds arrive on the winds. Birds find the island, bringing more seeds in their feathers and on their feet. In time the island may become a place where people can live and which they settle. That is what happened with this island, Santa Cruz de Tenerife, which is one of the Canary Islands, in the Atlantic Ocean. At its center, with a light dusting of snow, is Tiedi, an inactive volcano.

The Hawaiian Islands were also built by undersea volcanoes. The big island of Hawaii was originally two islands,
one built by the volcano Mauna Loa, the other by Mauna
Kea. Huge lava flows from Mauna Loa linked the two
islands and made them one. The clouds in this photograph
are moving from right to left. Those to the left were disturbed and broken up as they passed over the islands.

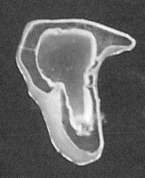

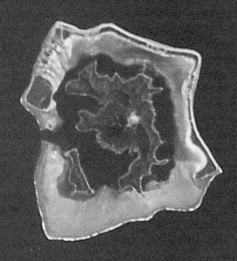

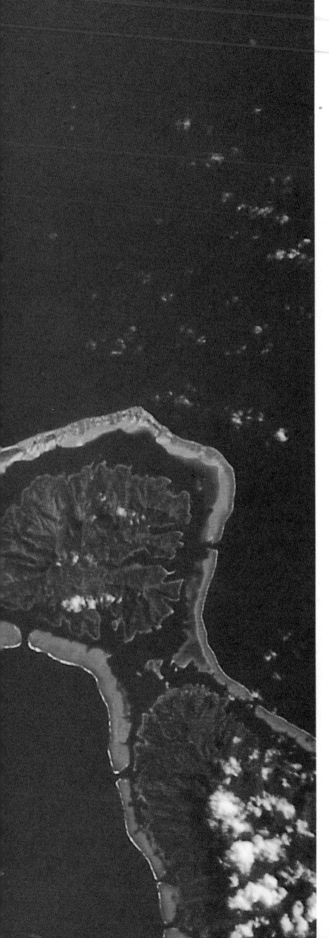

Bora-Bora, center in the picture at left, is a Pacific island that is changing. The middle of the island was built by a volcano. Where the shores of the island shelved off into the ocean, the waters were warm and shallow. Here colonies of corals took hold. Each coral was a tiny animal with a hard skeleton on the outside of its body. At first corals attached themselves to rocks, later to the skeletons of earlier generations. As time passed, they formed a reef around the island. The photograph shows the reef, as well as the lagoon that circles the island inside the reef. Now the volcano is cold and dead. It is slowly sinking back into the Earth. In time it will disappear, leaving a ring of coral and sand with a lagoon at the center. The ring of coral will be the kind of island called an atoll. The same thing is happening to the islands of Raiatea and Tahaa (lower right). Tapai (upper left) has already become an atoll.

The islands of Tarawa (partly cloud-covered) and
Abaiang, shown below, also became atolls many years ago.

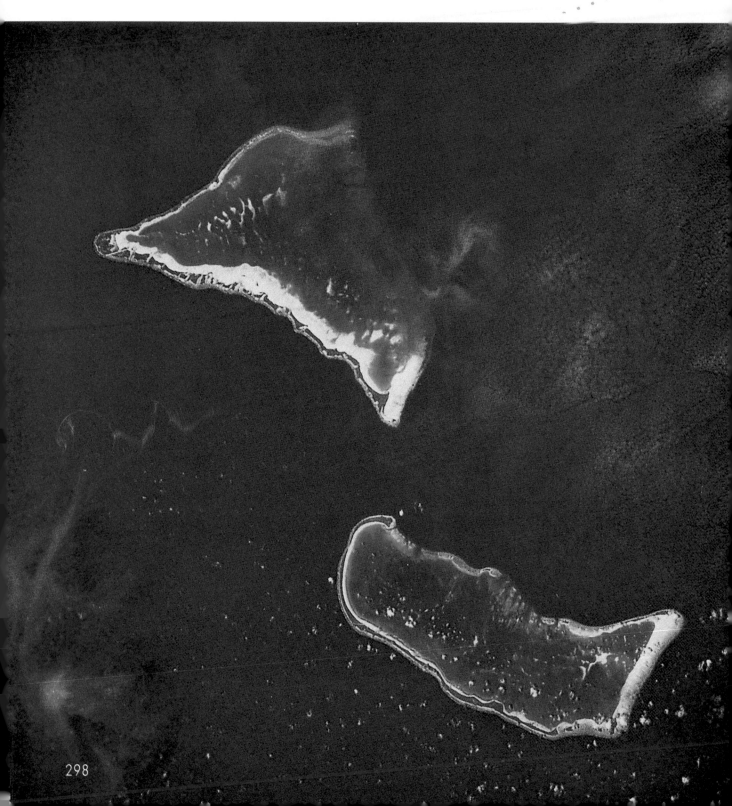

The Earth's crust is broken into huge pieces, or plates, that are in motion. Moving at a rate of an inch or two a year, they carry along whatever is on top of them—ocean floor, islands, whole continents. Millions of years ago, the plate carrying India collided with the plate carrying Asia. When the two land masses were pressed together, the Himalaya Mountains began to crumple out of the crust. As the plates went on pressing together, the mountains grew taller and taller. Today they are still among the Earth's young, growing mountains, and their folded, tilted rock tells of an ancient, great collision.

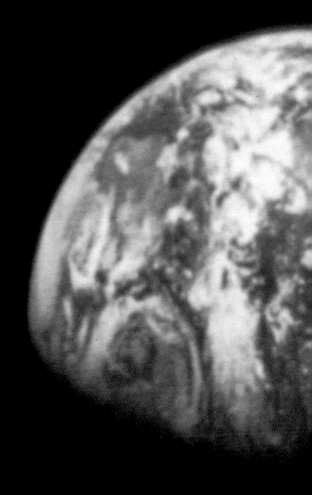

The ability to see Earth from space helps scientists to understand both how the planet works and how human activities are affecting the Earth. It helps all of us to share the feelings of the men and women who have gone into space.

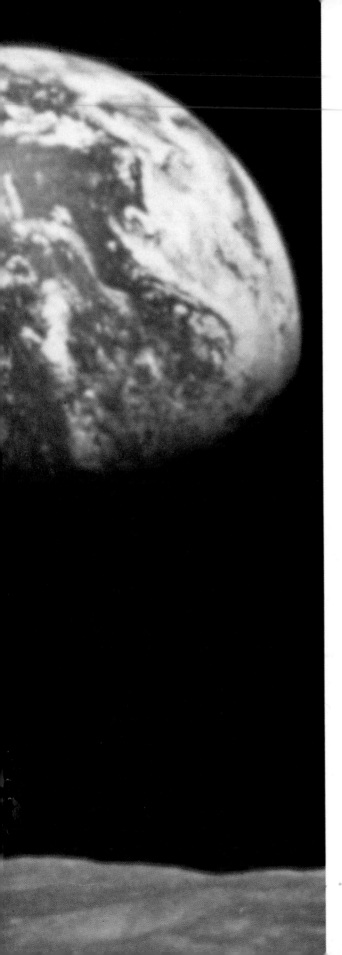

SPACESHIP EARTH

The Apollo astronauts who landed on the moon found themselves in a strange new world. No one had walked this ground before; the only footprints were their own. Nowhere was there a trace of life other than their own, only craters, seas of hardened lava, hills, and rocks. Above them stars and planets shone with a brilliance never seen on Earth, for the moon has no atmosphere to dim their light. Yet for the astronauts the most exciting sight was Earth. It was more than home.

Seen from the surface of the airless, barren moon or from the orbiting spacecraft, Earth was an island of life in the black sea of space, the only outpost of life to be seen.

All the men and women who have flown in space—
Americans, Soviets, foreign guests—have been awed by the
beauty of the Earth. They have also been surprised
by its size. To a person standing on its surface, the Earth
appears both large and sturdy. From space it seems
small and fragile.

These men and women are often concerned by the
man-made changes they see on the Earth. They look down
at the island of Madagascar (below), where tropical forests
are being felled. They see that the ocean around it is
red-brown, colored by soil eroding from land without
trees and carried to the sea by rivers.

They look down and see the slick of an oil spill in the sea.
They think about the birds and fishes and mammals and
plants that will die and about beaches with tarry sands.

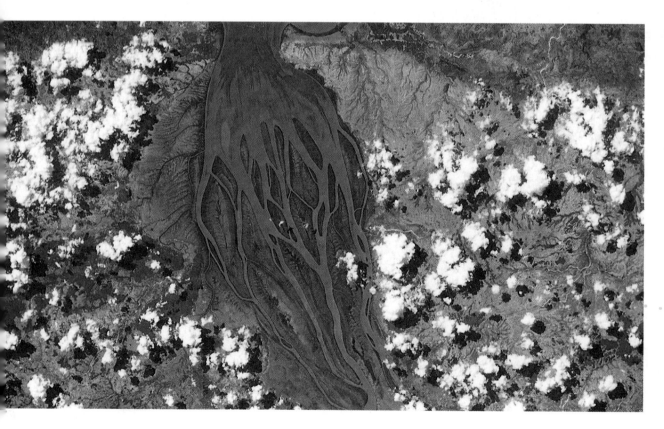

They know that from Earth the atmosphere seems to be boundless, an ocean of air that we take for granted and breathe without thinking about it. From space they see that the atmosphere is only a thin shell surrounding the Earth. Just before sunrise and just after sunset they can see it—the red layer is the air we breathe; above it is the stratosphere; the blue layer is the ionosphere. Beyond the shell is space, black and empty.

Space travelers often return with their thinking changed. On Earth we think of boundaries. The view from space is different. Rivers meander or rush from country to country without stopping, on their way to the sea. Forests reach from one country into another.

Sand and dust from the Sahara spread across the Atlantic (left) and blow toward the Americas. Smoke travels hundreds of miles on the winds. An ocean stretches from continent to continent, and the same waters wash the shores of both.

Space travelers see that the Earth is one planet, small and fragile, wondrous and lovely. It is the space-ship in which we journey around the sun, and our life-support system is its air and waters and lands. We are all, every person in the world, aboard the same ship. And so we must all, in ways large and small, treasure and protect it.

Think About It

❶ Of the main points made in this selection, which are facts and which are opinions?

❷ Do you think it would be a good idea for adults, as well as for students, to read this selection? Explain.

❸ How do the photos help readers understand the text?

What inspired you to write "Seeing Earth from Space"?

This book grew out of my fascination with images of Earth as seen from space. It is one thing to read that Earth is a planet. It is quite something else to *see* Earth from space—to *see* that Earth is a planet.

How did you write the book?

First, I spent several years collecting information from newspapers, magazines, books, and NASA. I wanted to learn how images from space are used by scientists who study weather and climate, the oceans, crops, geology, forests, and ancient civilizations. Then I began to write and to collect images to illustrate what I was saying.

What did you want readers to learn from this book?

My hope was that readers would share the wonder astronauts feel as they look at our planet. I wanted them to see Earth as a place to be treasured and cared for.

Little O, small earth, spinning in space,
face covered with dizzy clouds, racing,
chasing sunlight through the Milky Way,
say your secrets, small earth, little O,
know where you lead, I follow. I go.

Patched together
With land and sea,
I am earth,
Great earth.
Come with me!

EARTH

MYRA COHN LIVINGSTON, POET

Huge continents lie on me, dry land,
sand grained from crumbled rock, now drifted,
sifted to powder. Silt, sand, red clay
weigh down my crust in layers of loam.
Roam everywhere—I am earth, your home.

Mountains rise above me, their slopes white,
bright with fresh snow, tall peaks glistering.
Blistering brown domes bend over, hunched,
bunched together. Some, chained in deep folds,
molded in waves, sleep, wrinkled and old.

SONGS

LEONARD EVERETT FISHER, PAINTER

Hot volcanoes breathe in me, my back
blackened with cinders, scars of old fires,
pyres of ash. My red mouth and throat burn,
churn with hot, liquid lava. Below
flow molten rivers. Turn away! Go!

307

Forests live on me. Tall evergreens
lean against my mountains. Stands of beech
reach to the sky. Huge timber and bark
darken my leaf-strewn floors. Oak, teak, and pine,
vine-twisted rain forests—all are mine.

Waters bathe me, splash over my shores.
Pouring down from springs, ribboned streams
gleam with rills, hurry downwards, dashing,
plashing. Rivers rise. Blue swells leap high.
Dry up my waters and I will die.

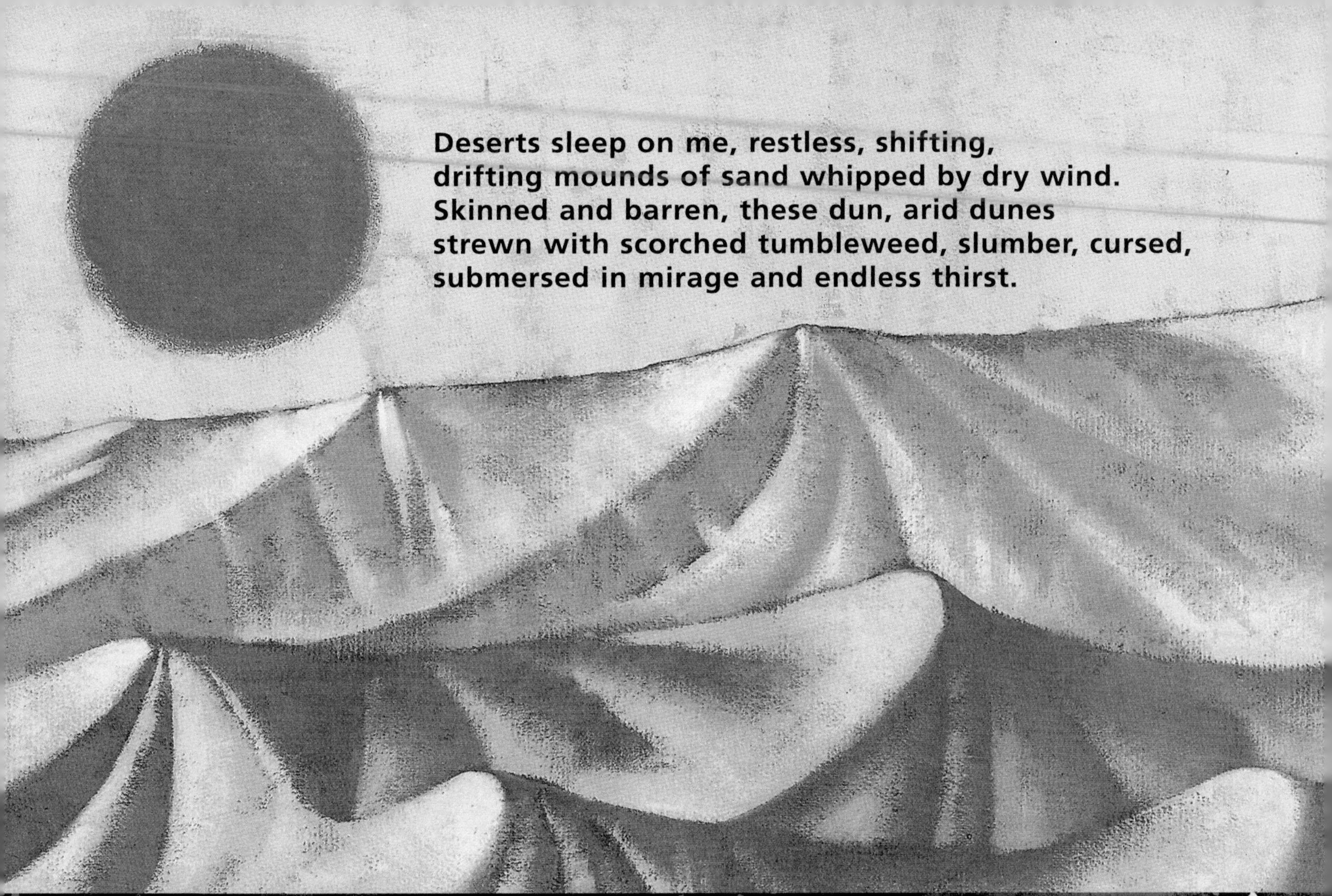

Deserts sleep on me, restless, shifting,
drifting mounds of sand whipped by dry wind.
Skinned and barren, these dun, arid dunes
strewn with scorched tumbleweed, slumber, cursed,
submersed in mirage and endless thirst.

Big O, great planet, spinning in space,
face covered with dizzy clouds, racing,
chasing sunlight through the Milky Way,
say your secrets again, giant O.
Know where you lead, I follow. I go.

Patched together
With land and sea,
I am earth,
Little O.
Come with me!

RESPONSE ACTIVITIES

ASTRONAUT THOUGHTS

ROLE-PLAY A BROADCAST Work with a small group.
Imagine that you are a team of astronauts planning
a live broadcast from space. Each of you will
describe something special you have seen from
your spacecraft. Tell what new ideas this has given
you about our life on Earth.

HOW TO HELP

WRITE DIRECTIONS Write a set of helpful tips
for taking care of Spaceship Earth. These should
be ideas that people can use in their everyday
lives to help protect our planet. Keep the
tips brief, and include simple illustrations
for some of them.

WHAT IT MEANS

PRESENT AN EXPLANATION How could you explain the meaning of the term "Spaceship Earth" to children in the first grade? Prepare a live presentation, or make a videotape that you could show to the children. Use drawings, photographs, or both to help explain the term.

MAKING CONNECTIONS

EXCHANGE ILLUSTRATIONS Choose a photograph from "Seeing Earth from Space" that could be paired with a passage from "Earth Songs." Choose a painting from "Earth Songs" to illustrate a passage from "Seeing Earth from Space." Display each illustration, and read aloud to classmates the passage you paired with it. Explain why you paired the illustrations and passages as you did.

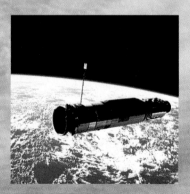

THEME WRAP-UP

What Is the Message?

WRITE ABOUT THE AUTHOR'S MESSAGE The title of this theme is "A Changing Planet." Choose two selections in the theme. How do you think each author feels about the topic he or she wrote about? Write a paragraph that explains what each author is saying about how Earth is changing.

We Want to Know

RESEARCH THE TOPIC In a group, brainstorm topics about Earth, the oceans, Yellowstone Park, or space. List questions that your group would like answered. Then decide on one or two questions to research. Use sources such as your textbooks, other nonfiction books, the Internet, and CD-ROMs to find information. After completing the research, organize the information you learned and present it on a poster, in a chart, or as a report. Share with the class what you learned.

I Didn't Know That!

FIND INFORMATION   What new discoveries did you make about Earth when you read the selections in "A Changing Planet"? List these new discoveries in a chart. In the first column, write the title of the selection. In the second column, write the page number where you found the information. In the third column, write what you learned. Share your chart with a partner. Tell why you were surprised by this new information.

Selection Title	Page Number	What I Learned

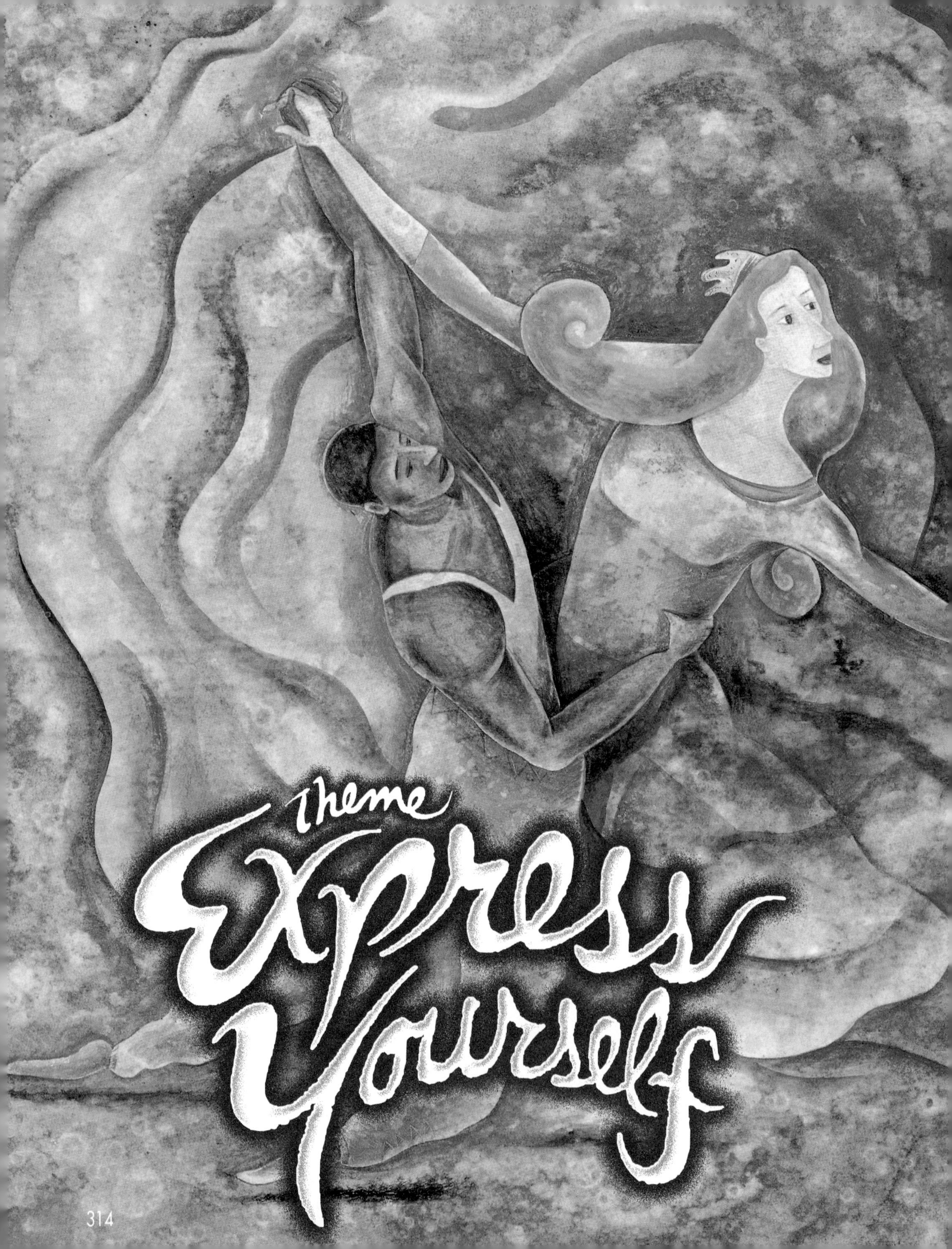

theme

Express Yourself

Contents

Reader's Choice

The Young Artist
by *Thomas Locker*

FICTION

When the king orders Adrian to paint untrue portraits of his royal court, the young artist faces a challenging dilemma.

Award-Winning Author

READER'S CHOICE LIBRARY

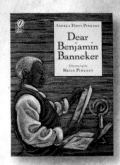

Dear Benjamin Banneker
by *Andrea Davis Pinkney*

BIOGRAPHY

Learn about the wisdom of Benjamin Banneker. This eighteenth-century tobacco farmer, scientist, mathematician, and astronomer used his skills to write a very popular almanac.

Notable Social Studies Trade Book

READER'S CHOICE LIBRARY

Zin! Zin! Zin! a Violin
by Lloyd Moss

FICTION

Instruments of the orchestra take the stage in this rhyming tribute to music.

Caldecott Honor; ALA Notable Book; *SLJ* Best Book; *New York Times* Best Illustrated Book

The Violin Man
by Maureen Brett Hooper

FICTION

Antonio joins in a search for a lost Stradivarius violin in his tiny Italian village.

Live Writing
by Ralph Fletcher

NONFICTION

Find out what fascinating tools writers use to make their work come alive.

Award-Winning Author

317

The following two selections, "Hattie's Birthday Box" and "The Empty Box," both appear in a book titled *Birthday Surprises: Ten Great Stories to Unwrap.*

Johanna Hurwitz, the editor, asked a variety of authors to take part in a special writing project. She gave them only one rule to follow: Write a story about a child who receives a beautifully wrapped birthday present that turns out to be empty!

Notable
Trade Book
for the
Language
Arts

HATTIE'S
BIRTHDAY BOX

written by Pam Conrad
illustrations by Tim Ladwig

from Birthday Surprises

The sign stretching across the ceiling of the nursing home's rec room says HAPPY ONE HUNDREDTH BIRTHDAY, SPENCER McCLINTIC, and on the wall in bright numbers and letters it says JULY 5, 1847 to 1947. Spencer McClintic is my great-great-grandfather, and our whole family is coming to celebrate.

Momma and I got here early because Momma wanted me to help her blow up balloons and tack up the decorations before everyone arrived. She says now that the war is over and most everyone is back home and rations are a thing of the past, we're going to *really* celebrate.

But Grandaddy's nervous. He sits in his chair by the window, rubbing his hands together and asking my mother over and over, "Now who-all is coming, Anna?"

And she keeps reciting the list of everyone who's coming, and he ticks them off on his fingers, but before she's even through, he asks impatiently, "But is Hattie coming? My baby sister? Are you sure she's coming?"

"Hattie's coming, Grandaddy. Don't you worry. Hattie will be here."

Momma doesn't hear, but I hear him. He mumbles, "Oh, no, oh, no, not Hattie. She's gonna skin me alive."

I pull up a stool near Grandaddy. "Don't you like Aunt Hattie, Grandaddy?"

"Oh, I love her to pieces," he answers. "But she's gonna have my hide. Last time I saw Hattie, she was a bride of sixteen, heading out in a wagon with her new husband to homestead in Nebraska. And I did a terrible thing, a terrible thing."

All the decorations are up, and now that Momma's sure everything is all set, she tells me to stay with Grandaddy and keep him calm while she runs home to get the cake and soda.

But there is no way to keep Grandaddy calm. "What'd you do that was so bad, Grandaddy? What was it?"

I watch Grandaddy wringing his hands and tapping his slippered feet nervously. He keeps glancing out the window to the road outside, like he's waiting for some old lynch mob to come riding over the hill. This is the story I finally got out of him.

It had been a warm May morning in 1873, and Grandaddy's sister Hattie McClintic Burden was a new bride ready to set out for a life on the distant, promising plains of Nebraska. The sun hadn't quite risen yet, and she and her new husband, Otto, were loading the final things into the wagon. While it was a happy occasion in that Hattie and her husband were heading out for a new life, it was also a sad day, because no one knew when they'd ever see them again. Grandaddy, who was a young man at the time, didn't know it would be seventy-four years before he would finally see her. But no one ever knew that back then. No one knew how long it would be before they saw each other or if they would ever see each other at all. There were no telephones, no airplanes, just the U.S. mail, slow but reliable, carrying recipes for pumpkin bread and clippings of hair from new babies, and sad messages of deaths.

The night before Hattie and Otto left, everyone had tried to smile and be happy for them. There was a combination going-away party and birthday party for Hattie, who was just sixteen. Everyone brought special gifts — blankets and lanterns and bolts of cotton, a pair of small sewing scissors, a bottle of ink, and even a canary in a shiny cage.

My grandaddy, who was then a young man of twenty-six, had stewed and brooded. He had been ten years old when Hattie was born, and she had always been his favorite. More than once he had carried her out into the barn on crystal clear nights to show her a calf being born. He had taught her to swim in the cool spring. And he had chased away the young boys when they had first started to come sniffing around. His heart was breaking that his little sister was going away, and he had wanted to give her the most special gift. The best gift of all. So she would always remember him and know how much he had loved her.

He would have given her a gold necklace, or a bracelet with diamonds, or earrings with opal jewels, but it had been a rough year, with a few of the cattle dying in a storm and a few others lost to a brief sickness. He had no money, nothing to trade, no real gift to give her. Not knowing what the gift would be, he had lovingly hammered together a small wooden box and carved her initials in it, thinking that whatever it would be, it would be about this size.

It was at the party that night that he realized there was nothing to give her and he concocted his tale. Finding her alone at the punch bowl, Spencer had clasped Hattie's small shoulders in his rough hands, looked straight in her face, and lied boldly.

"I got you something special, Hattie, something so special I think you'd better not open it right away. I want you to just hold on to the box, and don't open it unless times get hard, not unless things get to be their very worst, you hear me? And it will see you through."

Hattie had looked at him with such love and trust. He memorized her face, the same small face she had turned to him when a birth-wet calf had finally struggled to its feet, or when he had carried her out on snowy nights to turn her tongue to the swirling night sky. Her face was soft with love, and he knew she must have thought his gift was something precious that she could sell if crops failed or some other disaster happened. But he lied, he lied.

So that morning before the sun rose, he helped Otto hook up the team to the wagon, and once Hattie was high on her perch beside her husband—looking for all the world like a little child playing farmhouse— my young grandaddy had slipped the sealed and empty wooden box into her lap and backed away. He waved goodbye and never saw her again.

Until today. Aunt Hattie's flying in from Nebraska with cousin Harold and his wife, Mary. Since she was sixteen, Hattie has never set foot off Nebraska soil.

"I meant to finally buy her something to put in the box, I really did," Grandaddy keeps saying. "I thought that as soon as things got a little better, as soon as I had a little money, I'd buy those earrings or that necklace and send it right off to her, explaining everything. But then I don't know. Soon I got married myself, and then there were my own children, and Hattie just never mentioned it in any of her letters." Grandaddy groans and lowers his head into his upturned hands. "Oh, mercy, Hattie's coming."

People are starting to arrive now, and the room is filling with children, laughter, and presents. Many of the people are my relatives who live right nearby, and a few came up from Jersey and Washington, people I'd normally see on holidays and such but never all together like this in one place.

And Grandaddy won't even look at them. He just gets up and walks slowly to another seat far from the window. Out the window I see an airport taxi pull up.

I post myself behind Grandaddy and watch. His hands are

324

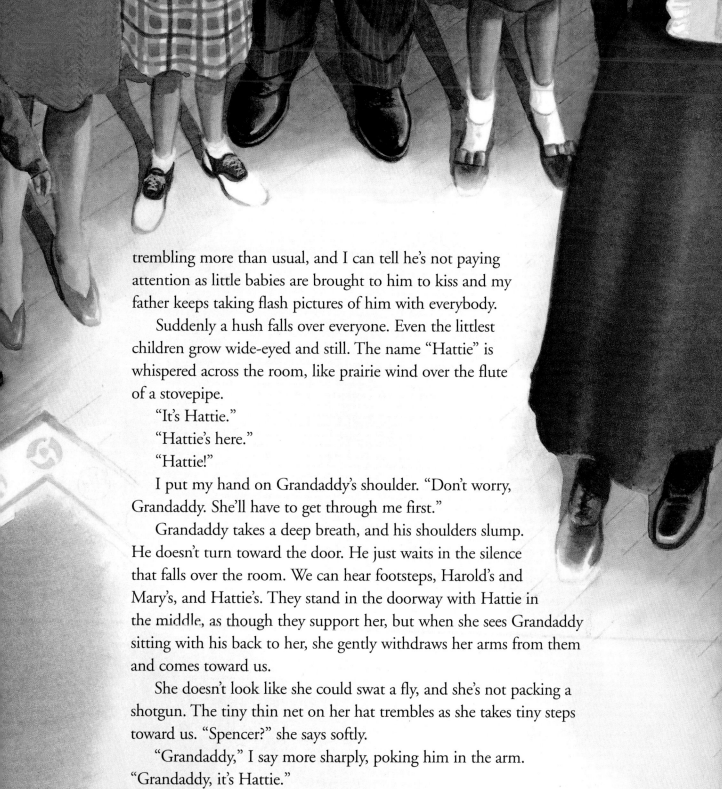

trembling more than usual, and I can tell he's not paying
attention as little babies are brought to him to kiss and my
father keeps taking flash pictures of him with everybody.

Suddenly a hush falls over everyone. Even the littlest
children grow wide-eyed and still. The name "Hattie" is
whispered across the room, like prairie wind over the flute
of a stovepipe.

"It's Hattie."

"Hattie's here."

"Hattie!"

I put my hand on Grandaddy's shoulder. "Don't worry,
Grandaddy. She'll have to get through me first."

Grandaddy takes a deep breath, and his shoulders slump.
He doesn't turn toward the door. He just waits in the silence
that falls over the room. We can hear footsteps, Harold's and
Mary's, and Hattie's. They stand in the doorway with Hattie in
the middle, as though they support her, but when she sees Grandaddy
sitting with his back to her, she gently withdraws her arms from them
and comes toward us.

She doesn't look like she could swat a fly, and she's not packing a
shotgun. The tiny thin net on her hat trembles as she takes tiny steps
toward us. "Spencer?" she says softly.

"Grandaddy," I say more sharply, poking him in the arm.
"Grandaddy, it's Hattie."

He turns then, ready to meet his Maker, I guess, but I'm right there,
right next to them, able to see both their faces, and there is nothing but
pure love, pure and powerful and undeniable love.

"Why, Spencer, they told me you were an old man."
She holds out her hands to him, and he takes them.

Tears stream down his cheeks and drip from his chin.
"But no one told me you were still such a pretty young
lady," he says. Still lying, my grandaddy.

"Oh, Spencer, Spencer," she says, "there's been too
much time and space." And I watch her gather him
into her skinny little arms, and he lays his face against
her shoulder. No one in the room is breathing. Then
all of a sudden, one of the cousins starts to clap, and
everyone, one at a time, joins in, until everyone is
laughing and wiping tears, patting Grandaddy on the
shoulder, and hugging Hattie.

I'm not about to leave Grandaddy's side. If
she's ever going to give him the business about
the empty box, I want to hear it. Someone
brings her a chair and sits her down right next
to him, and no one stops me so I sit down
between them right at their feet. And then I
notice it. On her lap is a small wooden
box, and the lid is off. Delicately carved into
its varnished top are the initials HMcB. She
holds the box in her hands, and I can see the
varnish worn dull in spots where her fingers
touch and must have touched for years.

Grandaddy sees it, too, and groans. "Oh,
Hattie, do you hate me? Can you ever forgive me?"

"Forgive you for what?"

"For the empty box."

"Forgive you? Why, Spencer, it was the best present
I've ever gotten."

"An empty box?" Grandaddy is stunned.

"It wasn't an empty box. It was a box full of
good things."

"How d'you figure that?" Grandaddy asks.

"Well, I put it in a safe place, you know. First I hid it under the seat in the wagon, and when we finally got our soddy built, I had Otto make a special chink in the wall where I hid it and where it stayed for years. And I always knew it was there if things got really bad.

"Our first winter, we ran out of food, and I thought to open the box then and see if it would help us, but there were kind neighbors who were generous with us, and I learned to let people be neighborly.

"And then one summer we lost our whole crop in a prairie fire, and I thought of the box, but Otto was sure we could make it on our own, and I learned to let him have his pride. Then when our son drowned, just out of despair I almost opened it, but you had said to open it only if things got their worst, and I knew I still had my daughter, and there was another baby already stirring in me.

"No matter how bad things got, Spencer, they never got their worst. Even when Otto finally died a few years ago. Your box taught me that."

"But you did open it." He points to the box, open and empty in her lap.

327

"I opened it when I knew I'd be seeing you. I always thought maybe there'd be a brooch or a gold stickpin or something." Hattie smiles. I can almost imagine her with her open face turned up to a snowy sky. She laughs. "I was going to wear it for you!"

"I always meant to fill it, Hattie—"

"Hush now," she says. "They're bringing your cake."

And sure enough, Momma's wheeling over a metal table that has a big iced sheet cake on it. Hattie slips the cover back on her empty box and places it on the floor beside her feet, beside me. I stand to get out of the way of the rolling table and take the box.

Grandaddy and Aunt Hattie hold hands while everyone sings "Happy Birthday." Their hands are like old wisteria vines woven into each other. I hold the empty box. I bring it to my face. I look inside. Nothing. It is empty. And then I smell it. At first I think it smells like wood, and then I smell all the rest—a young farmer's stubbornness, a pioneer mother's sorrow, and a wondrous wild and lasting hope.

Think About It

❶ How and why do Grandaddy's feelings change from the beginning of the story to the end?

❷ How does the author create a feeling of suspense?

❸ Why do you think Hattie brings the box to the party? Explain your answer.

ABOUT the AUTHOR

*P*am Conrad was an award-winning author who wrote picture books and novels. She said that even though her books are not autobiographies, "they are each about my life in one disguise or another." She also said that her books for young readers are based on her own children's lives and are her gifts to them.

Pam Conrad published more than two dozen books and won many national awards before she lost her life to cancer at the age of forty-eight.

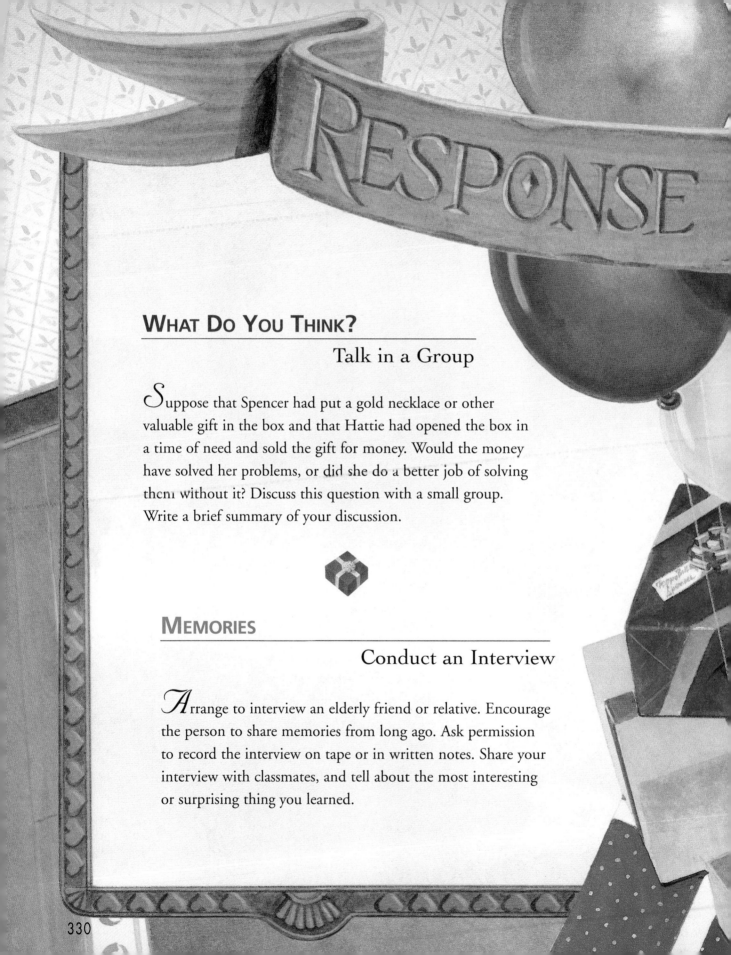

RESPONSE

WHAT DO YOU THINK?

Talk in a Group

Suppose that Spencer had put a gold necklace or other valuable gift in the box and that Hattie had opened the box in a time of need and sold the gift for money. Would the money have solved her problems, or did she do a better job of solving them without it? Discuss this question with a small group. Write a brief summary of your discussion.

MEMORIES

Conduct an Interview

Arrange to interview an elderly friend or relative. Encourage the person to share memories from long ago. Ask permission to record the interview on tape or in written notes. Share your interview with classmates, and tell about the most interesting or surprising thing you learned.

ACTIVITIES

SPECIAL GIFTS

Write a Letter

Hattie says that the empty box is full of good things. Think of some good things someone has given you that could be kept in an empty box. Write a letter to let that person know how much you appreciate the special gifts he or she has given you.

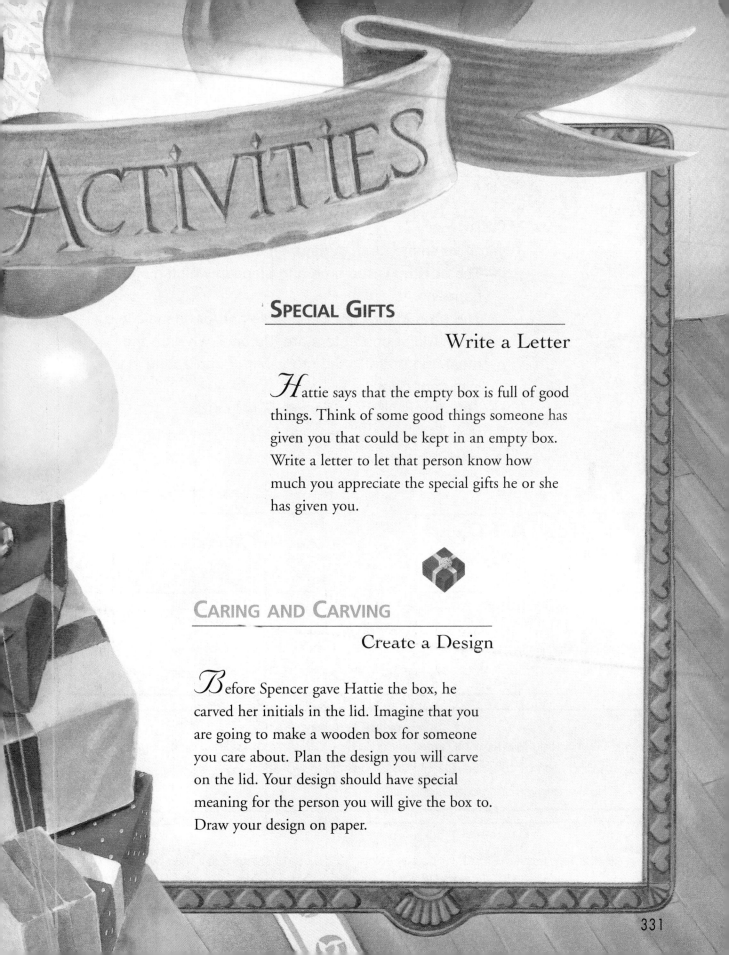

CARING AND CARVING

Create a Design

Before Spencer gave Hattie the box, he carved her initials in the lid. Imagine that you are going to make a wooden box for someone you care about. Plan the design you will carve on the lid. Your design should have special meaning for the person you will give the box to. Draw your design on paper.

Narrative Elements: Plot, Character, Setting

Like every story, "Hattie's Birthday Box" has the narrative elements of setting, characters, and plot.

- The **setting** is the time and place in which a story happens.
- The **characters** are the people and/or animals in a story. Major characters are the ones who are the most important to the story. Minor characters are less important.
- The **plot** is all the story's events in order.

You can use a diagram like this one to identify the narrative elements in "Hattie's Birthday Box."

Characters

Spencer McClintic/Grandaddy, Anna/Momma, a young girl/narrator, Aunt Hattie

Setting

A nursing home
July 5, 1947

Plot

Problem

The whole family is coming to Grandaddy's 100th birthday party, including his "baby sister" Hattie. Grandaddy hasn't seen her in 74 years, and he thinks she'll be mad at him.

Important Events

- Grandaddy tells how he once gave Hattie an empty box for her birthday, telling her not to open it until things "got their worst."
- Hattie arrives and hugs Grandaddy.

Solution

Hattie tells Grandaddy that not opening the box until things "got their worst" made her realize that things were not as bad as they could be.

When you read, you can usually find out right away whom the story is about and where and when it takes place. This information helps you follow the plot, or the sequence of events. Read the following story opener, and identify the characters, setting, and plot.

The wagon train left Ogallala, Nebraska. Wilfred had heard that soon they'd have to lower the wagon down a steep cliff. Papa said they'd have to be careful. Mama couldn't help. She'd have to watch the younger children to keep them from running into a rattlesnake or getting caught beneath a neighbor's wheels. That meant it would all be up to Papa and young Wil. Just thinking about it made Wil's knees begin to knock.

WHAT HAVE YOU LEARNED?

1. In "Hattie's Birthday Box," Grandaddy tells a story of something that happened when he was a young man. What is the plot of Grandaddy's story?

2. All stories have plots, including stories you've heard from older friends and family. Choose a favorite story and tell the characters, setting, and plot.

TRY THIS • TRY THIS • TRY THIS

Rewrite a story you have read recently. Keep the same plot but change either the characters or the setting. Share your revised story with classmates. Discuss how changing the characters or setting affected the story.

 Visit *The Learning Site!*
www.harcourtschool.com

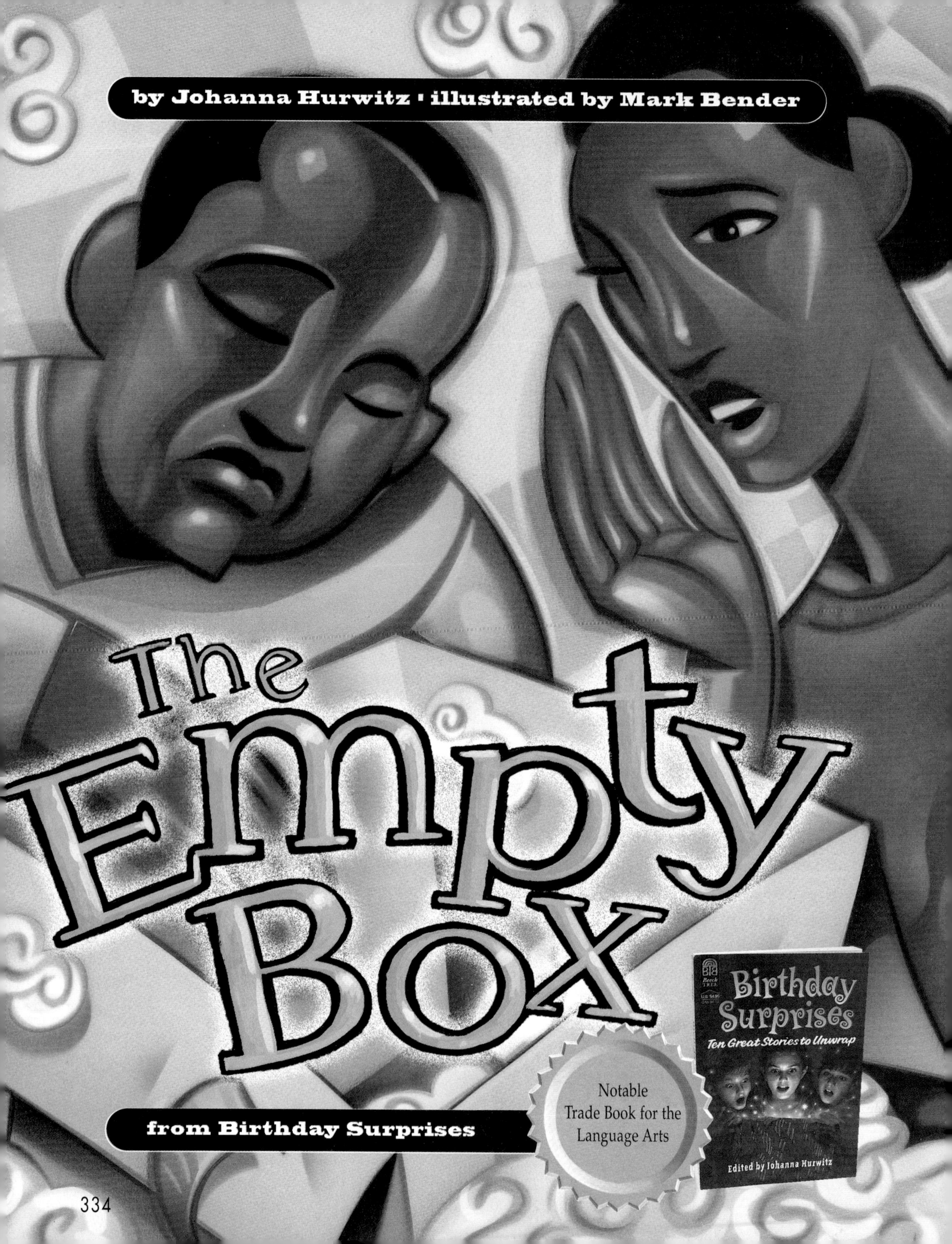

by Johanna Hurwitz · illustrated by Mark Bender

The Empty Box

from Birthday Surprises

Birthday Surprises
Ten Great Stories to Unwrap

Edited by Johanna Hurwitz

Notable
Trade Book for the
Language Arts

February 17
Nature's Wonder & Co.

To Whom It May Concern:

Two weeks ago I ordered the "tadpole in a bottle" kit advertised in your catalog. The package arrived yesterday, just in time for my son Jason's twelfth birthday, which was today. I didn't open your package to check it. Why should I? I had no reason to suspect that the tadpole wouldn't be inside. I covered your brown cardboard box with gift wrap and presented it to Jason this morning.

Jason ripped the paper off the box with great anticipation. He pulled out all the Styrofoam popcorn that was inside. The kitchen floor was covered with that awful stuff, but as it was Jason's birthday, I didn't scold him. However, within a minute the whole family stood ankle deep in the Styrofoam, and it was clear that there had been a packing error on your part. There was no bottle, with or without a tadpole, inside the package. You sent an empty box!

Of course Jason was very disappointed. It's a mean trick to give an empty box to a child on his birthday. I've explained to Jason that you must have accidentally forgotten to include his bottle and that you will ship it to him immediately. I tried phoning your 800 number all afternoon, but the line has been busy. I assume that this means your business is booming and not that your phone was off the hook. I would never have guessed so many people wanted to own tadpoles. Jason is anxiously awaiting his bottle.

Sincerely,

Lillian Peacock

Lillian Peacock
(Jason's mother)

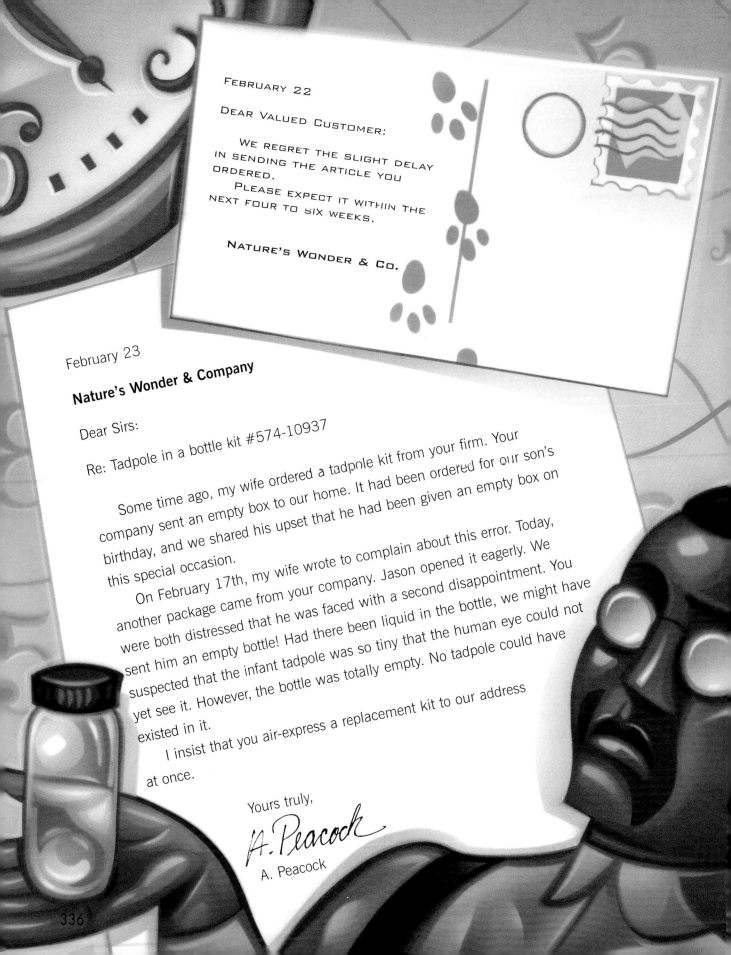

FEBRUARY 22

DEAR VALUED CUSTOMER:

WE REGRET THE SLIGHT DELAY IN SENDING THE ARTICLE YOU ORDERED.

PLEASE EXPECT IT WITHIN THE NEXT FOUR TO SIX WEEKS.

NATURE'S WONDER & CO.

February 23

Nature's Wonder & Company

Dear Sirs:

Re: Tadpole in a bottle kit #574-10937

Some time ago, my wife ordered a tadpole kit from your firm. Your company sent an empty box to our home. It had been ordered for our son's birthday, and we shared his upset that he had been given an empty box on this special occasion.

On February 17th, my wife wrote to complain about this error. Today, another package came from your company. Jason opened it eagerly. We were both distressed that he was faced with a second disappointment. You sent him an empty bottle! Had there been liquid in the bottle, we might have suspected that the infant tadpole was so tiny that the human eye could not yet see it. However, the bottle was totally empty. No tadpole could have existed in it.

I insist that you air-express a replacement kit to our address at once.

Yours truly,

A. Peacock

A. Peacock

Dear Sir: February 28

I regret to inform you that Nature's Wonder & Company cannot supply you with a peacock or its eggs. However, if you consult the enclosed catalog you will see that we have chicken and duck eggs at very reasonable prices. In fact, there is an *early spring special* of twelve fertilized chicken eggs at half the usual cost.

Please fill out the enclosed order form or place your order by calling our 800 number.

We are glad to be of service to you.

Sincerely,

Ellen George

Ellen George
Asst. Sales Manager

P.S. We are negotiating with a new distributor and hope in the future to also be able to supply turtle eggs.

March 1

Nature's Wonder & Co.

Dear Mr. Nature's,

When my class studied about writing letters, I told my teacher Mrs. Shea that all my friends lived nearby. I didn't think I would ever have to bother writing a real letter. Mrs. Shea said everyone needs to write a letter at some time or other. I guess she is right because now I am writing to you.

My birthday was on February 17. It was a pretty good day. I got some neat stuff, and Mom made my favorite dinner, which is sloppy joes. The present I most wanted and kept talking about was a tadpole in a bottle kit. I really was hoping to get it. When I opened my presents I saved the biggest package for last, because I was sure that the tadpole in a bottle would be inside.

Well guess what? The box was empty (unless you count all that junk you put in a package to keep the stuff inside from breaking). My dog got sick eating all that plastic stuff. But that's not the worst thing. I am worried about my tadpole. Where is it? It wasn't in the empty bottle you sent either.

Please look for it at your company and send it to my home right away. I want to watch the tadpole turn into a frog. If you don't hurry it will be too late.

Your friend,

Jason

Jason Peacock

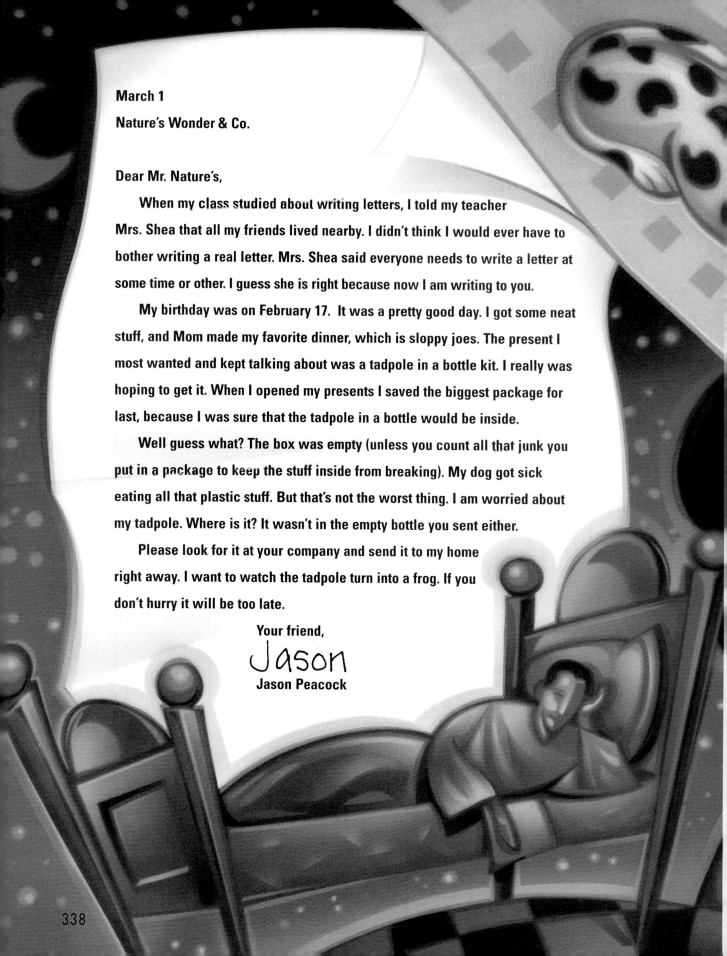

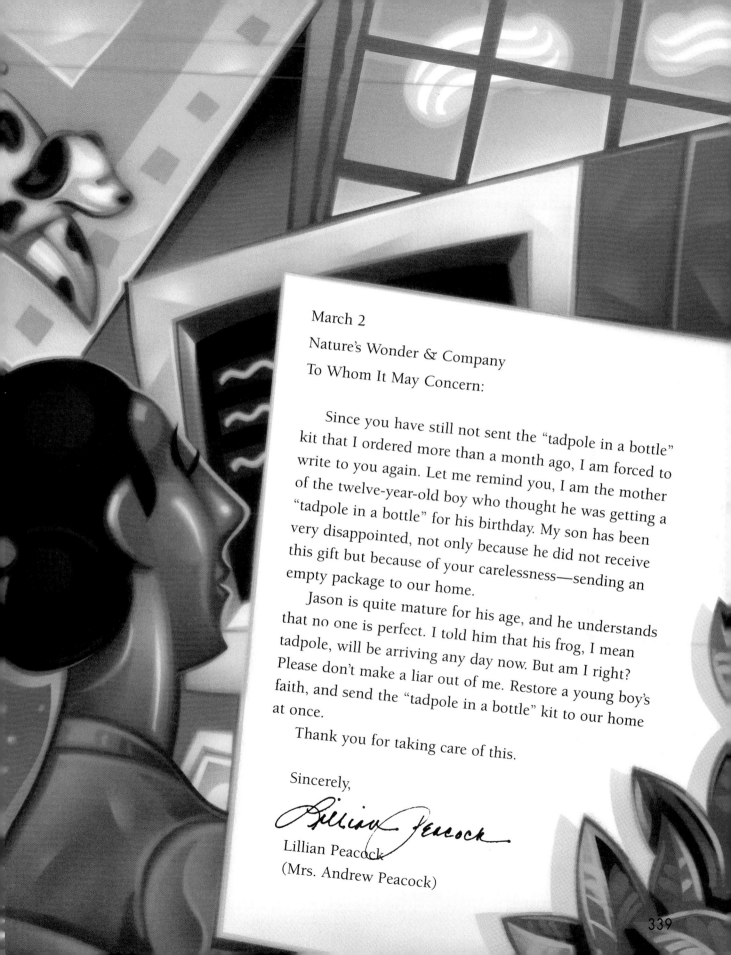

March 2

Nature's Wonder & Company

To Whom It May Concern:

Since you have still not sent the "tadpole in a bottle" kit that I ordered more than a month ago, I am forced to write to you again. Let me remind you, I am the mother of the twelve-year-old boy who thought he was getting a "tadpole in a bottle" for his birthday. My son has been very disappointed, not only because he did not receive this gift but because of your carelessness—sending an empty package to our home.

Jason is quite mature for his age, and he understands that no one is perfect. I told him that his frog, I mean tadpole, will be arriving any day now. But am I right? Please don't make a liar out of me. Restore a young boy's faith, and send the "tadpole in a bottle" kit to our home at once.

Thank you for taking care of this.

Sincerely,

Lillian Peacock
(Mrs. Andrew Peacock)

March 5
Nature's Wonder & Co.

Dear Ms. Ellen George:

Re: Tadpole in a bottle kit #574-10937

This is my last warning that if you don't immediately send a tadpole in a bottle kit to our home, I shall contact the Better Business Bureau. I hate to think how many other people, in addition to my young son, have been disappointed by the inefficient packaging done by your company. I don't know why you think I would want to order chicken eggs from you. They are easily available by the dozen at my local supermarket.

Yours truly,

A. Peacock

A. Peacock

MARCH 7

DEAR VALUED CUSTOMER:

WE REGRET THE SLIGHT DELAY IN SENDING THE ARTICLE YOU ORDERED.
PLEASE EXPECT IT WITHIN THE NEXT FOUR TO SIX WEEKS.

NATURE'S WONDER & CO.

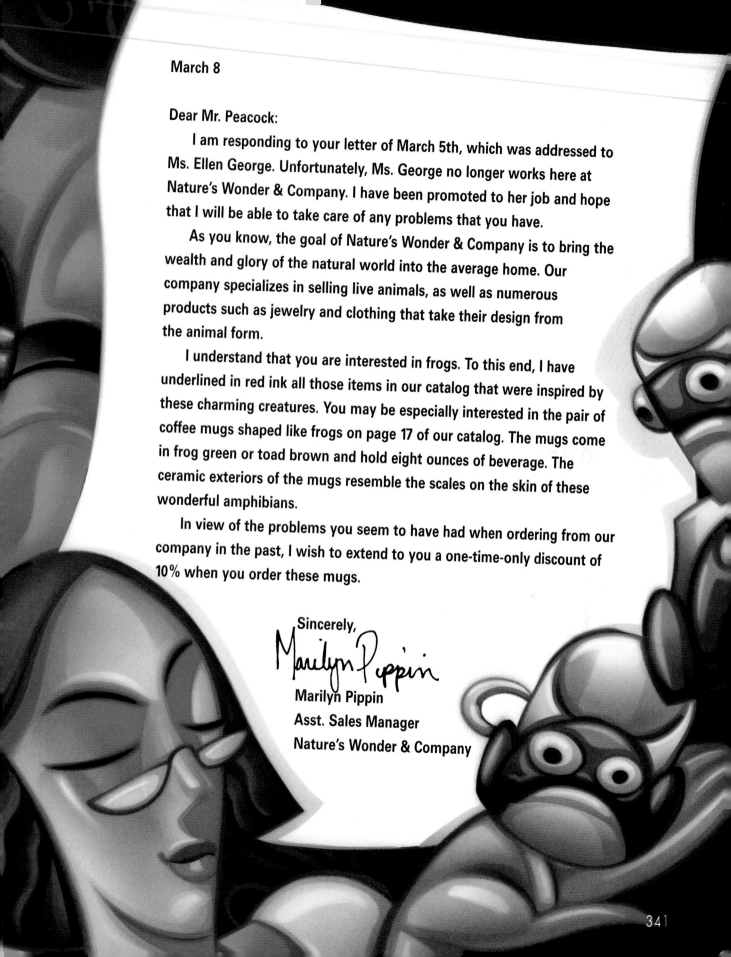

March 8

Dear Mr. Peacock:

I am responding to your letter of March 5th, which was addressed to Ms. Ellen George. Unfortunately, Ms. George no longer works here at Nature's Wonder & Company. I have been promoted to her job and hope that I will be able to take care of any problems that you have.

As you know, the goal of Nature's Wonder & Company is to bring the wealth and glory of the natural world into the average home. Our company specializes in selling live animals, as well as numerous products such as jewelry and clothing that take their design from the animal form.

I understand that you are interested in frogs. To this end, I have underlined in red ink all those items in our catalog that were inspired by these charming creatures. You may be especially interested in the pair of coffee mugs shaped like frogs on page 17 of our catalog. The mugs come in frog green or toad brown and hold eight ounces of beverage. The ceramic exteriors of the mugs resemble the scales on the skin of these wonderful amphibians.

In view of the problems you seem to have had when ordering from our company in the past, I wish to extend to you a one-time-only discount of 10% when you order these mugs.

Sincerely,

Marilyn Pippin

Marilyn Pippin
Asst. Sales Manager
Nature's Wonder & Company

March 10

Nature's Wonder & Co.

Dear Mr. Wonder:

    I was supposed to get a tadpole in a bottle kit for my birthday last month. I have been waiting for it for a long time. I'm worried that if you don't hurry and send it to my home, the tadpole will already be a frog. Then I won't be able to watch how it grows. I heard it was a very educational experience and I don't want to miss it.

    Please hurry and send my tadpole.

Your friend,

Jason

Jason Peacock

P.S. How does the frog get out of the bottle?

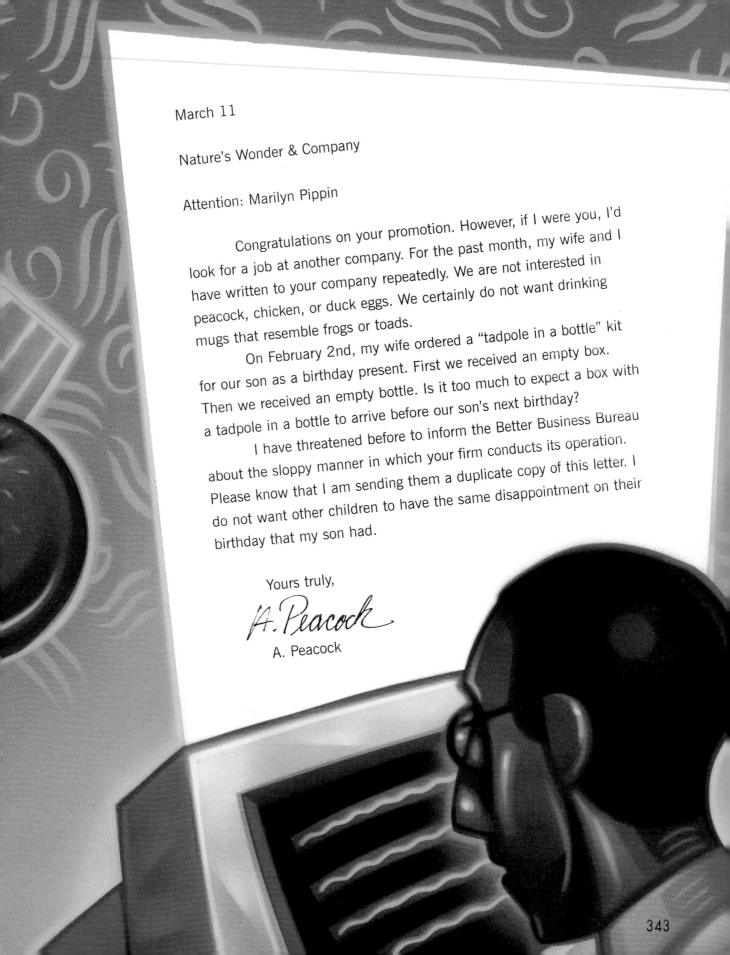

March 11

Nature's Wonder & Company

Attention: Marilyn Pippin

Congratulations on your promotion. However, if I were you, I'd look for a job at another company. For the past month, my wife and I have written to your company repeatedly. We are not interested in peacock, chicken, or duck eggs. We certainly do not want drinking mugs that resemble frogs or toads.

On February 2nd, my wife ordered a "tadpole in a bottle" kit for our son as a birthday present. First we received an empty box. Then we received an empty bottle. Is it too much to expect a box with a tadpole in a bottle to arrive before our son's next birthday?

I have threatened before to inform the Better Business Bureau about the sloppy manner in which your firm conducts its operation. Please know that I am sending them a duplicate copy of this letter. I do not want other children to have the same disappointment on their birthday that my son had.

Yours truly,

A. Peacock

A. Peacock

March 18

Dear Mr. Peacock,

I know you will be disappointed to hear that Nature's Wonder & Company has decided to discontinue shipping live tadpoles in bottles to its customers. We now plan to limit our stock to stuffed frogs (made out of cloth, not real frog), ceramic frogs, frog posters, and a large and unusual stone frog, which can be used as a garden seat.

In view of the problems you have had in the past weeks in trying to obtain a "tadpole in a bottle" kit for your son, I have arranged that the company ship all remaining stock of such bottles to your address. I'm sorry they won't arrive in time for your son's birthday— either this year's or next—but I know that young boys are delighted to get gifts at any time of the year.

Most sincerely,

Marilyn Pippin

Marilyn Pippin
Sales Manager
Nature's Wonder & Company

April 1

Nature's Wonder & Co.

Dear Mr. Nature's Wonder,

This has been the best day of my life. It's spring break so I was home from school when the United Parcel truck came to my house this morning. The driver brought two big boxes, and they were addressed to *me*. Then he went back to his truck and brought two more. Altogether there were twenty-four boxes!

Underneath those plastic pieces that you put in the boxes to keep the stuff inside from breaking was a tadpole in the bottle kit in each box. I never dreamed I would ever own twenty-four tadpoles. The tadpoles were pretty big. In fact, they were practically frogs. They had legs and feet and only the tiniest bit of tail left. It's too bad that I missed watching them grow up, but I don't care. It's great to have twenty-four frogs.

My friend Allan came over to my house, and very, very carefully, we broke the bottles so that the frogs could get out. At the moment they are all in my bathtub hopping about. I'm not sure how we are going to get washed. I think if we all took showers without using any soap it will work out fine.

Thanks a lot for sending all the frogs. I know I'm going to learn a lot just watching them.

Your friend,

Jason

Jason Peacock

P.S. Do dogs eat frogs? I hope not.
P.P.S. If my mother says I can't keep them all, I'm going to give them to my friends as birthday surprises.

Think About It!

1. How do Jason and his parents try to solve their problem? How does it finally get solved?
2. How are the letters from Jason, his mother, and his father different?
3. What do you think is the funniest thing that happens in the story? Explain.

Johanna Hurwitz

Dear Reader,

Thank you for reading "The Empty Box" from the book of short stories titled *Birthday Surprises: Ten Great Stories to Unwrap.*

I got the idea for this story from something that used to happen at the library where I worked years ago. Each year during the holiday season we decorated a Christmas tree and had a Hanukkah Menorah. To make the scene more festive, we wrapped empty boxes to make it look like presents waiting to be opened. When a child asked, "What's inside the box?" we answered, "Nothing."

But each year, we saw evidence that some child did not truly believe us. Hidden in a bathroom or stuffed into a wastebasket, we found the remains of opened gift boxes. Some child had thought there was really something inside each gift box and had secretly opened one to discover that "Nothing" was a truthful answer.

I hope you enjoyed my story, and I also hope all of your birthday packages have something wonderful inside.

Sincerely,

Johanna Hurwitz

Johanna Hurwitz

PANDORA'S BOX

by · Anne Rockwell
illustrations by · Rafael López

THE ROBBER BABY
※ STORIES FROM ※
THE GREEK MYTHS

BY ANNE ROCKWELL

$\mathcal{P}$andora was made, not born as other people are. Hephaestus[1] modeled her out of clay. He made her a young woman as beautiful as his wife, Aphrodite[2], the goddess of love and beauty.

Each of the gods and goddesses gave Pandora a gift. Then Athene, the goddess of wisdom, breathed life into her. Most of the gifts the gods gave her were good ones. But unfortunately Hermes[3], as always full of tricks and mischief, gave her more curiosity than was good for her.

Pandora was sent to live on earth. She had no trouble finding a good husband, for the gods and goddesses had given her the gifts of smiles and sweetness and wit and winning ways. Besides that, she was rich, for as a wedding gift the gods and goddesses gave her a box that had been made by Hephaestus. It was as beautiful as Pandora and very valuable, too.

"Never, never open that box!" all the gods and goddesses warned Pandora. She promised to obey them, but as time went on Pandora grew more and more curious about what was in the box that she had promised never to open.

In those days, there was no sadness among the mortals on earth. And why should it have been otherwise? There was no sickness, no hunger, no jealousy, no laziness, no greed, no anger, no cruelty. Even death was like a long and gentle sleep when people were very tired. There was no suffering of any kind.

Perhaps things would have remained that way if tricky Hermes had not given Pandora so much curiosity. But every day Pandora grew more and more curious about just what was in that box. At last, when she could no longer sleep for wondering what her box contained, she said to herself early one morning, "I will just take a little peek!"

---

[1] hə•fes′təs   [2] af•rə•dī′tē   [3] hər′mēz

So she opened the box, just to take a little peek. And out of that box flew dreadful things. Greed and Envy came out first and soared up into the clean, bright air. Pandora tried to slam the box shut, but she could not. Out flew Hatred and Cruelty with terrible force. Hunger and Poverty followed. Then Sickness came, and Despair, and all the other terrible things that the gods and goddesses knew should remain safely hidden in that box.

Pandora had set them all free.

"Come back! Come back where you belong!" Pandora called out to the terrible things as they flew around her. She grabbed at them in the air, but they soared out of her reach and up into the sky. None came back. They are still out there bringing misery and trouble to people on earth.

But the gods and goddesses had not put only dreadful things in Pandora's box. Hidden in among the terrible things was something small and fragile-winged and good. This thing was Hope. Who was the kindly god or goddess who thought to put Hope in among all the miseries and misfortunes? No one knows.

But because Hope was hidden in Pandora's box, whenever there is too much trouble and sadness among us mortals, Hope makes us think that tomorrow will be better.

And soon Pandora dried her tears.

"I hope I will never be too curious again!" she said.

And she never was.

Think About It

The myth "Pandora's Box" offers a creative explanation for how bad things came into our world. What is that explanation?

351

Response Activities

Customer Service

WRITE A BUSINESS LETTER   Jason's teacher says that everyone needs to write a letter at some time or other. Have you ever been unhappy with something you bought? Write to a company explaining how they could improve their product or service. Use the proper form for a business letter.

Frog Alert!

EXTEND THE STORY   How will Jason's parents feel about the frogs in their bathtub? From what you know about the characters' personalities, what do you think they will say and do? With a small group, plan a skit and act out what happens when Jason's mother and father get home.

Frogs, Frogs, Frogs

DEVELOP A PLAN Jason writes that he might give some of the frogs to his friends as birthday presents. If you had to find homes for twenty-four frogs, how would you solve your problem? Write down a plan of action. Use your imagination!

Making Connections

WRITE A SENTENCE Why is hope also hidden in Pandora's box? How does Jason show hope in "The Empty Box"? Write a few sentences on the subject of hope. Explain briefly how hope is involved in both stories.

THE
W I L L I
S C R

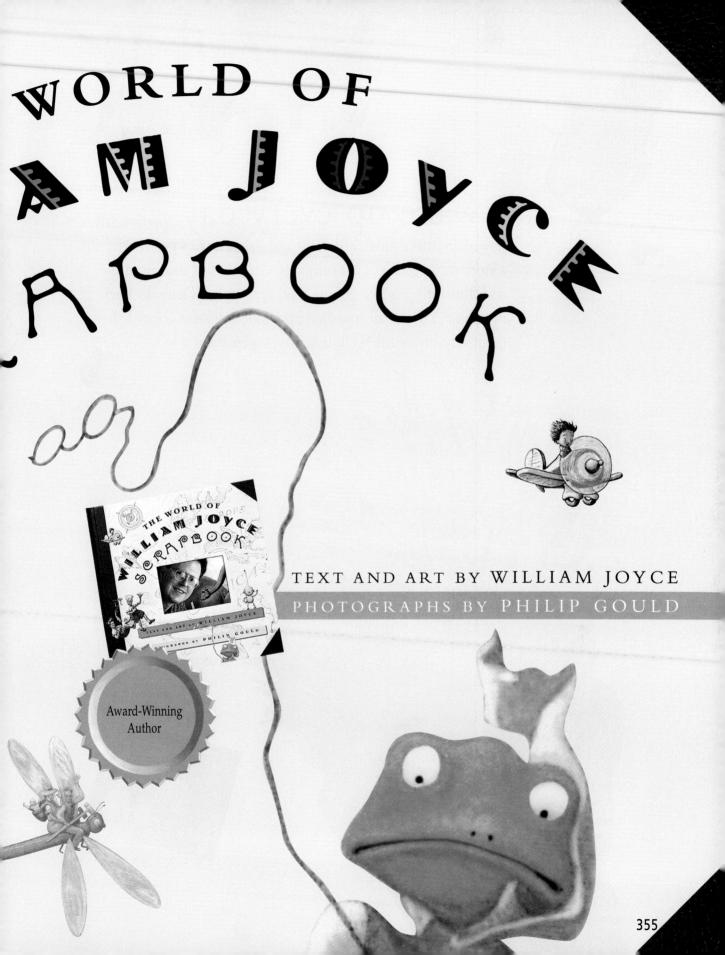

WORLD OF

M JOYCE

APBOOK

TEXT AND ART BY WILLIAM JOYCE

PHOTOGRAPHS BY PHILIP GOULD

Award-Winning
Author

I wake up every day (pretty early, now that I have kids) and draw and think until I get an idea for a story or a picture. That's my job. On the best days, writing and illustrating is like getting paid for recess. Where do I get my ideas? They're all smushed up inside my head. How'd they get inside my head? Well, it started when I was a kid. . . .

When I was a kid, I didn't

have many books, just a Mother Goose book, a fairy-tale book, and a book called *Where the Wild Things Are*.

But I did play with my toys and watch TV a lot. TV was different then. There were only three channels and all the shows were in black and white, but there was plenty of cool stuff to watch.

On summer nights, my sisters and I would watch cartoons, westerns, and monster movies all night long (or until we fell asleep).

I loved the stories in those old movies and I loved the drawings in *Where the Wild Things Are*. They really got my imagination going. So I started making up my own stories and drawing pictures to go with them. At first they were just about monsters and cars and spaceships and dinosaurs eating my sisters.

357

My first drawings were pretty simple. But I kept drawing and painting and telling stories with my pictures. My parents let me have art lessons, and I had a couple of teachers and librarians who encouraged me. I read lots of books and tried all different mediums—watercolors, oils, pencils, pastels, charcoal, crayons, felt-tipped pens, pen and ink—you name it. The older I got, the more I learned. I had favorite artists that I studied and even copied. I didn't copy them to make it easier to draw a picture. I copied them to learn how they drew. My favorite artists were Maurice Sendak, who did *Where the Wild Things Are*, Beatrix Potter, who did *Peter Rabbit*, and N.C. Wyeth, who did lots of famous stories like *Robin Hood* and *Treasure Island*. There were times when my drawings looked too much like theirs, but in time I found my own style.

AGE 5

AGE 17

AGE 8

AGE 9

BOOK BEGINNINGS

I had even learned to draw realistically, but drawing real life wasn't very exciting for me. I missed doing spaceships, bugs, dinosaurs, and monsters. I wanted to draw places that I'd never seen, adventures I'd never had, and people I'd always wanted to meet. I didn't care if they were real or not, because making them up was the most fun and made me happy.

So when I was in high school I decided I wanted to write and illustrate books about all the stuff I liked. Once I decided to do that, I had plenty of ideas.

How I Do a Book

It takes a long time to do a book, so I have to like the story or the idea a whole lot. The shortest time I spent on a book was two months. That was on my first book, *Tammy and the Gigantic Fish*. But I spent almost two years on my book *Santa Calls*.

First I plan the whole book with a series of pencil drawings. I figure out what the people and places will look like and where the words will fit. These first drawings are often very loose, but they help me figure out how to do my paintings. The color paintings take the most time to do, so the more I plan, the less likely I am to make a mistake. If you look closely and compare the sketches and paintings, you can see that I change my mind a lot. I move people around and make their hair or clothes different.

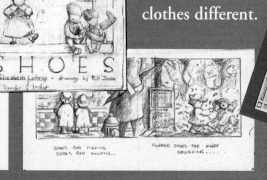

I usually paint using very watery layers. First I do yellow, then red, then blue, and then brown or black. Using these four colors, I can mix any color there is.

blue

black

Red

GEORGE SHRINKS

The first book that I both wrote and drew the pictures for was *George Shrinks*. Ever since I was a little kid I loved stories about people who were the wrong size. King Kong was way too big for everything, and Stuart Little was way too small. One day I found some of my old toys in a box. Mixed up with all the dinosaurs and army men was a little airplane that had a tiny pilot, and that got me thinking.

What if a boy named George (George is my Dad's middle name) shrank one day while his parents were away? What would he do? Would it be fun? Would it be scary? What would he eat?

So that's what I made *George Shrinks* about—how fun and scary and neat it would be if, just for a day, you were the same size as your toys. And of course I had George fly in that toy airplane.

But I don't make *everything* up. I used some real toys in the book like my old teddy bear—he's on the title page. I even used some of my real books and other stuff like my desk and a table fan and a potted plant.

GEORGE IS SHRINKING...

SHRINKING...

SHRINKING...

SHRINKING...

SHRINKING...

SHRINKING...

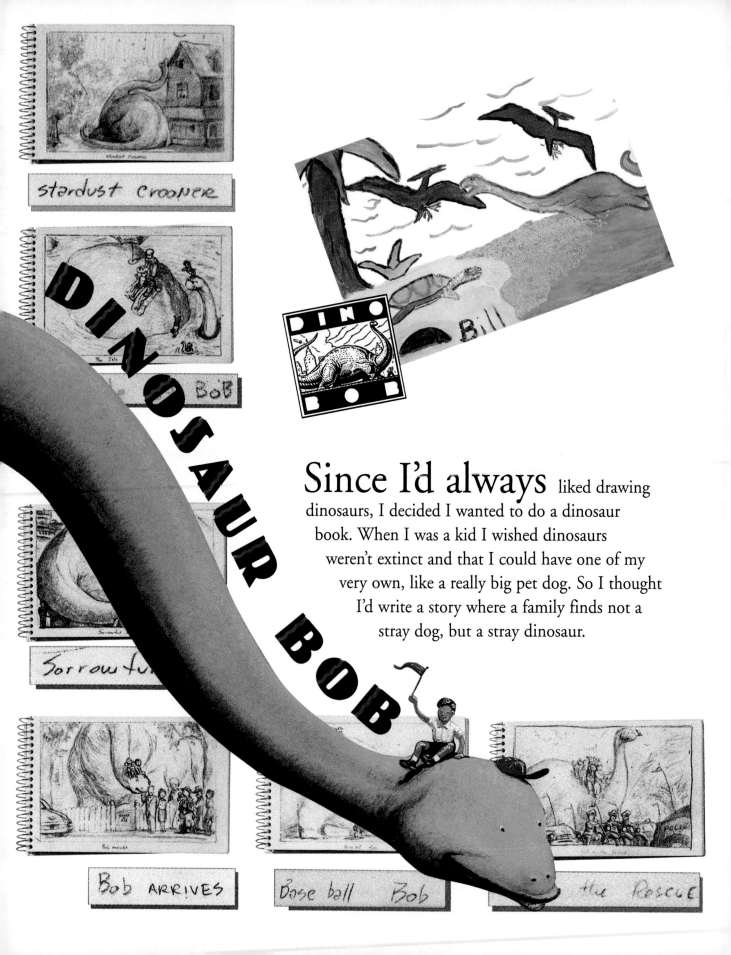

stardust crooner

DINOSAUR BOB

Bill

Sorrowful

Bob

Since I'd always liked drawing dinosaurs, I decided I wanted to do a dinosaur book. When I was a kid I wished dinosaurs weren't extinct and that I could have one of my very own, like a really big pet dog. So I thought I'd write a story where a family finds not a stray dog, but a stray dinosaur.

Bob ARRIVES

Base ball Bob

the Rescue

I thought about King Kong and the American tall tales like "Paul Bunyan," which was the story of a giant, and "Mighty Casey at the Bat," which was about a baseball player. I sort of combined them all and came up with a dinosaur named Bob who could play baseball and the trumpet and dance the Hokey Pokey.

So that's sort of the story of how I do what I do. I still draw all the time, just like when I was a kid. I sit at my desk, and I never know where the page will take me, or who I'll meet, or what adventure we may go on.

THE END

THINK ABOUT IT

1. Why does William Joyce enjoy writing and illustrating books?

2. Why do you think William Joyce includes drawings he made when he was young as well as illustrations from his books?

3. Which of the photographs and drawings in the scrapbook do you like best? Explain your answer.

WILLIAM JOYCE

William Joyce talks about why he wrote "The World of William Joyce Scrapbook."

When I go to schools, I get asked a lot of questions. *How do you do a book? Where do you get your ideas? How did you learn to draw? How long does it take to do a book? Do you put your family in your books? Do you get to sleep late? What was the first book you ever wrote?* Most people don't know any author/illustrators, and you can't find them listed in the phone book like doctors or plumbers or landscape architects.

Every author has his own way of doing a book. On these pages, I've tried to answer the questions about how I do mine.

RESPONSE ACTIVITIES

I Like Your Style

WRITE A PARAGRAPH Before William Joyce found his own style, he imitated the work of artists he admired. Is there an artist, writer, dancer, musician, or other person in the arts whose work you greatly admire? Write a paragraph telling why you like this person's style.

Do It Yourself

ILLUSTRATE A STORY Try using William Joyce's technique. Think of a little story you can illustrate with three or four pictures, and draw pencil sketches. Then use paints or oil pastels to create your illustrations. Display your sketches and illustrations together so classmates can compare them.

Hello, Mr. Joyce

ROLE-PLAY A VISIT Suppose you had an opportunity to visit with William Joyce. What would he be like in person? What would the two of you talk about? Write a list of questions you would like to ask. Work with a partner to role-play a visit with William Joyce in his home or studio.

The World of You

PLAN A SCRAPBOOK Imagine that you have grown up to become a writer and illustrator. Now you are preparing a scrapbook like William Joyce's about your world. Include drawings you made in fifth grade. Tell how you get ideas for your books and how you express your ideas in your work.

Fact and Opinion

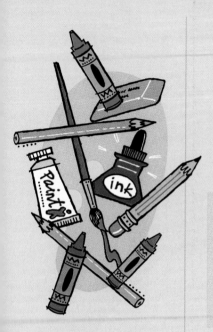

In "The World of William Joyce Scrapbook," the author tells you about his life as an artist. In telling you about his life, he gives you both facts and opinions. A **fact** is a statement that can be proved. An **opinion** is someone's belief about something. An opinion cannot be proved. Read the following paragraph from the selection.

> **I wake up every day (pretty early, now that I have kids) and draw and think until I get an idea for a story or a picture. That's my job. On the best days, writing and illustrating is like getting paid for recess.**

You can use a chart like the one below to identify facts and opinions.

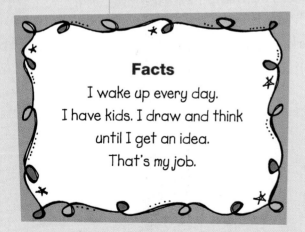

Facts
I wake up every day.
I have kids. I draw and think
until I get an idea.
That's *my* job.

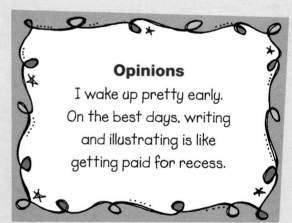

Opinions
I wake up pretty early.
On the best days, writing
and illustrating is like
getting paid for recess.

It is important for you to be able to tell the difference between a fact and an opinion when you read. Sometimes authors state opinions as if they were facts. Authors may also mix facts and opinions in their writing to try to persuade readers to accept opinions as facts. If you can tell facts from opinions when you read, you will be able to form your own ideas about the subject.

Read the paragraph below. Which statements are opinions and which are facts? How do you know?

I never know when I'll get an idea for a drawing, so I keep my sketchbook in my backpack all the time. It's a beautiful sketchbook, with a lion on the front. Sometimes I have to wait in my mom's office for her to finish a project. Waiting is really boring, so I draw. I often get my best ideas when I'm riding in the car.

WHAT HAVE YOU LEARNED?

1. What are some of the facts you learned about William Joyce? What are some of your opinions about the author and his work?

2. Read an article in a magazine or newspaper. List some of the facts and opinions that you find in the article.

TRY THIS • TRY THIS • TRY THIS

Write a paragraph about your favorite artist or musician. Tell why you like his or her work. Exchange papers with a partner. Underline all the facts in your partner's paragraph with one line. Put a double line under the opinions.

Visit *The Learning Site!*
www.harcourtschool.com

Satchmo's BLUES

Teachers' Choice

BY ALAN SCHROEDER
ILLUSTRATED BY FLOYD COOPER

The city of New Orleans sits along the mighty Mississippi River in southeastern Louisiana. It is home to red beans and rice, jazz music, and a musician named Louis Armstrong.

On hot summer nights, young Louis sat outside Economy Hall and listened to the Eagle Band play some of the best jazz music in town. He watched his favorite musician, Bunk Johnson, blow his cornet until the roof trembled. Louis hoped that someday he could blow his own horn that way and send the stars spinning.

Louis and his family lived on Perdido Street, "back o' town." It was a tough neighborhood, full of broken bottles and mangy dogs and kicked-in fences. But Louis didn't mind. At night when the lanterns were lit and Willie Reed brought out his fiddle, it was just like being at Economy Hall, with everyone clapping and dancing on boards:

"Mr. Jefferson Lord—
Play that barbershop chord!"

"Back o' town," everyone had a musical instrument of some kind—a clarinet, or a banjo, or maybe just an old pot someone had turned into a drum. But Louis didn't want a clarinet or a banjo. He wanted to blow a horn, just like Bunk Johnson. A real cornet, brass, with valves so quiet they whispered. But that took money, and Mama didn't have any. Not enough for a cornet anyway.

"You're gonna have to wait," she told Louis. "Now come on, help me hang up this washin'."

One day, right off Bourbon Street, Louis saw a horn sitting in a pawnshop window. It was a humdinger, all bright and sassy, just begging to be bought. The cardboard sign said $5. Louis turned away. He could never come up with that much money.

"It's not fair!" he thought. Everyone else had a musical instrument. Even Santiago, the pie man, had a little horn hanging from his wooden cart. People came flocking when they heard his familiar *toot-toot-ta-toot-toot*.

The next time Santiago came "back o' town," Louis ran up and tugged on his sleeve.

"Can I blow that horn, mister?" he asked eagerly.

The pie man handed it to him with a grin. Louis whipped the horn up to his lips and blew.

Nothing happened. Just a flat, spitting sound. *Ppphhhh....*

Everybody laughed, especially Santiago. Louis tried again. This time, the noise was even worse.

Santiago reached down and took the horn away.

"I thought you said you could blow it, Louis."

Louis frowned. "I thought I could."

That made everyone laugh even harder.

But Louis didn't give up. He wanted to turn that awful *ppphhhh* into something wonderful—something so hot and jazzy that everyone would come running.

"And I'm gonna do it, too," he said to himself.

Two weeks later, the horn was still in the pawnshop window. Louis wanted to go inside, but the man behind the counter didn't look any too friendly. The cardboard sign still said $5.

"That horn is mine," Louis whispered, pressing his nose against the window. "It's gotta be mine!"

Every afternoon, when he got home from school, Louis stood in front of the mirror and practiced his blowing. He pretended he was Bunk Johnson, raising the roof with his high C's.

"What's you doin' with your lips?" Mama asked. "You look like a fish."

"I'm blowin' my horn," Louis told her.

Mama shook her head. "I don't see any horn."

But Louis could—and it was a beauty.

Anytime there was a parade in New Orleans, Louis joined right in.

"Go on, get out of here, boy," the marchers told him, but that didn't stop Louis. He'd kick out his legs and fall in right behind the Excelsior Brass Band. One time, Bunk Johnson saw him from the sidewalk and waved. Louis's grin must have stretched from ear to ear. He didn't have a uniform—he didn't even have a horn—but Louis just had to be the proudest stepper in the whole parade.

That spring, he did everything he could to earn five dollars. He sold rags and coal, and ran errands for the neighbors. Twice a week, he went "front o' town" to the produce markets and poked through the trash barrels.

"You're not going to find a horn that way," his sister Beatrice said, laughing.

"Go away," Louis said. He wasn't looking for a horn—he was hunting for spoiled onions. Using a little knife, he'd cut out the rotten parts, dump the good parts in a sack, and sell them to the restaurants on Perdido Street. Five cents a bag.

"Where'd you get these onions, boy?" a man asked suspiciously.

"I grow 'em," Louis said. "I eat 'em, too. Want to smell my breath?"

The man stared at him for a moment, then laughed. "Why, you're sassier'n blazes! I like that! I'll take two bags."

Every Sunday, Mama took Louis and Beatrice to Elder Cozy's church. Louis could hardly sit still, listening to the rich gospel music around him. Mama closed her eyes and rocked back and forth, clapping her hands. During the sermon, Louis pretended he was messing with his horn.

"Quit makin' that fish face!" Mama whispered.

But Louis couldn't quit. Blowing that horn was all he could think about. Any week now, he'd walk into that pawnshop and plunk down his money. He had four dollars now—only one dollar to go.

Still, that was a lot of onions to sell.

On Decoration Day, Louis took the trolley to the Girod Cemetery. There, he pulled weeds and polished the tombstones for tips. He earned fifty-five cents that day. Heading home, Louis felt tired but happy. He'd have his horn by the end of the week!

He was surprised to see Mama waiting for him out on the front stoop. She looked worried.

"Today is your sister's birthday," she said quietly. "You know every year I make a mess of jambalaya, but that costs money, and right now I'm low. I need a quarter, Louis."

She held out her hand. For a second, Louis felt like bursting into tears. Why was she asking for a whole quarter? Didn't she know he was trying to save his money? Didn't she care?

"But Mama—"

"It's not for me, it's for your sister."

Louis pointed to his mother's apron pocket, where she kept her money. "You have enough," he said.

"I may and I may not. I think you need to chip in, Louis. You can't always be thinkin' about yourself and what you want." She touched his shoulder gently. "And, Louis . . . you know how much you love my jambalaya."

It was a hard choice. Louis stuck his hand in his pants pocket and fished around for a quarter. Why, why was Mama asking him to do this?

"Here," he said, quickly handing her the money. And before Mama could say thank you, Louis ran into the house, tears streaming down his cheeks.

That evening, Mama fixed a huge pot of her best jambalaya: shrimp and crab, and thick slices of spicy Cajun sausage.

"This'll keep your jaws a-jumpin'." She laughed, spooning the jambalaya into three big soup bowls.

Louis ate till his stomach was fixing to burst. He was glad now he'd given Mama the quarter. There was nothing "back o' town" to beat the taste of good jambalaya.

An hour later, after the dishes had been washed, Mama came out onto the stoop. Louis was sitting there quietly, looking up at the sky.

"I 'preciate what you did," Mama told him. "I know you were savin' that quarter for somethin' else." She paused, like she wasn't sure what to say next. "Here, I have something to give you. Hold out your hand."

Louis did. Mama dropped a silver dollar into his palm.

"I'm tired of seein' that fish face," she said to him, grinning. "It's time you got a real horn."

At last, Louis had his five dollars! He didn't even wait to put on his shoes. He ran as fast as he could down to the pawnshop and flung his money on the counter. The nickels spun like crazy on the wood.

"What do you want?" the owner asked. "I'm closin'."

"I want that horn in the window," Louis said.

The man grunted. "That horn is five dollars, sonny."

"That horn is mine!" Louis said proudly.

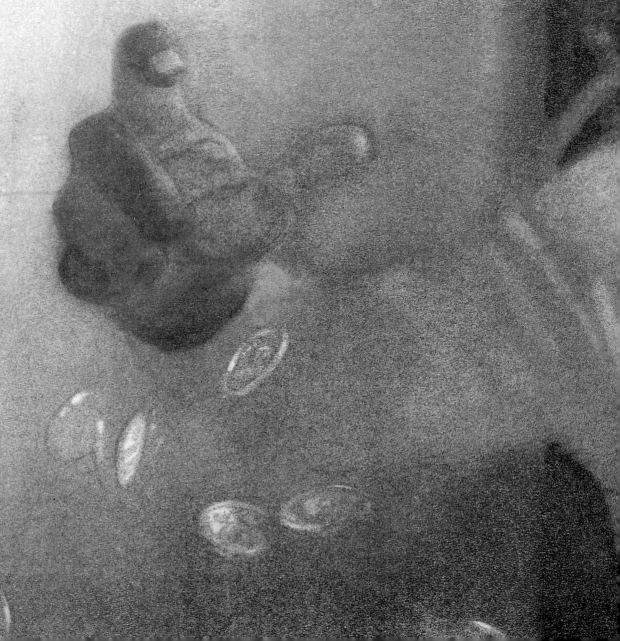

Leaving the pawnshop, Louis felt ten feet tall. Underneath a streetlamp, he got a good look at his horn. Sure, it was full of dings and dents, but he didn't care. A little elbow grease and it'd be as good as new.

The air that night was rich with honeysuckle and jazz. Louis leaned up against an old packing crate, pressed his lips to the mouthpiece, and blew.

A moment later, a wonderful sound filled the alley: music. One note, then two, three, four, then a whole cluster, all tripping out over each other. Louis' cheeks puffed out like air bags. He loved the sound he was hearing. It wasn't "Dixie Flyer," but it wasn't *ppphhhh*, either.

"Lou-is!" Mama was calling him in the distance. But he wasn't ready to go home yet. Not by a long shot. He'd waited a long time for this moment.

Leaning back, Louis pointed his horn straight up at the moon.

"Hold on, stars," he whispered. "Someday, I'm gonna blow you right out of the sky."

He propped his elbows on his knees, closed his eyes, and began to play.

Think About It

❶ How did Louis use imagination and creativity to help him reach his goal?

❷ Why do you think Louis's mother took his quarter and then gave him a silver dollar?

❸ Which scene in the story do you like the best? Why?

LOUIS ARMSTRONG

FROM THE AUTHOR
ALAN SCHROEDER

Louis Armstrong went on to become the most famous trumpeter in the history of popular music.

Leaving New Orleans at the age of twenty-one, he traveled north to Chicago, where he began his long and successful recording career. The microphone, and the public, loved Louis. Over the years, his string of hits included "Ain't Misbehavin'," "Tiger Rag," "West End Blues," and "Hello, Dolly!" The film industry was quick to spot Louis's remarkable talent. He appeared in numerous musicals, and by the 1950s he had become an international celebrity, known around the world as Satchmo or Ambassador Satch.

Louis was also a talented composer, writing, among other pieces, "Coal Cart Blues," "Cornet Chop Suey," and "Struttin' with Some Barbecue." His autobiography, *Satchmo: My Life in New Orleans*, appeared in 1954.

Louis Armstrong, the Trumpet King of Swing, died in New York City on July 6, 1971. His gravelly voice and dynamic trumpet playing will never be forgotten.

FLOYD COOPER

" . . . When I was three years old, my father added extra rooms to our house and had huge pieces of Sheetrock to use for the walls. I thought the Sheetrock looked like big chalkboards and drew a very large duck on one sheet. My duck lasted through repeated washings with soap and water. But I wasn't discouraged that my father tried to get rid of my artwork. I kept right on drawing. When I was nine, I sold my first painting. A family friend paid me $16.00 for artwork and hung it in his place of business. I began to paint and draw more than ever.

After college I worked for a greeting card company, but I didn't feel that I could be creative. Then I discovered the world of children's book illustrating. I like that it allows me to be creative. As I read a story that I am going to illustrate, I try to imagine it. I ask myself: What is the weather like? What time of day is it? What sounds can I hear? What are the smells? Then I try to make the story look as real as possible. "

ALAN SCHROEDER

FLOYD COOPER

Brass Instruments

from *Oxford Children's Encyclopedia*

Brass instruments are long, funnel-shaped tubes with a mouthpiece, coiled to make them easier to hold. The longer and wider the funnel, the deeper the notes it can produce.

To play a note on a brass instrument, you have to make your lips vibrate in the mouthpiece[1]: it is a bit like trying to blow a raspberry. On simple instruments like the bugle, you play different notes by changing the shape of your lips. Instruments like the trumpet and trombone have valves or slides that open up extra lengths of tubing, so that you can play more notes.

▼ The French horn is always held by the player with one hand inside the bell. The sound the French horn makes can be changed by removing the hand from the bell.

1 A good brass player can fit a mouthpiece to any tube—for example a garden hose, or even a kettle spout—and play it.

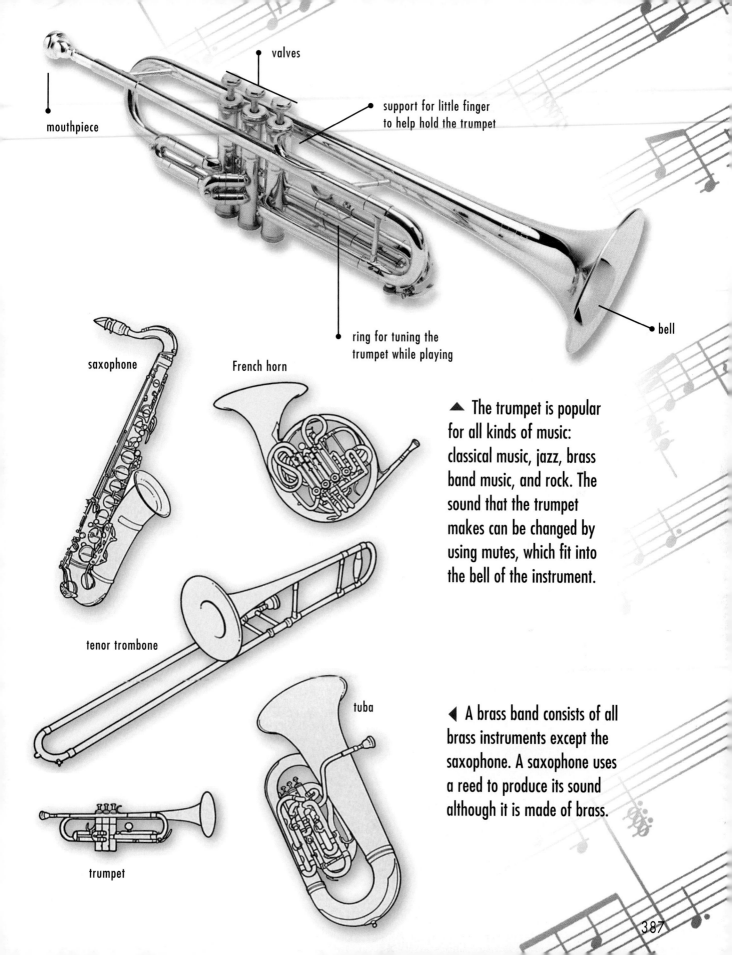

valves

support for little finger
to help hold the trumpet

mouthpiece

ring for tuning the
trumpet while playing

bell

saxophone

French horn

▲ The trumpet is popular
for all kinds of music:
classical music, jazz, brass
band music, and rock. The
sound that the trumpet
makes can be changed by
using mutes, which fit into
the bell of the instrument.

tenor trombone

tuba

◄ A brass band consists of all
brass instruments except the
saxophone. A saxophone uses
a reed to produce its sound
although it is made of brass.

trumpet

JAZZ MOVES

MOVE TO MUSIC With a small group, listen to a jazz recording, perhaps one by Louis Armstrong. As a group, talk about the music and develop dance movements to go with it. Move in creative ways to show the feelings you hear expressed in the music.

ReSponse

BETTER THAN NEW

WRITE A POEM
Louis didn't care that his horn was old and dented. Have you ever owned something that you loved, even though it wasn't in the best of shape? Write a poem about the object, telling what it meant to you.

LOUIS AND YOU

WRITE A DIALOGUE

Imagine that you live in New Orleans and Louis is a friend of yours. What might you say the first time you see his horn and hear him play? What do you think Louis would say to you? Write your conversation in the form of a dialogue, as if for a scene in a movie or a play.

Activities

MAKING CONNECTIONS

CREATE A HANDOUT

What facts from the encyclopedia article about brass instruments might have helped Louis when he first tried to play a horn? Create an illustrated list of suggestions that could be handed out to new horn players like Louis. You may want to use a word processing or desktop publishing program to create your handout.

Evelyn Cisneros
Prima Ballerina

by Charnan Simon

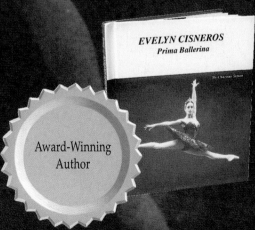

Award-Winning
Author

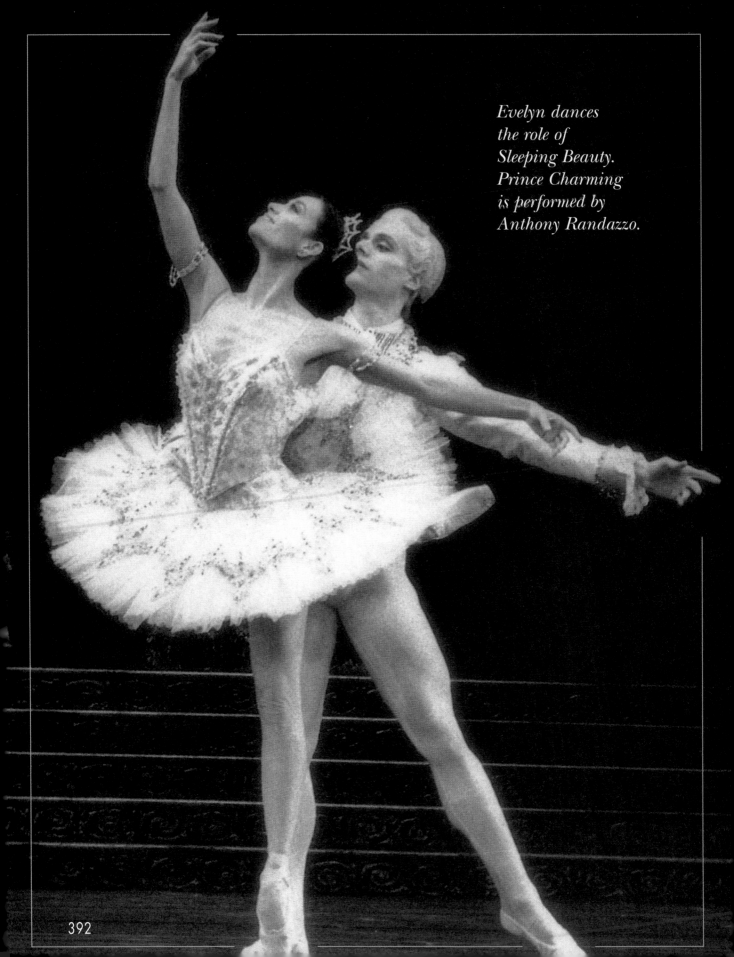

Evelyn dances the role of Sleeping Beauty. Prince Charming is performed by Anthony Randazzo.

As the curtain fell, the audience rose to its feet, clapping wildly. The San Francisco Ballet had just finished a performance of *Sleeping Beauty*. The princess found her prince and lived happily ever after. The audience, however, wasn't ready to let their princess go.

"Brava!" they shouted, throwing flowers to the stage. "Brava! Brava!"

The curtains rose, and Sleeping Beauty herself came to the center of the stage. She bowed gracefully and smiled. Evelyn Cisneros looked exactly like a princess.

Evelyn Cisneros is the prima ballerina for the San Francisco Ballet. She has danced on stages around the world. It is hard to imagine that she was once so shy she wouldn't even talk in school.

Evelyn Cisneros was born in Long Beach, California, on November 18, 1958. The Cisneros family soon moved to the seaside town of Huntington Beach. Evelyn, her younger brother Robert, and her parents were a warm and close-knit family. They were also the only Mexican American family in

Huntington Beach for a long time. Evelyn's father was a precision machinist whose parents had come to America from Mexico as migrant workers. Evelyn's mother's family had come to the United States from Durango, Mexico, in 1910 after the outbreak of the Mexican Revolution.

As the curtain fell, the audience rose to its feet, clapping wildly.

Belonging to such a loving family helped when neighborhood children teased Evelyn about how "different" she looked. Evelyn's dark skin, hair, and eyes made her stand out from her friends. Evelyn grew more and more timid. By the time she was seven, she was

Evelyn grew more and more timid.

afraid to even raise her hand or speak out in class.

Evelyn's mother thought perhaps dance classes would help cure her daughter's shyness. At first, Evelyn didn't like ballet class. She remembers, "I was very shy, and it was hard for me to stand in front of everyone in tights and leotard."

Evelyn's mother encouraged her to go to class for at least a year. By the end of the year, Evelyn had met Phyllis Cyr, who would be her first real ballet teacher. Phyllis Cyr taught Evelyn how to enjoy ballet. She showed Evelyn how to move to different kinds of music and to see the beauty of dance.

Evelyn worked hard at being a good dancer. She was naturally graceful, and turns and jumps came easily to her. But her left foot turned slightly inward, and Evelyn worked hours on stretching exercises to get the foot to turn out. Then, too, Evelyn's shoulders were naturally somewhat rounded. Again, Evelyn worked many long hours to develop flexibility and strength in her shoulders and back.

Hard work didn't bother Evelyn. With her family's support, Evelyn learned all that she could about dance. And not just ballet, either. Evelyn quickly mastered jazz, tap, and other styles of dancing.

Dance lessons were expensive, and for a long time the Cisneros family could afford only one

school district. Evelyn knew it would be hard to give up her school activities and devote herself to ballet. But it would be even harder to give up ballet. Evelyn chose dance.

From 7:30 in the morning until 2:30 in the afternoon, Evelyn went to junior high with her friends. After school she headed straight to the ballet studio. All afternoon she attended ballet class, demonstrated steps for other teachers, and taught tap class herself. After a quick dinner at home, she would go to the Pacific Ballet Theatre in Los Angeles. Evelyn danced at least five nights a week.

When she was fourteen, Evelyn's dance teachers encouraged her to try out for the San Francisco Ballet School. The teachers in San Francisco were impressed by Evelyn. To her surprise and delight, she was offered a full scholarship for the summer session.

Evelyn thrived under her new challenge. She practiced new and harder steps, and began acting some of the characters from famous ballets. More and more Evelyn was convinced that this was where she was meant to be.

By the time she was fourteen, Evelyn knew she had a decision to make.

The next year both the San Francisco Ballet School and the School of American Ballet in New York City offered Evelyn scholarships for their summer sessions. As much as she had loved San Francisco, Evelyn and her parents thought she should go to New York.

The summer proved to be scary, exciting—and disappointing. Fifteen-year-old Evelyn had never been away from her family for so long. She had never lived in such a huge, confusing city as New York. Still, she looked forward to studying with some of the finest dancers in the world. But when ballet school started, Evelyn was put in a very slow class. Evelyn recalls, "By the end

"I was just about ready to quit dancing."

of the summer, I was very discouraged. I felt very depressed, and so unsure of the talent I had that I was just about ready to quit dancing."

Evelyn's parents again helped. They suggested that she call the San Francisco Ballet School. The company invited her to join them for the last week of their summer session and to come back the following summer as well.

Evelyn worked hard at school all winter and returned to San Francisco the summer she was sixteen. At the end of that summer, the company offered to make her an apprentice. This would mean she would have to move to San Francisco and dance full time. At the end of the year, if she were good enough, she would be invited to join the company.

On February 1, 1976, Evelyn Cisneros moved to San Francisco. Within a year, she had joined the company as a full-fledged member of the ballet. She was just eighteen years old.

Evelyn quickly attracted the attention of the company's artistic director, Michael Smuin. In 1979 he created a major role for her in his ballet titled *A Song for Dead Warriors*. This ballet was broadcast nationally and turned out to be very controversial.

Helgi Tomasson, artistic director of the San Francisco Ballet, oversees rehearsals of Sleeping Beauty *with Evelyn and Anthony Randazzo.*

The ballet told about the mistreatment of Native Americans. Some people loved the ballet, and others hated it. Critics everywhere, however, praised Evelyn Cisneros's dancing ability.

In 1980, while the company was performing in New York City, the leading ballerina was injured. Evelyn was called on to take her place. Important writers from newspapers and magazines saw her dance and praised her performance. Almost overnight Evelyn Cisneros became a very famous dancer.

Triumph followed triumph in the next few years. In 1981,

Evelyn again appeared on television in the ballet *The Tempest.* In 1982, she danced both ballet and tap in a live telecast from the White House. Later that same year, she received more praise from both audiences and critics for her lead role in a new version of *Romeo and Juliet.*

Not everything went smoothly for the young ballerina, however. In 1978, when she was just nineteen, she married fellow dancer David McNaughton. Less than two years later, Evelyn and David were divorced. It was a sad time. Evelyn's close family hadn't prepared her for a personal upset such as this.

There were professional upsets as well. In 1985, Michael Smuin was replaced by Helgi Tomasson as director of the San Francisco Ballet. During his years in San Francisco, Smuin had worked closely with Evelyn. He had created some of his finest roles for her, and she had grown under his direction.

Helgi Tomasson, however, also appreciated Evelyn's talent and her popularity as a leading ballerina. He has continued to give her important roles and has even created two new ballets especially for her. "In the

> Evelyn Cisneros has truly earned the title of prima ballerina.

beginning it was very difficult," Evelyn admits. "But now we have a very reliable working relationship."

Evelyn Cisneros has truly earned the title of prima ballerina. One night she is the lovely, playful Princess Aurora in *Sleeping Beauty.* The next night she dazzles in the double role of Odette/Odile in *Swan Lake.* She shows off her brilliant technique in difficult modern ballets, and sparkles as the Sugar Plum Fairy in the Christmas favorite, *The Nutcracker Suite.*

Evelyn's dark Hispanic beauty, which was once a source of childhood teasing, is now admired by audiences everywhere. Today, Evelyn Cisneros is an international dancing star; she has never forgotten her roots. Evelyn is proud of her cultural heritage. Young Hispanics look up to her as an inspiration. She takes her responsibilities as a spokes-

Evelyn is proud of her cultural heritage.

person for the Hispanic community seriously.

Evelyn Cisneros received awards from Hispanic Women Making History in 1984 and the Mexican American Legal Defense Fund in 1985. In 1987, she was honored as an outstanding member of the Hispanic community by the National Concilio of America. The next year, in 1988, she was honored for her outstanding achievement in the performing arts by the California State League of United Latin American Citizens. That same year she also was a spokesperson for a Latino youth conference held at California State University.

Evelyn also talks often to school children about what her life is like. She tells young dancers, "When you do anything athletic—and ballet is very hard on your body—you have to take good care of yourself. You have to make sure you eat properly and get enough rest."

When Evelyn is not dancing she and her husband, former dancer Robert Sund, share their home with two cats, Chatito and Boris. They like to walk on the beach, invite friends over for dinner, and go to the movies. For vacations, she and Robert go to Hawaii, or to visit Evelyn's parents in Baja California.

The San Francisco Ballet production of Swan Lake.

403

... she is applauded wherever she goes.

Evelyn Cisneros has traveled a long way from being a shy little Mexican American girl in Huntington Beach. Today, she is comfortable on dance stages around the world. Instead of being teased and left out, she is applauded wherever she goes. Through hard work and determination, she has turned her talent into a treasure.

Think About It

❶ How did Evelyn Cisneros use her creativity to overcome difficulties in her life?

❷ Why do you think the author uses direct quotes from Evelyn Cisneros?

❸ What do you think was the turning point in Evelyn's career? Explain your answer.

Meet the Author
Charnan Simon

Charnan Simon grew up in Ohio, Oregon, and Washington. She holds a B.A. degree in English Literature from Carleton College in Northfield, Minnesota, and an M.A. in English Literature from the University of Chicago. Ms. Simon worked for a children's book company in Boston after college, and then spent five happy years editing *Cricket* magazine. It was during her *Cricket* years that she began studying ballet and tap. She loved it—and it was great preparation for writing about Evelyn Cisneros. Ms. Simon has written dozens of books and articles for young people and especially likes writing—and reading— history, biography, and fiction of all sorts. She wrote *Jane Addams: Pioneer Social Worker* and won the Notable Social Studies Trade Book award in 1997. Today Ms. Simon lives in Madison, Wisconsin with her husband and two daughters.

Celebration

I shall dance tonight.
When the dusk comes crawling,
There will be dancing
  and feasting.
I shall dance with the others
  in circles,
    in leaps,
    in stomps.
Laughter and talk
  will weave into the night,
Among the fires
  of my people.
Games will be played
And I shall be
  a part of it.

—Alonzo Lopez
Illustrated by Tomie dePaola

Eagle Flight

An eagle wings gracefully
through the sky.
On the earth I stand
and watch.
My heart flies with it.

—*Alonzo Lopez*
Illustrated by Tomie dePaola

Response Activities

A Big Decision

LIST PROS AND CONS   Evelyn Cisneros had to make a big decision about her life when she was only fourteen. What things do you think she considered? Make two columns on a sheet of paper. In one column, list the pros, or reasons for her choice. In the other, list the cons, or reasons against it. Keep in mind that Evelyn couldn't have known at that time how her life would turn out.

In Motion

CONSTRUCT A MOBILE   Use art materials and found objects to create a mobile. Try to capture the graceful movements of ballet. Some of the photographs used to illustrate the selection may give you ideas for your mobile.

Finding Out

MAKE A PRESENTATION   Gather information about a performing arts school near you. For example, you might talk to people you know who attend one of these schools. You might also use the yellow pages of the phone book to make telephone calls to performing arts schools, asking for advertisements and brochures. Use the information you gather to make an oral presentation about where these schools are located in your community, what kinds of programs they offer, and when their classes are held.

Making Connections

CREATE DANCE MOVEMENTS   A ballet is a dance that tells a story. Some ballets take their stories from fairy tales, folktales, legends, or poems. With a small group, choose one of the poems by Alonzo Lopez. Create dance movements that you can use to show the ideas and feelings expressed in the poem.

409

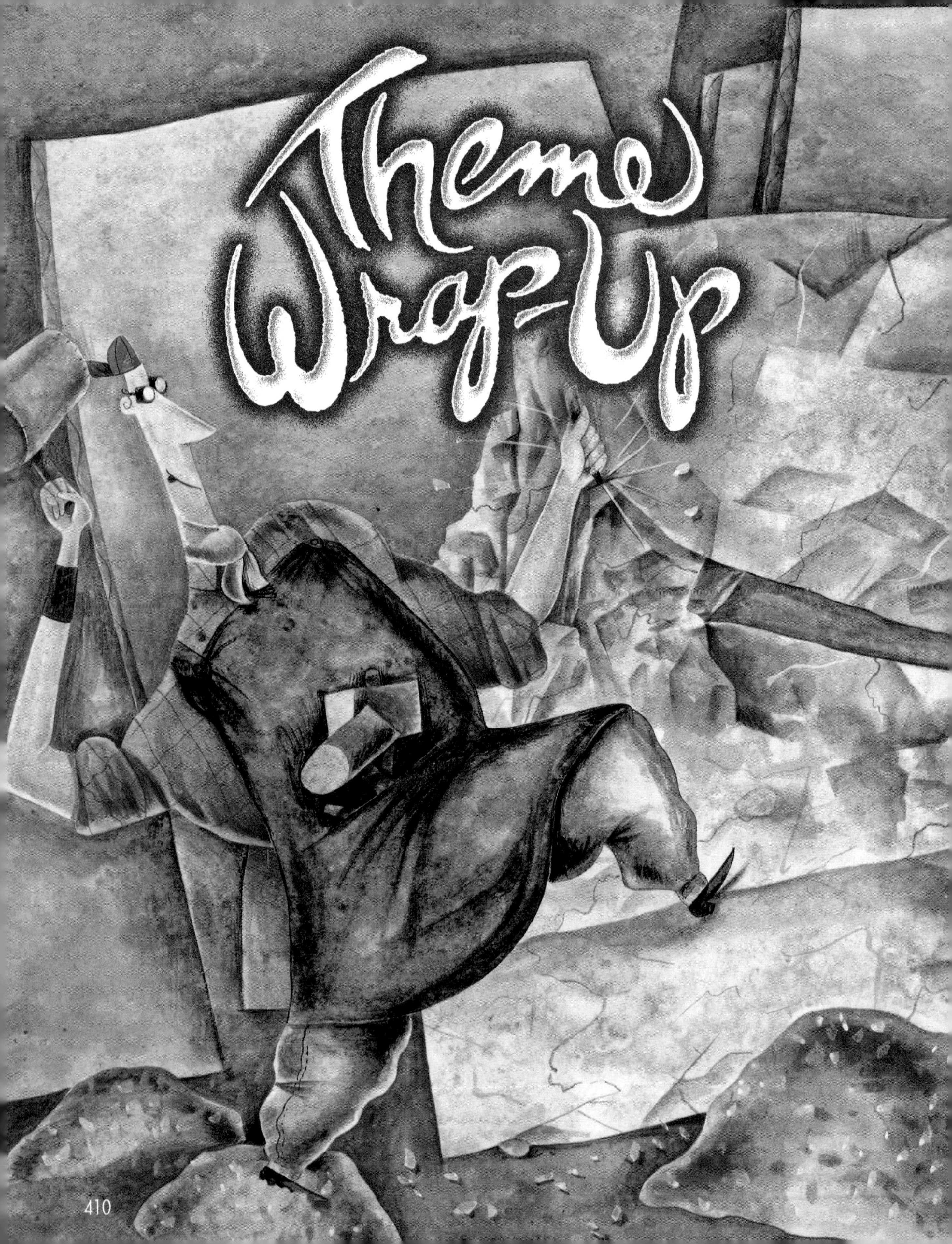
Theme
Wrap-Up

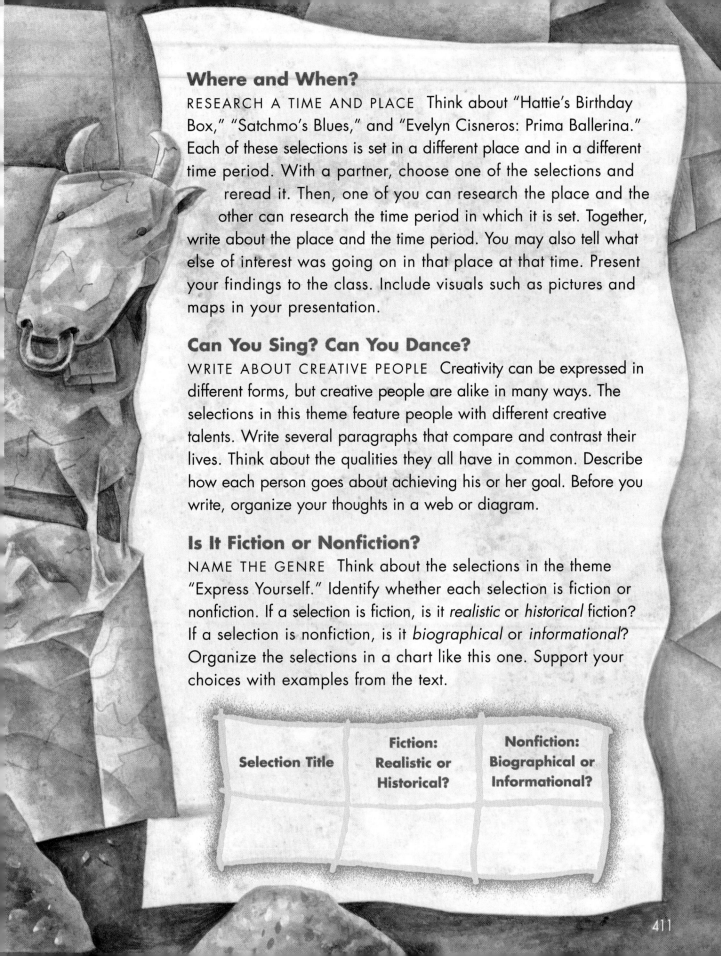

Where and When?

RESEARCH A TIME AND PLACE Think about "Hattie's Birthday Box," "Satchmo's Blues," and "Evelyn Cisneros: Prima Ballerina." Each of these selections is set in a different place and in a different time period. With a partner, choose one of the selections and reread it. Then, one of you can research the place and the other can research the time period in which it is set. Together, write about the place and the time period. You may also tell what else of interest was going on in that place at that time. Present your findings to the class. Include visuals such as pictures and maps in your presentation.

Can You Sing? Can You Dance?

WRITE ABOUT CREATIVE PEOPLE Creativity can be expressed in different forms, but creative people are alike in many ways. The selections in this theme feature people with different creative talents. Write several paragraphs that compare and contrast their lives. Think about the qualities they all have in common. Describe how each person goes about achieving his or her goal. Before you write, organize your thoughts in a web or diagram.

Is It Fiction or Nonfiction?

NAME THE GENRE Think about the selections in the theme "Express Yourself." Identify whether each selection is fiction or nonfiction. If a selection is fiction, is it *realistic* or *historical* fiction? If a selection is nonfiction, is it *biographical* or *informational*? Organize the selections in a chart like this one. Support your choices with examples from the text.

Selection Title	Fiction: Realistic or Historical?	Nonfiction: Biographical or Informational?

THEME

SCHOOL RULES

CONTENTS

Frindle

by Andrew Clements

FICTION

In this imaginative tale, Nick learns about words and where they come from. When he invents a new word, excitement spreads throughout the school and the town.

READER'S CHOICE LIBRARY

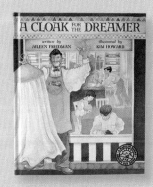

A Cloak for the Dreamer

by Aileen Friedman

FOLKTALE

Misha dreams of exploring the world, not following in his father's footsteps to become a tailor.

READER'S CHOICE LIBRARY

The Librarian Who Measured the Earth

by Kathryn Lasky

BIOGRAPHY

Everyone knew the Earth was round, but no one knew its size. Curiosity leads Eratosthenes to measure our planet.

***SLJ* Best Book**

Strider

by Beverly Cleary

REALISTIC FICTION

Leigh and Barry find a dog abandoned at the beach. They name him Strider and share custody of their new best friend.

Award-Winning Author

Math Curse

by Jon Scieszka

REALISTIC FICTION

Find out what happens when a girl's day is filled with arithmetic. Will she break her math curse?

Texas Bluebonnet Award; Children's Choice; *SLJ* Best Book

READER'S CHOICE

Off and

Miata Ramirez is running for fifth-grade president against Rudy, the class clown. Miata promises to plant flowers and clean up the school if elected. Rudy promises extra ice cream days and more recess time. When Rudy appears to be winning, Miata considers what she can do to get back in the race.

OFF AND RUNNING

GARY SOTO
ILLUSTRATED BY ERIC VELASQUEZ

Award-Winning
Author

Running

by Gary Soto   illustrated by Jerry Tiritilli

Saturday morning. There were only a few days to go until election day. Miata sat before the cluttered desk in her bedroom, surrounded by campaign posters and buttons. She stirred the water of her five-gallon aquarium with a pencil. One of the guppies darted and blew out a single bubble that rose to the surface and popped.

"Come on," Miata said into the telephone cradled between her ear and neck. She was calling a classmate to remind her to vote on Tuesday. She had called Dolores, Alma, Sandra, and Apple, whose real name was Apolonia.

"Belinda?" Miata asked when a voice answered.

"No, it's her mom," the thick voice replied. "She's still asleep."

"Would you please remind her to vote for me — this is Miata Ramirez."

The woman said that she would give the message to her daughter and hung up.

Then Miata's telephone rang. Miata answered in an official tone, "The Ramirez residence." Then she heard that *quack-quack* of duck laughter. Miata sat up straight and pulled some loose ends of hair behind her ear.

"Who is this?"

"Quack-quack."

"You think you're cute!"

"No. Rudy's cute. *Quack-quack.*"

"Are you a friend of Rudy's?"

"Better than a friend."

With this, the person hung up, leaving Miata repeating to herself, "Better than a friend. What does that mean?" Miata stared at the telephone. She picked up the receiver again and expected to hear the obnoxious *quack-quack* of laughter but got only the usual long *buzzzzzzzzz.*

When she heard her name being called, she left her bedroom and sniffed in the delicious scent of *chorizo con huevos*. She tried to get into a better mood. She skipped to the kitchen, where her father was already at the table.

"*Buenos días*," he greeted her, the sports page folded in front of him. "You been on the phone a lot, *mi'ja*." He sipped his coffee and asked, "*Pues*, so who's your *novio*?"

"Papi, I don't have a boyfriend! I was calling some girls to vote for me." She sat down, stomach growling, and clutched her napkin. She liked Saturday mornings. That was when her mother made tortillas.

"Dad," she asked, "you ever know anyone important?"

"Ever know anyone important?" her father repeated slowly. His eyes floated up to his wife, who was cracking an egg into the frying pan. "How 'bout your mommy? She's important."

Miata got up and hugged her mom's waist. "Mom is the best." She looked down at the eggs, now brownish red from the *chorizo*, and inhaled the flavorful smells of fried *papas*.

Her father sipped his coffee and said, "You mean someone well known?"

"Yeah." Miata returned and sat down, scooting her chair along the linoleum floor.

"Someone like a rock star or an actor?"

"Yeah, like that!"

"Someone like Eddie Olmos or Carlos Santana?"

"Yeah, Dad!"

"Like those *vatos* called Culture Clash?"

"Exactly!"

Miata's father tapped his wrench-thick finger on the table as he searched his memory. He finally shook his head and said, "Nah, can't say I have."

Miata's heart sank. She wanted to see if someone famous would endorse her campaign.

Joey came into the kitchen, still in his pajamas. His eyes were thick with sleep. He said, "Hi," and climbed into his chair.

Breakfast was now on the table. As Miata's family tore into the morning feast, her mom told her about a woman who had been mayor of a town in Mexico. It was Miata's *abuela's* sister-in-law. The woman had been mayor three times and was responsible for educating the young people.

"A real mayor?" Miata said with her mouth full. She swallowed and drank from her milk glass. Her mind began to turn. She thought that maybe that woman could tell her something about winning an election.

"Yeah, in a *pueblecito* near Aguascalientes. That was way before she moved here." Her mother wiped her plate with a piece of tortilla.

"Can you call her for me?" Miata asked.

"If you want, *mi'ja,*" Miata's mother said. "I think I have her number. But she's really old." Mrs. Ramirez got up and cleared away some of the dishes from the table.

Miata's father asked, "We're going to the *quinceañera, ¿que no?*" as he picked up his own plate. They had been invited to celebrate the fifteenth birthday of a friend's daughter.

"Of course, but I'll let Miata visit with *la señora* for a little bit first."

After breakfast Miata and her father did the dishes, soapsuds climbing to their elbows. By the time they were finished, Miata's mother had arranged to see the woman, who lived nearby. Her name was Doña Carmen Elena Vasquez. Miata's mother said the woman was very happy to talk with Miata but would she please buy her some bread and Doña Carmen would pay her later.

"What should I ask her?" Miata asked. Now she was uncertain about meeting the woman.

"I don't know, *mi'ja*," her mother said. She was standing in front of the mirror in the hallway, dabbing her puckered mouth with peach-colored

422

lipstick. "Come on. I'll give you a ride and you can walk home."

"Where are you going, Mom?" Miata asked. She pushed her face toward the mirror and glanced at her curls. She was starting to like her new hairdo.

"To Kmart."

Miata and her mother left, pulling away from the curb in their new used car, a Ford Thunderbird. They drove slowly up the street, the tires sweeping the fall leaves. They stopped at a convenience store to buy the bread.

They arrived at Doña Carmen's house.

"Don't let her pay you for the bread," Miata's mother told her. "Tell her it's a gift."

Miata got out of the car and eyed the small house, which was white with a toppled TV antenna on the roof. Geraniums, potted in coffee cans and milk cartons, lined the steps of the porch. A ceramic statue of *la Virgen de Guadalupe* stood in the middle of the lawn. On the bumper of Doña Carmen's old Ford LTD gleamed a sticker: YO ❤ JALISCO.

"Do I have to go by myself?" Miata asked.

"Yes. You wanted to meet someone important," Miata's mother replied through the window.

"Is she nice?"

"Of course she's nice. She's your *abuela's* sister-in-law. She's family."

Miata looked at the house. A cat was now stretching on the steps.

"When you're done talking, I want you to go straight home," her mother continued. "We have to be at the *quinceañera* at three." She touched a button and the window slowly rolled up with a sigh. The Thunderbird pulled away, scattering some leaves and an orange-colored cat washing itself in the middle of the street.

Miata approached the house, kicking at the fall leaves. She walked up the steps, knocked on the screen door, and peered in. An old woman was sitting on the edge of the couch. She was holding a lamp in one hand and a screwdriver in the other. A toolbox sat on the coffee table.

"Hello," Miata called brightly. "Am I disturbing you?"

"*¿Quién es?* Who is it?" the woman asked. She rose from the couch and unlatched the screen door.

"It's me—Miata Ramirez." She held up the loaf of bread. "I got it for you, Doña Carmen."

"*¡Ven acá, mi'ja!* Come in," Doña Carmen said in a singsong voice. She was a short woman, an inch taller than Miata, and walked with a slow shuffle. Her face was as soft as a pear, but her hair was steel gray.

Miata entered the house. A yellowish shaft of sunlight entered the corner of the living room, where a bookshelf sat. Portraits of the Kennedys and Cesar Chavez hung on the wall. A crucifix, made of bronze, hung on the wall.

"*¿Cómo te llamas?* What's your name?" Doña Carmen asked.

"Miata."

"Miata?" Doña Carmen regarded the young girl. "You gotta lot of curls."

Miata touched her hair. She wanted to explain the perm but thought the story was too complicated.

Doña Carmen told Miata in Spanish to sit down and apologized for the messiness of the house. She gestured to the toolbox on the coffee table.

"I'm fixing the lamp," Doña Carmen said. "It wouldn't close."

"You mean turn off?"

"*Sí.*" She sighed and said, "So you want to be *la jefa*, the leader, at your school?"

When Miata nodded her head, the curls bounced about her ears.

"Your *mami* probably told you. I used to be the mayor of *mi pueblo*." She sat up straight, hands on the lap of her print dress. "Yes, I beat *mi esposo*, my husband."

"You . . . ran against your husband?" Miata asked.

"*Sí, muchacha.*" Doña Carmen's eyes sparkled as she recalled her husband, dead now eight years. They had loved each other but had seldom thought the same way.

"*Pues*, he would argue, '*Vieja*, today is Tuesday,' and I would say, '*No, hombre*, it's Wednesday.' Then we would spend all week arguing if

Tuesday was really Wednesday. That's how we were. We went round and round. Imagine! We lived like that for forty-six years until God took him away."

"So you ran against him for mayor?" Miata was now more than curious. She had spied a portrait of the couple on top of the television. They were as young as fruit on a tree.

"Yes. The man didn't want to advance. When we had a chance to hire some smart young women from Mexico City to teach in the school, he was against it. He said that the young women had city ideas that would make the children bad." Doña Carmen laughed and slapped her lap. "But you know what? Our children were already bad!" She laughed again and said, "No, they weren't *really* bad. They just liked to play."

Immediately Miata pictured Rudy and Alex. They just liked to play, too.

Doña Carmen explained how she had run against her husband because she had seen the future. She knew that one day the children of her town

would need to advance, not stay in place.

"The days of working like donkeys were gone, *mi'ja*," Doña Carmen said. "And the *gente*—the people—could see this. So I won! I was the mayor for three terms!"

"That's great," Miata said. She was impressed and full of fire as she listened to Doña Carmen tell her

recess." Miata clicked her tongue. "Doesn't that sound ridiculous?"

Doña Carmen looked right into Miata's eyes and, it seemed to her, right into her heart. "*¿Y tú?* What are you promising?"

Miata looked away for a moment and bit her bottom lip. After listening to the old woman's story, Miata was afraid that she had nothing really to offer.

"I just want to do little things," Miata said.

"*¿Cómo?*"

Miata told her that her school was run-down. There was graffiti, broken equipment, a poor, muddy lawn, and no flowers in the flower beds. Her promise was to make things pretty.

"Good. I will help you."

"How?"

"I'll give you all the flowers and little snippings you need." Doña Carmen rose from the couch and pulled Miata by her arm. She led her through the kitchen and out the back door. They stood on the small porch overlooking hundreds of plants— geraniums, azaleas, rosebushes,

about the new school they had constructed and the numbers who had gone on to the university.

"You're running against a *muchacho* at school, *¿que no?*" Doña Carmen asked.

"Yeah, this boy named Rudy Herrera."

"What is he promising?"

"Ice cream every day and more

hydrangeas, and jasmine.

"It's almost winter, but in spring, *pues*, we'll have *muchas flores*!"

"Yeah," Miata whispered to herself, as she pictured in her mind the fragrant jasmine waving in the wind. She also pictured the azalea she had planted, dotted with white flowers.

"We're going to have a sweet-smelling school."

Think About It

❶ How does meeting Doña Carmen make a difference in Miata's life?

❷ How does the author's use of Spanish words add to the selection?

❸ What traits does Miata have that would make her a good school leader? Why are these traits important?

"I think I'm very childlike," says Gary Soto. "I like the *youth* in my poetry. For me that's really important."

It was Gary's youthful outlook on life that led him to start writing poetry and stories for young people. Most of his stories are about experiences he had growing up. He believes he can write best about the things he knows. The fun that he had pops up in many of his stories. The things that were not fun are there too, things such as chopping cotton and cutting grapes under the hot California sun. In Gary Soto's stories, you can share these experiences.

Response Act

VOTE FOR MIATA

CREATE A POSTER
Think of a good slogan that Miata could use in her campaign. Then create an eye-catching poster based on your slogan. The poster should tell voters what Miata stands for and why they should vote for her.

A BETTER SCHOOL

MAKE A CHART Miata runs for class president because she wants to make changes in her school. What kinds of changes would you like to see in your school? Make a chart that lists the changes you would like to make. Beside each change, list the materials or other resources you would need. In a third column, list the people or groups you would ask to help you.

ivities

CREATE A FACT SHEET Doña Carmen had been the mayor of her town in Mexico. Who is your mayor? Use local newspapers and other sources to find out about the mayor of your town or city. Make up a fact sheet telling about your mayor and what he or she has done for your community.

COME TO A *QUINCEAÑERA*

EXPLAIN THE CELEBRATION Miata's family is invited to a *quinceañera*, or fifteenth birthday party. Find out why this birthday is important in Spanish-speaking cultures. Maybe someone in your school or your community can tell you how it is celebrated. With a partner, role-play inviting someone to a *quinceañera*. The person being invited is unfamiliar with this kind of celebration, so briefly explain what it is.

Predict Outcomes

As you read "Off and Running," you probably tried to think about what would happen next. When we read, we often **make predictions**. To do this, we combine what the author tells us with what we already know. Thinking about story events and the characters' actions and feelings will help you make logical predictions as you read.

Read the chart below to understand how you can combine story information with your own knowledge to make a prediction.

Information I Have Read		My Experiences		My Prediction
Miata wants to win an election. She is energetic and hardworking.	**+**	I know that energetic, responsible people usually find a way to succeed.	**=**	I predict Miata will listen to Doña Carmen's ideas and win the election.

Predicting outcomes gives you a purpose for reading. When you have made a prediction, you find yourself reading to find out whether you are right or wrong. Having a purpose for reading helps you remember more of what you read.

Read the following paragraph. Then make and complete a chart like the one shown.

Rosa tapped the coffee can lightly against the patio. Leaning the can to one side, she pulled gently on the cluster of stems and eased out the marigolds. Cradling the root ball in her hands, she lowered the plants into the dirt. The soil was damp yet crumbly. Carefully, she spooned potting soil into the hole.

Information		Experience		Prediction
	+		=	

WHAT HAVE YOU LEARNED?

1 Doña Carmen went to a friend's house for the weekend and didn't water her plant. What do you predict will happen to the plant?

2 Think of an event being planned by your class or school. What do you predict will happen? Why do you think as you do?

Visit The Learning Site!
www.harcourtschool.com

TRY THIS • TRY THIS • TRY THIS

Write the beginning of a mystery story. Give readers enough information to make a logical prediction. Readers can use a chart like the one below to make predictions.

Information		Experience		Prediction
	+		=	

Little by Little

by Jean Little

illustrated by Allen Garns

LITTLE BY LITTLE

A Writer's Education

JEAN LITTLE

ALA Notable Book

Boston Globe — Horn Book Honor

Nine-year-old Jean Little enjoys reading, though she has problems with it. The words jiggle before her eyes and are badly blurred. To make matters worse, some children are mean to her about these problems. But Jean is determined to fit in, especially today, the first day in fifth grade.

I looked up from my grade five reader and smiled. I liked Miss Marr a lot. And, even though we had only met an hour ago, I thought she liked me, too.

She was young and pretty and she had a gentle voice. But that was not all. Like Mr. Johnston, she had had polio. As I listened to her passing out books behind me, I could hear

limping, first a quick step, then a slow one. The sound made me feel a little less lonely. My teacher would understand how it felt to be the only cross-eyed girl in Victory School.

"This is your desk, Jean," she had said.

It sat, all by itself, right up against the front blackboard. I was supposed to be able to see better there. I had not yet managed to make anyone understand that if I wanted to read what was written on the board, I would have to stand up so that my face was only inches away from the writing. Then I would have to walk back and forth, following the words not only with my eyes but with my entire body. If the writing were up at the top of the board, I would have to stand on tiptoe or even climb on a chair to be able to decipher it. If it were near the bottom, I would have to crouch down.

I remembered Miss Bogart printing large, thick, yellow letters on a green chalkboard. That had been so different. These dusty grey boards looked almost the same colour as the thin, white scratches Miss Marr's chalk made. Her small, neat words were composed of letters that flowed into each other, too, which made reading them even harder.

I would not explain. How could I? She might make me climb and crouch to read the words.

I stood out far too much as it was. All the desks except mine were nailed to the floor in five straight rows. The seats flipped up when you slid out of them. They were attached to the desk behind. On top was a trough for your pencil, and in the right-hand corner, an inkwell which Miss Marr kept filled from a big ink bottle with a long spout. All the desk lids were a dark wine colour.

My desk was new and varnished a shiny golden brown. It had been provided for me because, in theory, it could be moved to wherever I could see best. It was, however, far too heavy and unwieldy for Miss Marr or me to shift. All that special desk did was single me out even more.

I turned sideways in my new desk so that I could watch Miss Marr and caught sight of Shirley Russell instead. If only she would notice me!

Shirley had about her the magic of a story. She and her brother Ian had come from England to stay with their aunt and uncle and be safe from the bombing. She had joined our class near the end of grade four. Shirley had a lovely voice, with an accent like the child movie actress Margaret O'Brien's. She also had golden ringlets, longer and fairer than Shirley Temple's. She was a War Guest. She was different, too, but everybody wanted to be her friend.

"Face front, Jean," Miss Marr said. "Here are your spelling words."

She had typed them for me on a big print typewriter. I bent over them, drawing each letter on the roof of my mouth with the tip of my tongue. I had discovered that this helped me to remember them. It also helped fill in time.

When the bell rang for recess, Miss Marr astonished me by saying to Shirley Russell, "This is Jean Little, Shirley. She can't see well. Would you be her friend and help her get into the right line when it's time to come back inside?"

Shirley smiled sweetly and nodded her golden head. I could not believe this was really happening. Shirley Russell was actually going to be my friend. At last I was going to have a girl to do things with, and not just any girl. The War Guest herself!

We marched down the stairs and went out into the girls' side of the playground. I turned to Shirley, my smile shy, my heart singing.

Shirley scowled. Just under her breath, so that nobody but me could hear, she snarled, "You keep away from me. Get lost!"

Then she turned and ran.

"Be my partner, Shirley, and I'll give you my Crackerjack prize," I heard one girl call out.

There was a hubbub of offered bribes and vows of eternal friendship. Nobody looked in my direction.

I stood where I was, stunned into immobility. I should have guessed, perhaps, that our teacher had asked the impossible of the English girl. She was popular at the moment, but if she had me trailing after her, her accent might suddenly cease to be interesting and just be weird. She was a foreigner, after all, and she knew it.

Before any of them had time to notice me watching them, I walked away to the far side of the playground. I leaned up against a tall tree and stared off into the distance, as though I had my mind on things other than silly grade five girls. To keep myself from crying, I began talking to the tree that was supporting me.

"Are you lonely, too, tree?" I murmured. "If you are, I'll come every day and talk to you. We could be friends."

As I drew a shaking breath, much like a sob, I heard a gentle rustle above my head. I glanced up. The leafy branches seemed to nod to me.

You can count on a tree, I told myself. A tree is better than a person.

But I knew it was not true.

When we were supposed to line up to march in again, I heard Shirley's laugh and tagged on the end of the right line. I counted my steps on the way in. I'd find it tomorrow without any help from Shirley Russell.

Back at my desk, I heard Miss Marr ask two people to pass out pieces of paper. Staring down at the blank sheet, I hoped we were going to draw or write a composition.

"We're going to have a mental arithmetic test," Miss Marr said.

"Write down the numbers 1 to 10 on your paper."

I bent my arm around my sheet, shielding it from prying eyes, even though the others were not close

to me. I had a sinking feeling the
test she was talking about would
involve those horrible times tables
everybody but me had mastered in
grade three. I picked up the special fat
pencil Miss Marr had given me and
did as I had been told. As I waited
for the first question, I clutched the
pencil so tightly that my knuckles
whitened.

"Question one," said Miss Marr.
"8 × 3."

I began to add. Eight and eight
were . . . sixteen? Or was it fourteen?

Three and three are six, I muttered
inside my head, changing my method
of attack. I turned down two fingers so
that I would know when I reached
eight.

"Question two," Miss Marr said.
"6 × 4."

I gave up on question one and
began to add fours. I had reached
twelve and four are sixteen when she
went on to question three.

When she reached question ten, I stared down at my paper in dismay. All that was written on it were the numbers 1 to 10 in a neat column. I had not managed to get even one answer.

"Since this is the first day, you can each mark your own paper," she said. "What is it, Ruth?"

"Can I sharpen my pencil?" Ruth Dayton's voice asked.

"Yes. But hurry up. You are keeping us all waiting."

As she passed behind me, Ruth glanced over my shoulder. I did not notice her small hiss of astonishment as she took in the fact that I had not answered a single question.

"The answer to question one is twenty-four," the teacher said as Ruth regained her seat.

I knew that behind my back, forty pencils were checking the answer. I had to do something to look busy. With painstaking neatness, I pencilled in 24 beside the number 1.

"If you have 24 beside the number 1," said my new teacher, "check it right."

I stared down at my page. There, right next to the 1 was written 24. Feeling a little like a sleepwalker, unable to stop herself, I put a check mark next to the answer my teacher had just dictated. After all, she had *not* said, "If you got the answer right . . ." She had said, "If you have the number 24 beside the number 1 . . ." And I did.

"The correct answer for Number 2 is also 24," she said then. I wrote that down.

"If you have the answer 24 beside the number 2, check it right."

We worked our way down the sheet. First she would tell us the answer. I would write it down. Then she would instruct us to "check it right," and I would put a neat check mark on the paper.

When the others had finished marking their answers right or wrong, Miss Marr said, "Raise your hand if you have ten answers checked right."

I looked at my arithmetic paper. There they were, all ten answers checked right. I raised my hand. As I did so, I expected something dramatic to happen, a thunderbolt to strike me dead or a huge voice to roar, *"Jean Little, what have you done?"* Nothing of the kind disturbed Miss Marr's classroom. The teacher looked around at the eight or nine raised hands.

"Good for you," she said.

I snatched my hand down and stared hard at a broken piece of chalk lying in the chalk trough. I did not check to see whether anybody admitted to having none checked right. I was sure I was the only one who would have missed them all.

As she began a geography lesson, I felt relief wash over me. Mental arithmetic was at an end, for that day, at least. Perhaps everything was going to be all right.

My happiness lasted until noon.

Ruth and Stella came marching up to my desk while I was putting away my books. They stared at me with contempt.

"I saw you," Ruth said.

"What a cheat!" Stella put in. Her eyes were gleaming.

"Saw me what?" I said feebly. "I don't know what you're talking about. I didn't cheat."

"You might as well save your breath," Stella sneered. "Ruth *saw* you and so did I. You copied down the answers after she said them out loud."

"Are you going to tell on me?" I heard, and despised, the bleat of panic in my voice. They had me at their mercy and we all knew it.

"Do you think we would tattle?" Stella said, as though such a thing had never been known to happen. "We won't tell."

I cheered up too soon. She had not finished.

"But if you don't tell her yourself what a cheater you are, nobody in this class will ever speak to you again. We don't intend to be friends with a cheater."

I had no choice. I longed for friends. In spite of Shirley's snub, I still hoped that someday it might happen. I couldn't risk turning the entire class against me.

Miss Marr was at her desk. I walked up to stand beside it, moving slowly, trying hard to think of a way to confess that would satisfy my class and not make Miss Marr hate me.

Ruth and Stella lurked near enough to hear what I said. I stood by my teacher's elbow until she looked up. Then I took a deep breath and began. I stammered and stuttered, but at last she took in what I was mumbling. She told me to sit down. Then she waved Stella and Ruth away.

"You two are supposed to be on your way home," she said, her voice a little sharp. "Run along."

They went as slowly as they dared, but until they were well out of earshot, Miss Marr ignored me. She sharpened a pencil, then two. Finally she turned and looked at me.

"I saw what you did, Jean," she said.

I gasped. Had she watched me cheat and said nothing? I could not believe it.

She sat down near me and went on quietly.

"I don't think you meant to cheat, did you? It just happened . . . when you could not get the answers fast enough to keep up. Wasn't that the way it was?"

"Yes. That's just what happened," I told her, staring at the floor and trying not to cry. "I'm no good at my times tables . . ."

447

"You won't ever do it again, will you?"

I shook my head violently.

"Never ever!"

"Then we'll just forget it this time," she told me. "And you'd better get busy learning your tables."

"I will," I promised. "Oh, I will."

Think About It

1. What problems does Jean face, and what does she learn?

2. Do you think Ruth and Stella are right to treat Jean as they do? Why or why not?

3. Why do you think the author called her autobiography "Little by Little"?

Meet the Author

Jean Little

When did you decide to become a writer? I always wanted to become a writer, but I thought writers had a difficult time making a living. So I became a teacher. After teaching for a while, I decided to give writing a try. I wrote a book, *Mine for Keeps*, which was a story about a young girl with cerebral palsy.

Do you use any special tools to help you when writing? Yes. I write on a talking computer, and I use a scanner that magnifies print.

How do you try to capture the interest of your readers? I like to start a story at a point where the main character is facing a change or a challenge of some sort. I never start with the main character cozily waking up. He or she is usually puzzled, afraid, irritated, or sad.

449

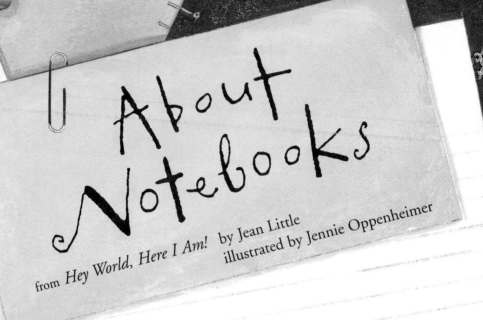

About Notebooks

from *Hey World, Here I Am!* by Jean Little
illustrated by Jennie Oppenheimer

I love the first page of a new notebook.
I write the date crisply.
My whole name marches exactly along the line.
The spaces are always even.
The commas curl just so.
I never have to erase on the first page.
Never!

When I get to the middle, there are lots of eraser holes.
The corners are dog-eared.
Whole paragraphs have been crossed out.
My words slide off the lines and crowd together.
I wish it was done.

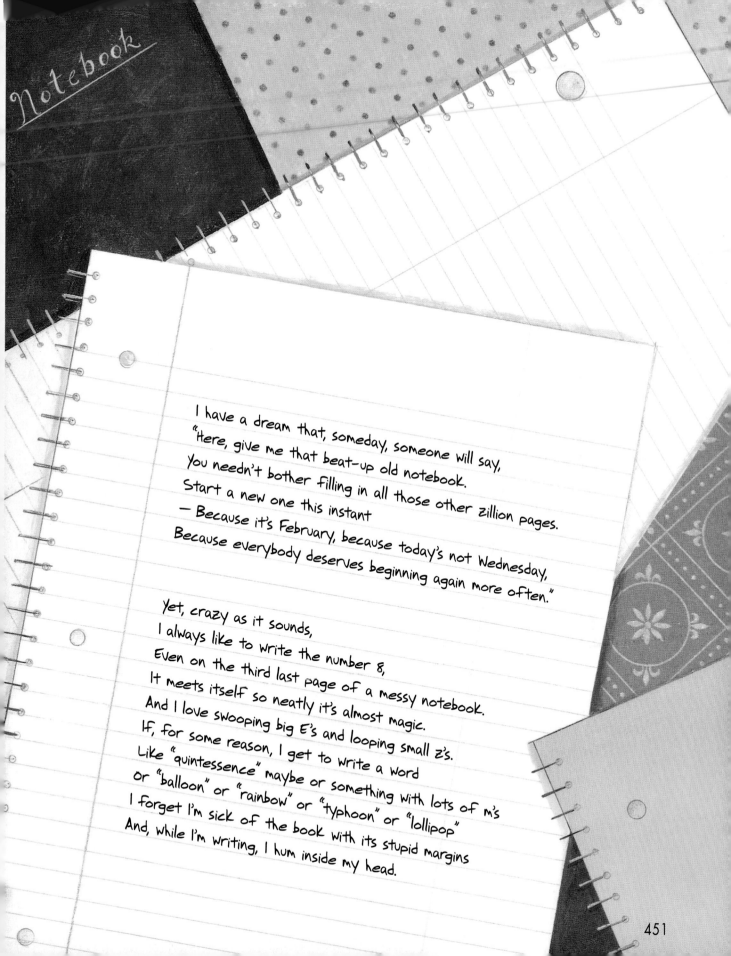

I have a dream that, someday, someone will say,
"Here, give me that beat-up old notebook.
You needn't bother filling in all those other zillion pages.
Start a new one this instant
— Because it's February, because today's not Wednesday,
Because everybody deserves beginning again more often."

Yet, crazy as it sounds,
I always like to write the number 8,
Even on the third last page of a messy notebook.
It meets itself so neatly it's almost magic.
And I love swooping big E's and looping small z's.
If, for some reason, I get to write a word
Like "quintessence" maybe or something with lots of m's
Or "balloon" or "rainbow" or "typhoon" or "lollipop"
I forget I'm sick of the book with its stupid margins
And, while I'm writing, I hum inside my head.

ReSponse

PAINT A PICTURE Imagine how you would feel if you experienced the same problems that Jean Little did in the fifth grade. Use paints or watercolors to create a picture that shows your feelings. Your painting may show a realistic scene, or it may use shapes and colors to express emotions.

WRITE A LETTER Many years have passed since Jean Little was in school. Do you think students today would treat her the same way that her classmates did then? Write a letter to Jean Little. Tell her what you think her experiences might be like if she were a fifth grader in your school today. Explain why they might be the same as or different from her experiences then.

Activities

WHAT HAPPENS NEXT?

ROLE-PLAY A CONVERSATION Miss Marr told Ruth and Stella to run along so she could speak with Jean in private. What might Ruth and Stella say to Jean after she talks to Miss Marr? What might Jean tell them? In a small group, role-play the events following Jean's talk with Miss Marr.

MAKING CONNECTIONS

WRITE A PARAGRAPH In the poem "About Notebooks," Jean Little describes some of her habits of writing. Choose something important from the poem that best describes Jean Little as a writer. Explain your answer.

DEAR MR. HENSHAW

by Beverly Cleary
illustrated by David Goldin

Leigh Botts has been keeping a diary and writing to his favorite author, Mr. Boyd Henshaw, since second grade. Now, as a sixth grader, Leigh has new problems:

Newbery Medal
ALA Notable Book
SLJ Best Book

❶ His mother and his father, a truck driver, are divorced.

❷ His father's girlfriend has a son his age that Leigh calls the pizza boy.

❸ Someone at school is stealing the best part of Leigh's lunch every day.

❹ His story for the Young Writers' Yearbook is not going well.

Can Leigh find solutions to any of these problems?

Thursday, March 1

I am getting behind in this diary for several reasons, including working on my story and writing to Mr. Henshaw (really, not just pretend). I also had to buy a new notebook because I had filled up the first one.

The same day, I bought a beat-up black lunchbox in the thrift shop down the street and started carrying my lunch in it. The kids were surprised, but nobody made fun of me, because a black lunchbox isn't the same as one of those square boxes covered with cartoon characters that first and second graders carry. A couple of boys asked if it was my Dad's. I just grinned and said, "Where do you think I got it?" The next day my little

slices of salami rolled around cream cheese were gone, but I expected that. But I'll get that thief yet. I'll make him really sorry he ate all the best things out of my lunch.

Next I went to the library for books on batteries. I took out a couple of easy books on electricity, really easy, because I have never given much thought to batteries. About all I know is that when you want to use a flashlight, the battery is usually dead.

I finally gave up on my story about the ten-foot wax man, which was really pretty dumb. I thought I would write a poem about butterflies for Young Writers because

a poem can be short, but it is hard to think about butterflies and burglar alarms at the same time, so I studied electricity books instead. The books didn't have directions for an alarm in a lunchbox, but I learned enough about batteries and switches and insulated wires, so I think I can figure it out myself.

Friday, March 2

Back to the poem tonight. The only rhyme I can think of for "butterfly" is "flutter by." I can think up rhymes like "trees" and "breeze" which are pretty boring, and then I think of "wheeze" and "sneeze." A poem about butterflies wheezing and sneezing seems silly, and anyway a couple of girls are already writing poems about monarch butterflies that flutter by.

Sometimes I start a letter to Dad thanking him for the twenty dollars, but I can't finish that either. I don't know why.

Saturday, March 3

Today I took my lunchbox and Dad's twenty dollars to the hardware store and looked around. I found an ordinary light switch, a little battery and a cheap doorbell. While I was looking around for the right kind of insulated wire, a man who had been watching me (boys my age always get watched when they go into stores) asked if he could help me. He was a nice old gentleman who said, "What are you planning to make, son?" *Son*. He called me son, and my Dad calls me kid. I didn't want to tell the man, but when he looked at the things I was holding, he grinned and said, "Having trouble with your lunch, aren't you?" I nodded and said, "I'm trying to make a burglar alarm."

He said, "That's what I guessed. I've had workmen in here with the same problem."

It turned out that I needed a 6-volt lantern battery instead of the battery I had picked out. He gave me a couple of tips and, after I paid for the things, a little slap on the back and said, "Good luck, son."

457

I tore home with all the things I bought. First I made a sign for my door that said

KEEP OUT

MOM

THAT MEANS YOU

Then I went to work fastening one wire from the battery to the switch and from the other side of the switch to the doorbell. Then I fastened a second wire from the battery to the doorbell. It took me a while to get it right. Then I taped the battery in one corner of the lunchbox and the doorbell in another. I stood the switch up at the back of the box and taped that in place, too.

Here I ran into a problem. I thought I could take the wire clamp meant to hold a thermos bottle inside the lunchbox lid and hook it under the switch if I reached in carefully as I closed the box. The clamp wasn't quite long enough. After some thinking and experimenting, I twisted a wire loop onto it. Then I closed the box just enough so I could get my hand inside and push the wire loop over the button on the switch before I took my hand out and closed the box.

DOORBELL

BATTERY

CONNECT to SWITCH

Monday, March 5

Today Mom packed my lunch carefully, and we tried the alarm to see if it still worked. It did, good and loud. When I got to school, Mr. Fridley said, "Nice to see you smiling, Leigh. You should try it more often."

I parked my lunchbox behind the partition and waited. I waited all morning for the alarm to go off. Miss Martinez asked if I had my mind on my work. I pretended I did, but all the time I was really waiting for my alarm to go off so I could dash back behind the partition and tackle the thief. When nothing happened, I began to worry. Maybe the loop had somehow slipped off the switch on the way to school.

Then I opened the box. My burglar alarm worked! That bell inside the box went off with a terrible racket that brought Mom to my door. "Leigh, what on earth is going on in there?" she shouted above the alarm.

I let her in and gave her a demonstration of my burglar alarm. She laughed and said it was a great invention. One thing was bothering me. Would my sandwich muffle the bell? Mom must have been wondering the same thing, because she suggested taping a piece of cardboard into the lid that would make a shelf for my sandwich. I did, and that worked, too.

I can't wait until Monday.

Lunchtime came. The alarm still hadn't gone off. We all picked up our lunches and went off to the cafeteria. When I set my box on the table in front of me, I realized I had a problem, a big problem. If the loop hadn't slipped off the switch, my alarm was still triggered. I just sat there, staring at my lunchbox, not knowing what to do.

"How come you're not eating?" Barry asked with his mouth full. Barry's sandwiches are never cut in half, and he always takes a big bite out of one side to start.

Everybody at the table was looking at me. I thought about saying I wasn't hungry, but I was. I thought about taking my lunchbox out into the hall to open, but if the alarm was still triggered, there was no way I could open it quietly. Finally I thought, Here goes. I unsnapped the two fasteners on the box and held my breath as I opened the lid.

Wow! My alarm went off! The noise was so loud it startled everybody at the table including me and made everyone in the cafeteria look around. I looked up and saw Mr. Fridley grinning at me over by the garbage can. Then I turned off the alarm.

I began to feel like some sort of **HERO**. Maybe I'm not so medium after all.

L U N C H B O X   H E R O

Suddenly everybody seemed to be noticing me. The principal, who always prowls around keeping an eye on things at lunchtime, came over to examine my lunchbox. He said, "That's quite an invention you have there."

"Thanks," I said, pleased that the principal seemed to like my alarm.

Some of the teachers came out of their lunchroom to see what the noise was all about. I had to give a demonstration. It seems I wasn't the only one who had things stolen from my lunch, and all the kids said they wanted lunchboxes with alarms, too, even those whose lunches were never good enough to have anything stolen. Barry said he would like an alarm like that on the door of his room at home. I began to feel like some sort of hero. Maybe I'm not so medium after all.

One thing bothers me, though. I still don't know who's been robbing my lunch.

Tuesday, March 6

Today Barry asked me to come home with him to see if I could help him rig up a burglar alarm for his room because he has a bunch of little sisters and stepsisters who get into his stuff. I thought I could, because I had seen an alarm like that in one of the electricity books from the library.

Barry lives in a big old house that is sort of cheerful and messy, with little girls all over the place. As it turned out, Barry didn't have the right kind of battery so we just fooled around looking at his models. Barry never uses directions when he puts models together, because the directions are too hard and spoil the fun. He throws them away and figures out how the pieces fit by himself.

I still don't know what to write for Young Writers, but I was feeling so good I finally wrote to Dad to thank him for the twenty dollars because I had found a good use for it even if I couldn't save it all toward a typewriter. I didn't say much.

I wonder if Dad will marry the pizza boy and his mother. I worry about that a lot.

Thursday, March 15

This week several kids turned up with lunchboxes with burglar alarms. You know that song about the hills ringing with the sound of music? Well you might say our cafeteria rang with the sound of burglar alarms. The fad didn't last very long, and after a while I didn't even bother to set my alarm. Nobody has robbed my lunchbox since I set it off that day.

I never did find out who the thief was, and now that I stop to think about it, I am glad. If he had set off the alarm when my lunchbox was in the classroom, he would have been in trouble, big trouble. Maybe he was just somebody whose mother packed bad lunches—jelly sandwiches on that white bread that tastes like Kleenex. Or maybe he had to pack his own lunches and there was never anything good in the house to put in them. I have seen people look into their lunches, take out the cookies and throw the rest in the garbage. Mr. Fridley always looks worried when they do this.

I'm not saying robbing lunchboxes is right. I am saying I'm glad I don't know who the thief was, because I have to go to school with him.

Friday, March 16

Tonight I was staring at a piece of paper trying to think of something to write for Young Writers when the phone rang. Mom told me to answer because she was washing her hair.

It was Dad. My stomach felt as if it was dropping to the floor, the way it always does when I hear his voice. "How're you doing, kid?" he asked.

"Fine," I said, thinking of the success of my burglar alarm. "Great."

"I got your letter," he said.

"That's good," I said. His call took me so by surprise that I could feel my heart pounding, and I couldn't think of anything to say until I asked, "Have you found another dog to take Bandit's place?" I think what I really meant was, Have you found another boy to take my place?

"No, but I ask about him on my CB," Dad told me. "He may turn up yet."

"I hope so." This conversation was going no place. I really didn't know what to say to my father. It was embarrassing.

Then Dad surprised me. He asked, "Do you ever miss your old Dad?"

I had to think a minute. I missed him all right, but I couldn't seem to get the words out. My silence must have bothered him because he asked, "Are you still there?"

"Sure, Dad, I miss you," I told him. It was true, but not as true as it had been a couple of months ago. I still wanted him to pull up in front of the house in his big rig, but now I knew I couldn't count on it.

"Sorry I don't get over your way more often," he said. "I hear the sugar refinery in Spreckels is closing down."

"I read about it in the paper," I said.

"Is your mother handy?" he asked.

"I'll see," I said even though by then she was standing by the phone with her hair wrapped in a towel. She shook her head. She didn't want to talk to Dad.

"She's washing her hair," I said.

"Tell her I'll manage to send your support check sometime next week," he said. "So long, kid. Keep your nose clean."

"So long, Dad," I answered. "Drive carefully." I guess he'll never learn that my name is Leigh and that my nose is clean. Maybe he thinks I'll never learn that he drives carefully. He doesn't really. He's a good driver, but he speeds to make time whenever he can avoid the highway patrol. All truckers do.

After that I couldn't get back to thinking about Young Writers, so I picked up *Ways to Amuse a Dog* and read it for the thousandth time. I read harder books now, but I still feel good when I read that book. I wonder where Mr. Henshaw is.

Saturday, March 17

Today is Saturday, so this morning I walked to the butterfly trees again. The grove was quiet and peaceful, and because the sun was shining, I stood there a long time, looking at the orange butterflies floating through the gray and green leaves and listening to the sound of the ocean on the rocks. There aren't as many butterflies now. Maybe they are starting to go north for the summer. I thought I might write about them in prose instead of poetry, but on the way home I got to thinking about Dad and one time when he took me along when he was hauling grapes and what a great day it had been.

Tuesday, March 20

Yesterday Miss Neely, the librarian, asked if I had written anything for the Young Writers' Yearbook, because all writing had to be turned in by tomorrow. When I told her I hadn't, she said I still had twenty-four hours and why didn't I get busy? So I did, because I really would like to meet a Famous Author. My story about the ten-foot wax man went into the wastebasket. Next I tried to start a story called *The Great Lunchbox Mystery*, but I couldn't seem to turn my lunchbox experience into a story because I don't know who the thief (thieves) was (were), and I don't want to know.

Finally I dashed off a description of the time I rode with my father when he was trucking the load of grapes down Highway 152 through Pacheco Pass. I put in things like the signs that said STEEP GRADE, TRUCKS USE LOW GEAR and how Dad down-shifted and how skillful he was handling a long, heavy load on the curves. I put in about the hawks on the telephone wires and about that high peak where Black Bart's lookout used to watch for travelers coming through the pass so he could signal to Black Bart to rob them, and how the leaves on the trees along the stream at the bottom of the pass were turning yellow and how good tons of grapes smelled in the sun. I left out the part about the waitresses and the video games. Then I copied the whole thing over in case neatness counts and gave it to Miss Neely.

Saturday, March 24

Mom said I had to invite Barry over to our house for supper because I have been going to his house after school so often. We had been working on a burglar alarm for his room which we finally got to work with some help from a library book.

I wasn't sure Barry would like to come to our house which is so small compared to his, but he accepted when I invited him.

Mom cooked a casserole full of good things like ground beef, chilies, tortillas, tomatoes and cheese. Barry said he really liked eating at our house because he got tired of eating with a bunch of little sisters waving spoons and drumsticks. That made me happy. It helps to have a friend.

Barry says his burglar alarm still works. The trouble is, his sisters think it's fun to open his door to set it off. Then they giggle and hide. This was driving his mother crazy, so he finally had to disconnect it. We all laughed about this. Barry and I felt good about making something that worked even if he can't use it.

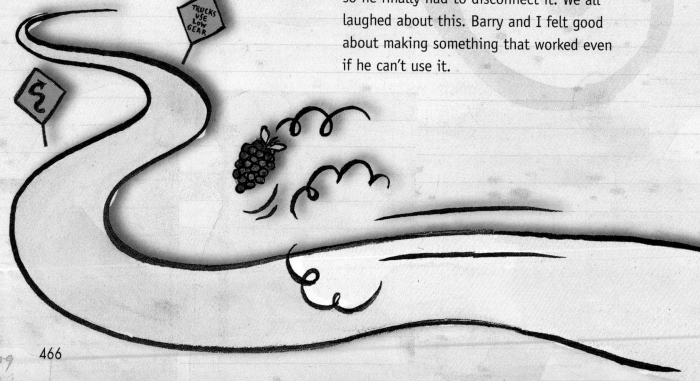

Barry saw the sign on my door that said KEEP OUT MOM THAT MEANS YOU. He asked if my Mom really stays out of my room. I said, "Sure, if I keep things picked up." Mom is not a snoop.

Barry said he wished he could have a room nobody ever went into. I was glad Barry didn't ask to use the bathroom. Maybe I'll start scrubbing off the mildew after all.

Sunday, March 25

I keep thinking about Dad and how lonely he sounded and wondering what happened to the pizza boy. I don't like to think about Dad being lonesome, but I don't like to think about the pizza boy cheering him up either.

Tonight at supper (beans and franks) I got up my courage to ask Mom if she thought Dad would get married again. She thought awhile and then said, "I don't see how he could afford to. He has big payments to make on the truck, and the price of diesel oil goes up all the time, and when people can't afford to build houses or buy cars, he won't be hauling lumber or cars."

I thought this over. I know that a license for a truck like his costs over a thousand dollars a year. "But he always sends my support payments," I said, "even if he is late sometimes."

"Yes, he does that," agreed my mother. "Your father isn't a bad man by any means."

Suddenly I was mad and disgusted with the whole thing. "Then why don't you two get married again?" I guess I wasn't very nice about the way I said it.

Mom looked me straight in the eye. "Because your father will never grow up," she said. I knew that was all she would ever say about it.

Tomorrow they give out the Young Writers' Yearbook! Maybe I will be lucky and get to go have lunch with the Famous Author.

467

Monday, March 26

Today wasn't the greatest day of my life. When our class went to the library, I saw a stack of Yearbooks and could hardly wait for Miss Neely to hand them out. When I finally got mine and opened it to the first page, there was a monster story, and I saw I hadn't won first prize. I kept turning. I didn't win second prize which went to a poem, and I didn't win third or fourth prize, either. Then I turned another page and saw Honorable Mention and under it:

A DAY ON DAD'S RIG
by
LEIGH M. BOTTS

There was my title with my name under it in print, even if it was mimeographed print. I can't say I wasn't disappointed because I hadn't won a prize, I was. I was really disappointed about not getting to meet the mysterious Famous Author, but I liked seeing my name in print.

Some kids were mad because they didn't win or even get something printed. They said they wouldn't ever try to write again which I think is pretty dumb. I have heard that real authors sometimes have their books turned down. I figure you win some, you lose some.

Then Miss Neely announced that the Famous Author the winners would get to have lunch with was Angela Badger. The girls were more excited than the boys because Angela Badger writes mostly about girls with problems like big feet or pimples or something. I would still like to meet her because she is, as they say, a real live author, and I've never met a real live author. I am glad Mr. Henshaw isn't the author because then I would *really* be disappointed that I didn't get to meet him.

Friday, March 30

Today turned out to be exciting. In the middle of second period Miss Neely called me out of class and asked if I would like to go have lunch with Angela Badger. I said, "Sure, how come?"

Miss Neely explained that the teachers discovered that the winning poem had been copied out of a book and wasn't original so the girl who submitted it would not be allowed to go and would I like to go in her place? Would I!

Miss Neely telephoned Mom at work for permission and I gave my lunch to Barry because my lunches are better than his. The other winners were all dressed up, but I didn't care. I have noticed that authors like Mr. Henshaw usually wear old plaid shirts in the pictures on the back of their books. My shirt is just as old as his, so I knew it was OK.

Miss Neely drove us in her own car to the Holiday Inn, where some other librarians and their winners were waiting in the lobby. Then Angela Badger arrived with Mr. Badger, and we were all led into the dining room which was pretty crowded. One of the

librarians who was a sort of Super Librarian told the winners to sit at a long table with a sign that said Reserved. Angela Badger sat in the middle and some of the girls pushed to sit beside her. I sat across from her. Super Librarian explained that we could choose our lunch from the salad bar. Then all the librarians went off and sat at a table with Mr. Badger.

There I was face to face with a real live author who seemed like a nice lady, plump with wild hair, and I couldn't think of a thing to say because I hadn't read her books. Some girls told her how much they loved her books, but some of the boys and girls were too shy to say anything. Nothing seemed to happen until Mrs. Badger said, "Why don't we all go help ourselves to lunch at the salad bar?"

What a mess! Some people didn't understand about salad bars, but Mrs. Badger led the way and we helped ourselves to lettuce and bean salad and potato salad and all the usual stuff they lay out on salad bars. A few of the younger kids were too short to reach anything but the bowls on the first rows. They weren't doing too well until Mrs. Badger helped them out. Getting lunch took a long time, longer than in a school cafeteria, and when we carried our plates back to our table, people at other tables ducked and dodged as if they expected us to dump our lunches on their heads. All one boy had on his plate was a piece of lettuce and a slice of tomato because he thought he was going to get to go back for roast beef and fried chicken. We had to straighten him out and explain that all we got was salad. He turned red and went back for more salad.

I was still trying to think of something interesting to say to Mrs. Badger while I chased garbanzo beans around my plate with a fork. A couple of girls did all the talking, telling Mrs. Badger how they wanted to write books exactly like hers. The other librarians were busy talking and laughing with Mr. Badger who seemed to be a lot of fun.

Mrs. Badger tried to get some of the shy people to say something without much luck, and I still couldn't think of anything to say to a lady who wrote books about girls with big feet or pimples. Finally Mrs. Badger looked straight at me and asked, "What did you write for the Yearbook?"

I felt myself turn red and answered, "Just something about a ride on a truck."

"Oh!" said Mrs. Badger. "So you're the author of *A Day on Dad's Rig*!"

Everyone was quiet. None of us had known the real live author would have read what we had written, but she had and she remembered my title.

"I just got honorable mention," I said, but I was thinking, She called me an author. *A real live author called me an author.*

"What difference does that make?" asked Mrs. Badger. "Judges never agree. I happened to like *A Day on Dad's Rig* because it was written by a boy who wrote honestly about something he knew and had strong feelings about. You made me feel what it was like to ride down a steep grade with tons of grapes behind me."

"But I couldn't make it into a story," I said, feeling a whole lot braver.

"Who cares?" said Mrs. Badger with a wave of her hand. She's the kind of person who wears rings on her forefingers. "What do you expect? The ability to write stories comes later, when you have lived longer and have more understanding. *A Day on Dad's Rig* was splendid work for a boy your age. You wrote like *you*, and you did not try to imitate someone else. This is one mark of a good writer. Keep it up."

I noticed a couple of girls who had been saying they wanted to write books exactly like Angela Badger exchange embarrassed looks.

"Gee, thanks," was all I could say. The waitress began to plunk down dishes of ice cream. Everyone got over being shy and began to ask Mrs. Badger if she wrote in pencil or on the typewriter and did she ever have books rejected and were her characters real people and did she ever have pimples when she was a girl like the girl in her book and what did it feel like to be a famous author?

I didn't think answers to those questions were very important, but I did have one question I wanted to ask which I finally managed to get in at the last minute when Mrs. Badger was autographing some books people had brought.

She called me an author. A real live author called **me** an author.

471

"Mrs. Badger," I said, "did you ever meet Boyd Henshaw?"

"Why, yes," she said, scribbling away in someone's book. "I once met him at a meeting of librarians where we were on the same program."

"What's he like?" I asked over the head of a girl crowding up with her book.

"He's a very nice young man with a wicked twinkle in his eye," she answered. I think I have known that since the time he answered my questions when Miss Martinez made us write to an author.

On the ride home everybody was chattering about Mrs. Badger this, and Mrs. Badger that. I didn't want to talk. I just wanted to think. A real live author had called *me* an author. A real live author had told me to keep it up. Mom was proud of me when I told her.

The gas station stopped pinging a long time ago, but I wanted to write all this down while I remembered. I'm glad tomorrow is Saturday. If I had to go to school I would yawn. I wish Dad was here so I could tell him all about today.

Think About It

❶ What events help Leigh feel happier about himself?

❷ Based on Leigh's journal entries, what do you think Beverly Cleary wants us to think about him?

❸ Leigh is glad he doesn't know the lunch thief's identity. What does this tell you about his character?

Meet the Author
Beverly Cleary

Did you know that you were going to write *Dear Mr. Henshaw* in journal style when you began?

Yes. I prefer to write in the third person, but I know that first-person books are popular with children. I decided that presenting this book in the form of a diary and letters might be an interesting change of pace for me.

There is a scene in *Dear Mr. Henshaw* in which a well-known author goes to lunch with several writing students. Did anything like this ever happen to you?

Even though I usually don't write so specifically from life, this incident did happen. I was asked to go to lunch with a group of about 20 children who had won a reading contest. We were only allowed to eat from the salad bar. One boy did not understand this and took just one piece of lettuce and tomato because he thought he was going back for roast beef and fried chicken. We had to set him straight, and the children had a good laugh.

RESPONSE ACTIVITIES

Meeting a Famous Author

ROLE-PLAY A CONVERSATION Leigh and the other students had many questions for Angela Badger. If you could meet Beverly Cleary, the author of "Dear Mr. Henshaw," what questions would you ask about her life and work? With a small group, brainstorm questions and possible replies. Then role-play a group of student writers having lunch with Beverly Cleary.

Keep Out!

DESIGN AN INVENTION Leigh and Barry invent a burglar alarm for Barry's room, but Barry's mother can't stand the noise. How else might Barry keep out unwanted visitors? Think of something that wouldn't bother his mother. Use your imagination. Draw a diagram or make a model of your invention.

Not Just Books

DELIVER A SPEECH What else do librarians do besides help people find books? Interview a librarian in your school or community library. You might ask what kind of training he or she needed for the job. What special events or projects has he or she taken part in? Use your interview notes to outline a speech on what you have learned. Then deliver your speech to your classmates.

A Great Day

WRITE A PERSONAL NARRATIVE Angela Badger likes the way Leigh wrote about the day he spent with his father. Think of a day that was special to you. Write a personal narrative, or true story, about your own special day. Keep Angela Badger's advice in mind as you write.

Author's Purpose and Perspective

In "Dear Mr. Henshaw," Leigh wrote in his diary for a reason — he wanted to record events in his life and express his feelings about them. The reason an author has for writing is called the **author's purpose**. The most common purposes authors have for writing are shown here.

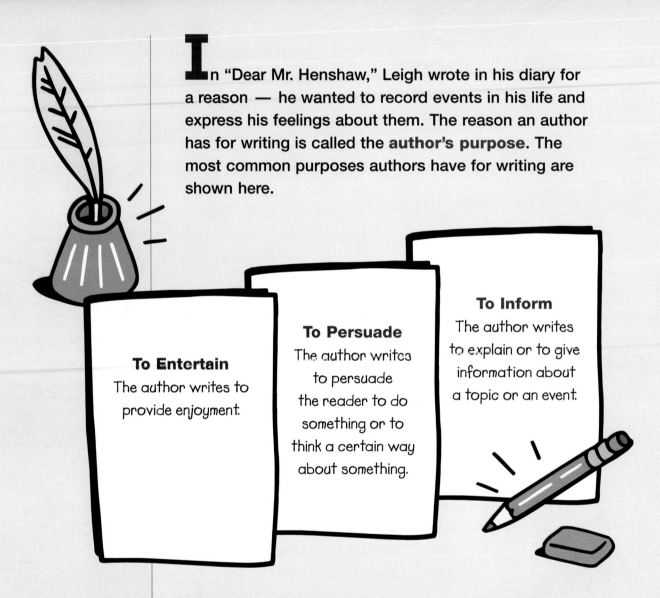

To Entertain
The author writes to provide enjoyment.

To Persuade
The author writes to persuade the reader to do something or to think a certain way about something.

To Inform
The author writes to explain or to give information about a topic or an event.

Authors often have an opinion or attitude about a subject. This is called the **author's perspective**. Knowing the author's perspective can help you determine the author's purpose for writing.

Thinking about the author's purpose and perspective can help you figure out whether an author has included personal opinions in his or her writing. If an author mentions both sides of an issue or includes only facts, then the writing is called objective. Sometimes an author leaves out information and presents only facts that support his or her opinion. Then the writing is called slanted, or biased.

What is the author's purpose and perspective in the paragraph below?

Everyone should write something for the Young Writers' Yearbook. Entering competitions is a good way for students to improve their writing skills. Also, I know that the winners will receive an excellent prize. Last year I won third place, and it was so much fun to have lunch with a real, published author.

WHAT HAVE YOU LEARNED?

1 List the author's purpose for each of the following: a comic strip, an advertisement, and a movie review.

2 Look back at another selection you've read this year. What was the author's perspective? What was the author's main purpose for writing the selection?

TRY THIS • TRY THIS • TRY THIS

Read a letter to the editor in a newspaper or magazine. What is the perspective, or opinion, of the person who wrote the letter? How can you tell?

Visit *The Learning Site!* www.harcourtschool.com

THE HUNDRED

BY ELEANOR ESTES   ILLUSTRATED BY SI HUYNH

DRESSES

THE
HUNDRED
DRESSES

ELEANOR ESTES
ILLUSTRATED BY
LOUIS SLOBODKIN

Newbery
Honor

....

Somehow Maddie could not buckle down to work.

She sharpened her pencil, turning it around carefully in the little red sharpener, letting the shavings fall in a neat heap on a piece of scrap paper, and trying not to get any of the dust from the lead on her clean arithmetic paper.

A slight frown puckered her forehead. In the first place she didn't like being late to school. And in the second place she kept thinking about Wanda. Somehow Wanda's desk, though empty, seemed to be the only thing she saw when she looked over to that side of the room.

How had the hundred dresses game begun in the first place, she asked herself impatiently. It was hard to remember the time when they hadn't played that game with Wanda; hard to think all the way back from now, when the hundred dresses was like the daily dozen, to then, when everything seemed much nicer. Oh, yes. She remembered. It had begun that day when Cecile first wore her new red dress. Suddenly the whole scene flashed swiftly and vividly before Maddie's eyes.

Somehow Wanda's desk, though empty, seemed to be the only thing she saw when she looked over to that side of the room.

It was a bright blue day in September. No, it must have been October, because when she and Peggy were coming to school, arms around each other and singing, Peggy had said, "You know what? This must be the kind of day they mean when they say, 'October's bright blue weather.'"

Maddie remembered that because afterwards it didn't seem like bright blue weather any more, although the weather had not changed in the slightest.

As they turned from shady Oliver Street into Maple, they both blinked. For now the morning sun shone straight in their eyes. Besides that, bright flashes of color came from a group of a half-dozen or more girls across the street. Their sweaters and jackets and dresses, blues and golds and reds, and one crimson one in particular, caught the sun's rays like bright pieces of glass.

A crisp, fresh wind was blowing, swishing their skirts and blowing their hair in their eyes. The girls were all exclaiming and shouting and each one was trying to talk louder than the others. Maddie and Peggy joined the group, and the laughing, and the talking.

"Hi, Peg! Hi, Maddie!" they were greeted warmly. "Look at Cecile!"

What they were all exclaiming about was the dress that Cecile had on—a crimson dress with cap and socks to match. It was a bright new dress and very pretty. Everyone was admiring it and admiring Cecile. For long, slender Cecile was a toe-dancer and wore fancier clothes than most of them. And she had her black satin bag with her precious white satin ballet slippers slung over her shoulders. Today was the day for her dancing lesson.

Maddie sat down on the granite curbstone to tie her shoelaces. She listened happily to what they were saying. They all seemed especially jolly today, probably because it was such a bright day. Everything sparkled. Way down at the end of the street the sun shimmered and turned to silver the blue water of the bay. Maddie picked up a piece of broken mirror and flashed a small circle of light edged with rainbow colors onto the houses, the trees, and the top of the telegraph pole.

And it was then that Wanda had come along with her brother Jake.

Maddie picked up a piece of broken mirror and flashed a small circle of light edged with rainbow colors ...

They didn't often come to school together. Jake had to get to school very early because he helped old Mr. Heany, the school janitor, with the furnace, or raking up the dry leaves, or other odd jobs before school opened. Today he must be late.

Even Wanda looked pretty in this sunshine, and her pale blue dress looked like a piece of the sky in summer; and that old gray toboggan cap she wore—it must be something Jake had found—looked almost jaunty. Maddie watched them absent-mindedly as she flashed her piece of broken mirror here and there. And only absent-mindedly she noticed Wanda stop short when they reached the crowd of laughing and shouting girls.

"Come on," Maddie heard Jake say. "I gotta hurry. I gotta get the doors open and ring the bell."

"You go the rest of the way," said Wanda. "I want to stay here."

Jake shrugged and went on up Maple Street. Wanda slowly approached the group of girls. With each step forward, before she put her foot down she seemed to hesitate for a long, long time. She approached the group as a timid animal might, ready to run if anything alarmed it.

Even so, Wanda's mouth was twisted into the vaguest suggestion of a smile. She must feel happy too because everybody must feel happy on such a day.

As Wanda joined the outside fringe of girls, Maddie stood up too and went over close to Peggy to get a good look at Cecile's new dress herself. She forgot about Wanda, and more girls kept coming up, enlarging the group and all exclaiming about Cecile's new dress.

"Isn't it lovely!" said one.

"Yeah, I have a new blue dress, but it's not as pretty as that," said another.

"My mother just bought me a plaid, one of the Stuart plaids."

"I got a new dress for dancing school."

"I'm gonna make my mother get me one just like Cecile's."

Everyone was talking to everybody else. Nobody said anything to Wanda, but there she was, a part of the crowd. The girls closed in a tighter circle around Cecile, still talking all at once and admiring her, and Wanda was somehow enveloped in the group. Nobody talked to Wanda, but nobody even thought about her being there.

Maybe, thought Maddie, remembering what had happened next, maybe she figured all she'd have to do was say something and she'd really be one of the girls. And this would be an easy thing to do because all they were doing was talking about dresses.

Maddie was standing next to Peggy. Wanda was standing next to Peggy on the other side. All of a sudden, Wanda impulsively touched Peggy's arm and said something. Her light blue eyes were shining and she looked excited like the rest of the girls.

"What?" asked Peggy. For Wanda had spoken very softly.

Wanda hesitated a moment and then she repeated her words firmly.

"I got a hundred dresses home."

"That's what I thought you said. A hundred dresses. A hundred!" Peggy's voice raised itself higher and higher.

"Hey, kids!" she yelled. "This girl's got a hundred dresses."

For now Peggy seemed to think a day was lost if she had not had some fun with Wanda, winning the approving laughter of the girls.

Silence greeted this, and the crowd which had centered around Cecile and her new finery now centered curiously around Wanda and Peggy. The girls eyed Wanda, first incredulously, then suspiciously.

"A hundred dresses?" they said. "Nobody could have a hundred dresses."

"I have though."

"Wanda has a hundred dresses."

"Where are they then?"

"In my closet."

"Oh, you don't wear them to school."

"No. For parties."

"Oh, you mean you don't have any everyday dresses."

"Yes, I have all kinds of dresses."

"Why don't you wear them to school?"

For a moment Wanda was silent to this. Her lips drew together. Then she repeated stolidly as though it were a lesson learned in school, "A hundred of them. All lined up in my closet."

"Oh, I see," said Peggy, talking like a grown-up person. "The child has a hundred dresses, but she wouldn't wear them to school. Perhaps she's worried about getting ink or chalk on them."

With this everybody fell to laughing and talking at once. Wanda looked stolidly at them, pursing her lips together, wrinkling her forehead up so that the gray toboggan slipped way down on her brow. Suddenly from down the street the school gong rang its first warning.

"Oh, come on, hurry," said Maddie, relieved. "We'll be late."

"Good-by, Wanda," said Peggy. "Your hundred dresses sound bee-you-tiful."

More shouts of laughter greeted this, and off the girls ran, laughing and talking and forgetting Wanda and her hundred dresses. Forgetting until tomorrow and the next day and the next, when Peggy, seeing her coming to school, would remember and ask her about the hundred dresses. For now Peggy seemed to think a day was lost if she had not had some fun with Wanda, winning the approving laughter of the girls.

Yes, that was the way it had all begun, the game of the hundred dresses. It all happened so suddenly and unexpectedly, with everybody falling right in, that even if you felt uncomfortable as Maddie had there wasn't anything you could do about it. Maddie wagged her head up and down. Yes, she repeated to herself, that was the way it began, that day, that bright blue day.

And she wrapped up her shavings and went to the front of the room to empty them in the teacher's basket.

THE CONTEST

Now today, even though she and Peggy had been late to school, Maddie was glad she had not had to make fun of Wanda. She worked her arithmetic problems absent-mindedly. Eight times eight …let's see …nothing she could do about making fun of Wanda. She wished she had the nerve to write Peggy a note, because she knew she'd never have the courage to speak right out to Peggy, to say, "Hey, Peg, let's stop asking Wanda how many dresses she has."

When she finished her arithmetic, she did start a note to Peggy. Suddenly she paused and shuddered. She pictured herself in the school yard, a new target for Peggy and the girls. Peggy might ask her where she got the dress she had on, and Maddie would have to say that it was one of Peggy's old ones that Maddie's mother had tried to disguise with new trimmings so that no one in Room 13 would recognize it.

If only Peggy would decide of her own accord to stop having fun with Wanda. Oh, well! Maddie ran her hand through her short blonde hair as though to push the uncomfortable thoughts away. What difference did it make? Slowly Maddie tore the note she had started into bits. She was Peggy's best friend, and Peggy was the best-liked girl in the whole room. Peggy could not possibly do anything that was really wrong, she thought.

As for Wanda, she was just some girl who lived up on Boggins Heights and stood alone in the school yard. Nobody in the room thought about Wanda at all except when it was her turn to stand up for oral reading. Then they all hoped she would hurry up and finish and sit down, because it took her forever to read a paragraph. Sometimes she stood up and just looked at her book and couldn't, or wouldn't, read at all.

The teacher tried to help her, but she'd just stand there until the teacher told her to sit down. Was she dumb or what? Maybe she was just timid. The only time she talked was in the school yard about her hundred dresses. Maddie remembered her telling about one of her dresses, a pale blue one with cerise-colored trimmings. And she remembered another that was brilliant jungle green with a red sash. "You'd look like a Christmas tree in that," the girls had said in pretended admiration.

Thinking about Wanda and her hundred dresses all lined up in the closet, Maddie began to wonder who was going to win the drawing and coloring contest. For girls, this contest consisted of designing dresses, and for boys, of designing motor boats. Probably Peggy would win the girls' medal. Peggy drew better than anyone else in the room. At least that's what everybody thought. You should see the way she could copy a picture in a magazine of some film star's head. You could almost tell who it was. Oh, Maddie did hope Peggy would win. Hope so? She was sure Peggy would win. Well, tomorrow the teacher was going to announce the winners. Then they'd know.

Thoughts of Wanda sank further and further from Maddie's mind, and by the time the history lesson began she had forgotten all about her.

The only time she talked was in the school yard about her hundred dresses.

The minute they entered the classroom they stopped short and gasped.

THE HUNDRED DRESSES

The next day it was drizzling. Maddie and Peggy hurried to school under Peggy's umbrella. Naturally on a day like this they didn't wait for Wanda Petronski on the corner of Oliver Street, the street that far, far away, under the railroad tracks and up the hill, led to Boggins Heights. Anyway they weren't taking chances on being late today, because today was important.

"Do you think Miss Mason will surely announce the winners today?" asked Peggy.

"Oh, I hope so, the minute we get in," said Maddie, and added, "Of course you'll win, Peg."

"Hope so," said Peggy eagerly.

The minute they entered the classroom they stopped short and gasped. There were drawings all over the room, on every ledge and window sill, tacked to the tops of the blackboards, spread over the bird charts, dazzling colors and brilliant lavish designs, all drawn on great sheets of wrapping paper.

There must have been a hundred of them all lined up!

These must be the drawings for the contest. They were! Everybody stopped and whistled or murmured admiringly.

As soon as the class had assembled, Miss Mason announced the winners. Jack Beggles had won for the boys, she said, and his design of an outboard motor boat was on exhibition in Room 12, along with the sketches by all the other boys.

"As for the girls," she said, "although just one or two sketches were submitted by most, one girl—and Room 13 should be very proud of her—this one girl actually drew one hundred designs—all different and all beautiful. In the opinion of the judges, any one of her drawings is worthy of winning the prize. I am happy to say that Wanda Petronski is the winner of the girls' medal. Unfortunately Wanda has been absent from school for some days and is not here to receive the applause that is due her. Let us hope she will be back tomorrow. Now, class, you may file around the room quietly and look at her exquisite drawings."

The children burst into applause, and even the boys were glad to have a chance to stamp on the floor, put their fingers in their mouths and whistle, though they were not interested in dresses. Maddie and Peggy were among the first to reach the blackboard to look at the drawings.

"Look, Peg," whispered Maddie, "there's that blue one she told us about. Isn't it beautiful?"

"Yeah," said Peggy, "and here's that green one. Boy, and I thought I could draw!"

THINK ABOUT IT

❶ How did Maddie's classmates influence her behavior, and how did Miss Mason try to influence her students?

❷ If you could give Maddie some advice, what would you tell her, and why? Explain your answers.

❸ Why do you think the author chose to tell the story from Maddie's point of view?

ELEANOR ESTES

The author of nineteen books, Eleanor Estes was known for writing stories that appealed to children. Estes once said, "I like to feel that I am holding up a mirror and I hope that what is reflected in it is a true image of childhood."

Estes worked as a children's librarian until the publication of her first book, *The Moffats*, which became a popular series. She based many of her stories on her memories of growing up in West Haven, Connecticut, a place that "had everything a child could want." Estes won several literary awards, including a Newbery Medal for *Ginger Pye* and three Newbery Honors prizes.

She died in 1988.

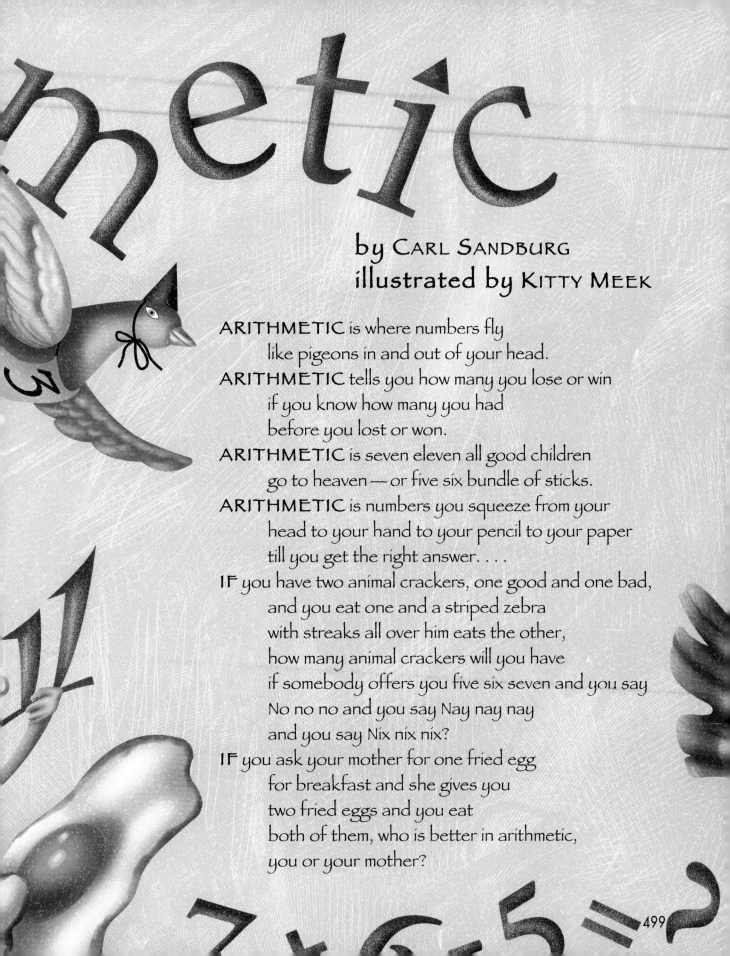

metic

by CARL SANDBURG
illustrated by KITTY MEEK

ARITHMETIC is where numbers fly
    like pigeons in and out of your head.
ARITHMETIC tells you how many you lose or win
    if you know how many you had
    before you lost or won.
ARITHMETIC is seven eleven all good children
    go to heaven — or five six bundle of sticks.
ARITHMETIC is numbers you squeeze from your
    head to your hand to your pencil to your paper
    till you get the right answer. . . .
IF you have two animal crackers, one good and one bad,
    and you eat one and a striped zebra
    with streaks all over him eats the other,
    how many animal crackers will you have
    if somebody offers you five six seven and you say
    No no no and you say Nay nay nay
    and you say Nix nix nix?
IF you ask your mother for one fried egg
    for breakfast and she gives you
    two fried eggs and you eat
    both of them, who is better in arithmetic,
    you or your mother?

499

RESPONSE ACTIVITIES

TEACHERS COUNT

CONDUCT AN INTERVIEW Like Miss Mason in the story, teachers in real life often attempt to teach their students important lessons in life, such as getting along together and appreciating each other. Interview a teacher, principal, school secretary, or other adult in your school community. Ask this person to tell you about a teacher who taught him or her a valuable lesson. Write a brief summary of your interview.

IDEAS, IDEAS

BRAINSTORM SUBJECTS Imagine that your class is going to have a drawing contest like the one in the story. Meet with classmates to brainstorm subjects for contestants to design and draw, such as T-shirts, skateboards, or uniforms for a sports team. Try to think of original ideas that will be fun and interesting for everyone to draw. Make a list of your ideas.

DO IT YOURSELF

MAKE SKETCHES After you have brainstormed subjects for the Ideas, Ideas activity, choose one that most interests you. Draw as many different designs for that subject as you wish, using interesting colors and combinations. You may choose to draw only one design or many.

MAKING CONNECTIONS

WRITE A POEM Suppose Miss Mason had a poetry contest instead of a drawing contest. Using "Arithmetic" as an example, write a short poem about your favorite school subject. Share your poem with your classmates.

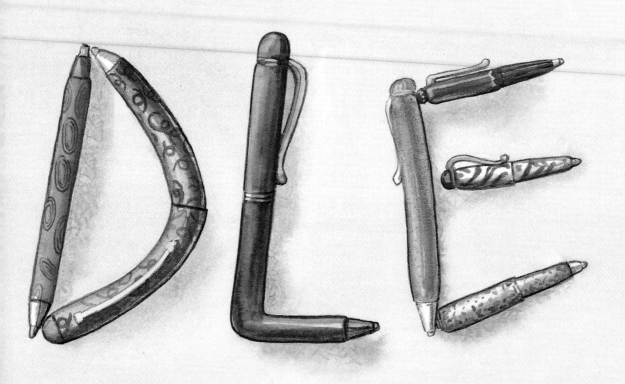

by ANDREW CLEMENTS
illustrated by SHEILA BAILEY

Nicholas Allen is known for his ideas. In third grade he transformed his classroom into a tropical island. In fourth grade he chirped like a blackbird during class and made the other students giggle. But now it's fifth grade and Nick knows he has to be very careful. He's in Mrs. Granger's language arts class, and she is as clever as she is strict. She loves the dictionary and she posts a "Word of the Day" on the blackboard each day. When Nick tries to avoid a homework assignment by asking a difficult question, she gives him an extra task — an oral report on where words come from. Nick presents an unusual report, but Mrs. Granger surprises him with an even more unusual reaction.

Mrs. Granger was beaming at him. Nick sank lower in his chair. This was worse than writing the report, worse than standing up to give it. He was being treated like—like the teacher's pet. And he had the feeling she was doing it on purpose. His reputation was in great danger. So he launched another question.

He raised his hand, and he didn't even wait for Mrs. Granger to call on him. "Yeah, but, you know, I still don't really get the idea of why words all mean different things. Like, who says that d-o-g means the thing that goes 'woof' and wags its tail? Who says so?"

And Mrs. Granger took the bait. "Who says *dog* means dog? You do, Nicholas. You and me and everyone in this class and this school and this town and this state and this country. We all agree. If we lived in France, we would all agree that the right word for that hairy four-legged creature was a different word—*chien*—it sounds like 'shee-en,' but it means what d-o-g means to you and me. And in Germany they say *hund*, and so on, all around the globe. But if all of us in this room decided to call that creature something else, and if everyone else did, too, then that's what it would be called, and one day it would be written in the dictionary that way. *We* decide what goes in that book." And she pointed at the giant dictionary. And she looked right at Nick. And she smiled again.

Then Mrs. Granger went on, "But of course, that dictionary was worked on by hundreds of very smart people for many years, so as far as we are concerned, that dictionary is the law. Laws can change, of course, but only if they need to. There may be new words that need to be made, but the ones in that book have been put there for good reasons."

Mrs. Granger took a look at the clock, eight minutes left. "Now then, for today you were to have done the exercises beginning on page twelve in your *Words Alive* book. Please get out your papers. Sarah, will you read the first sentence, identify the mistake, and then tell us how you corrected it?"

Mrs. Granger jammed the whole day's work into the last eight minutes, a blur of verbs and nouns and prepositions, and yes, there was another homework assignment.

And Nick didn't try to sidetrack Mrs. G. again. He had slowed her down a little, but had he stopped her? No way.

She was unstoppable . . . at least for today.

Three things happened later that same afternoon.

Nick and Janet Fisk had missed the bus because of a school newspaper meeting, so they walked home together. They were seeing who could walk along the curb without falling. It took a lot of concentration, and when Janet stepped off into the street, Nick said, "That's three points for me."

But Janet said, "I didn't fall. I saw something. . . . Look." She bent down and picked up a gold ballpoint pen, the fancy kind.

That was the first thing—Janet finding the pen.

They got back on the curb, and Nick followed Janet, putting one foot carefully in front of the other on the narrow concrete curb. And while he stepped along, he thought back over the school day, especially about his report. And what Mrs. Granger had said about words at the end of the period finally sank in.

That was the second thing—understanding what Mrs. Granger had said.

She had said, "Who says *dog* means dog? You do, Nicholas."

"You do, Nicholas," he repeated to himself.

I do? Nick thought, still putting one foot in front of the other, following Janet. *What does that mean?* And then Nick remembered something.

When he was about two years old, his mom had bought him one of those unbreakable cassette players and a bunch of sing-along tapes. He had loved them, and he played them over and over and over and over. He would carry the tape and the player to his mother or his big brother or his father and bang them together and say, "Gwagala, gwagala, gwagala," until someone put the cassette in the machine and turned it on.

And for three years, whenever he said "gwagala," his family knew that he wanted to hear those pretty sounds made with voices and instruments. Then when Nick went to preschool, he learned that if he wanted his teacher and the other kids to understand him, he had to use the word *music*. But *gwagala* meant that nice sound to Nick,

506

because Nick said so. Who says *gwagala* means music? "You do, Nicholas."

"No fair!" yelled Janet. They were at the corner of their own street, and Nick had bumped into her, completely absorbed in his thoughts. Janet stumbled off the curb, and the gold pen in her hand clattered onto the street.

"Sorry . . . I didn't mean to, honest," said Nick. "I just wasn't watching. . . . Here . . ." Nick stooped over and picked up the pen and held it out to her. "Here's your . . ."

And that's when the third thing happened.

Nick didn't say "pen." Instead, he said, "Here's your . . . frindle."

"Frindle?" Janet took her pen and looked at him like he was nuts. She wrinkled her nose and said, "What's a *frindle*?"

Nick grinned and said, "You'll find out. See ya later."

It was there at the corner of Spring Street and South Grand Avenue, one block from home on a September afternoon. That's when Nick got the big idea.

And by the time he had run down the street and up the steps and through the door and upstairs to his room, it wasn't just a big idea. It was a plan, a whole plan, just begging for Nick to put it into action. And "action" was Nick's middle name.

The next day after school the plan began. Nick walked into the Penny Pantry store and asked the lady behind the counter for a frindle.

She squinted at him. "A what?"

"A frindle, please. A black one," and Nick smiled at her.

She leaned over closer and aimed one ear at him. "You want *what*?"

"A frindle," and this time Nick pointed at the ballpoint pens behind her on the shelf. "A black one, please."

The lady handed Nick the pen. He handed her the 49¢, said "thank you," and left the store.

Six days later Janet stood at the counter of the Penny Pantry. Same store, same lady. John had come in the day before, and Pete the day before that, and Chris the day before that, and Dave the day before that. Janet was the fifth kid that Nick had sent there to ask that woman for a frindle.

And when she asked, the lady reached right for the pens and said, "Blue or black?"

Nick was standing one aisle away at the candy racks, and he was grinning.

Frindle was a real word. It meant *pen*. Who says frindle means pen? "You do, Nicholas."

Half an hour later, a group of serious fifth graders had a meeting in Nick's play room. It was John, Pete, Dave, Chris, and Janet. Add Nick, and that's six kids—six secret agents.

They held up their right hands and read the oath Nick had written out:

From this day on and forever, I will never use the word PEN again. Instead, I will use the word FRINDLE, and I will do everything possible so others will, too.

And all six of them signed the oath—with Nick's frindle. The plan would work.

Thanks, Mrs. Granger.

Think About It

❶ What is Nick's idea, and how does he make it work?

❷ Why is Mrs. Granger an important character in this story?

❸ If you were a friend of Nick's, would you want to help him carry out his plan? Why or why not?

Meet the Author
Andrew Clements

When Andrew Clements visits schools and talks to students, he gives the same speech his character Mrs. Granger gives to her students. "I tell kids that the dictionary is a work in progress, that words mean what they mean because we agree. If we stopped calling pens 'pens' and started calling them 'frindles,' eventually the dictionary would change." Then he asks the students to think about hooking words together. He explains, "A word is a word because it has meaning, and when we hook words together we're dealing with larger and larger chunks of meaning." He explains that writers must realize their work may have an audience, so their written ideas have to make sense. He also says, "Storytelling is the artistic exploration of an idea. And the best stories are honest."

CHILDREN

by Langston Hughes

Children are not nearly so resistant to poetry as are grown-ups. In fact, small youngsters are not resistant at all. But in reading my poems to children from kindergarten to junior high school age, I sometimes think they might want to know *why* people write poetry. So I explain to them:

> *If you put*
> *Your thoughts in rhyme*
> *They stay in folks' heads*
> *A longer time.*

Since most people want others to remember what they say, poetry helps people to remember.

For instance, I say, "Does your mother ever send you to the store and you forget what she sent you after? Or you bring back the wrong thing? That often happened to me when I was a boy. But if my mother had told me in verse what she wanted, for example:

> *Langston, go*
> *To the store, please,*
> *And bring me back*
> *A can of peas.*

AND POETRY

illustrated by Eric Westbrook

"I wouldn't have brought back a can of corn. *Please* and *peas* rhyme, which makes it easy to remember. Or if my mother had said:

> *Sonny, kindly*
> *Do me a favor*
> *And go get a bottle*
> *Of vanilla flavor.*

"Then I am sure I would not have gotten a bottle of vinegar. The word *flavor*, not simply *bottle*, would have stuck in my head because of its sound tag with *favor*. That is one reason why:

> *To make words sing*
> *Is a wonderful thing—*
> *Because in a song*
> *Words last so long.*

Think About It

In what other situations could you use rhyming poetry to help you remember something?

Response

Use Your Frindle

WRITE CLUES Invent your own new word, as Nick did. Write your word on a sheet of paper. Then write some good clues to help others guess what the word means. Don't make the clues too easy, but don't make them too hard, either. Exchange papers with a classmate, and see if you can figure out the meanings of each other's words.

In the Gym

CREATE A ROUTINE Work with a small group. Imagine that you are aerobics instructors. Each instructor should invent a new move and think of an original name for it. Make your move one that will be fun to do and that will build strength and energy. Your group should then combine members' moves to create an aerobic workout routine. Call out the names of the moves as you perform them.

Activities

You Can Look It Up

WRITE A DICTIONARY ENTRY Members of a family sometimes use words that only they can understand. Nick's family understands that the word *gwagala* means "music" because Nick made it up. Imagine that your family or a group of friends has a word like this. Write a complete dictionary entry for the word. Use a real dictionary as your guide for what to include in the entry.

Making Connections

WRITE A RHYME Imagine that a poet wanted to remember to take his or her frindle to school. Write a rhyme that he or she might make up as a reminder. If you can't think of a word to rhyme with *frindle*, keep in mind that poet Langston Hughes may not have been able to think of a word to rhyme with *vanilla* either, but he still made up a good rhyme.

THEME WRAP-UP

Today's Lesson

EXAMINE STORY CHARACTERS Each of the main characters in this theme learns a valuable lesson that changes him or her in some way. Reread one of the selections from this theme and find the turning point—the point in the story at which the main character learns a lesson. Read that part of the selection to a partner, and discuss how it shows that the character has changed.

What Do You Think?

WRITE ABOUT THE THEME The title of this theme is "School Rules." Recall the selections in this theme, and then write one or two paragraphs explaining what you think the theme title means. Use quotes from the stories to support your opinion. Share your explanation with your classmates.

A Favorite Character

HAVE A CHARACTER DEBATE Which of the main characters in this theme is your favorite? Work in a small group to hold a character debate. Each member should present a short speech describing a character and explaining why he or she thinks this person would make a good friend. Use examples from the selection to support your opinion. The other members of the group should take notes during each speech and then discuss why they agree or disagree. You may ask questions of the speaker to be sure you are understanding his or her message correctly.

THEME

AMERICAN
ADVENTURE

CONTENTS

READER'S CHOICE

Maria's Comet
by Deborah Hopkinson

HISTORICAL FICTION

Maria Mitchell longs to join her father on their rooftop to explore the stars through a telescope.

Award-Winning Author

READER'S CHOICE LIBRARY

And Then What Happened, Paul Revere?
by Jean Fritz

HISTORICAL FICTION

Paul Revere's famous ride to Lexington is only one of his many thrilling experiences. Find out what happens to Paul Revere next.

ALA Notable Book; *Boston Globe–Horn Book* **Honor**

READER'S CHOICE LIBRARY

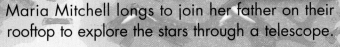

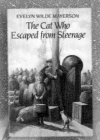

The Cat Who Escaped from Steerage
by Evelyn Wilde Mayerson

HISTORICAL FICTION

Young Chanah is packed in the steerage section of a ship with her family, but no one knows that she smuggled a cat aboard.

Notable Social Studies Trade Book

Surprising Myself
by Jean Fritz

BIOGRAPHY

Find out why this adventurous author keeps her manuscripts in the refrigerator for three weeks each year!

Award-Winning Author

Cattle Trails: "Git Along Little Dogies"
by Kathy Pelta

NONFICTION

Find out how real cowboys braved the western cattle trails and caught "trail fever" along the way.

Award-Winning Author

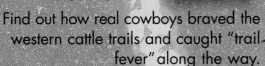

ACROSS
WIDE D...

THE DARK SEA

THE MAYFLOWER JOURNEY

by Jean Van Leeuwen
pictures by Thomas B. Allen

Award-Winning
Author

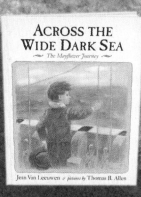

ACROSS THE
WIDE DARK SEA
The Mayflower Journey

Jean Van Leeuwen & pictures by Thomas B. Allen

Plymouth, England, 1620

I STOOD CLOSE TO MY FATHER as the anchor was pulled dripping from the sea. Above us, white sails rose against a bright blue sky. They fluttered, then filled with wind. Our ship began to move.

My father was waving to friends on shore. I looked back at their faces growing smaller and smaller, and ahead at the wide dark sea. And I clung to my father's hand.

We were off on a journey to an unknown land.

The ship was packed tight with people—near a hundred, my father said. We were crowded below deck in a space so low that my father could barely stand upright, and so cramped that we could scarcely stretch out to sleep.

Packed in tight, too, was everything we would need in the new land: tools for building and planting, goods for trading, guns for hunting. Food, furniture, clothing, books. A few crates of chickens, two dogs, and a striped orange cat.

Our family was luckier than most. We had a corner out of the damp and cold. Some had to sleep in the ship's small work boat.

The first days were fair, with a stiff wind.

My mother and brother were seasick down below. But
I stood on deck and watched the sailors hauling on ropes,
climbing in the rigging, and perched at the very top of the
mast, looking out to sea.

What a fine life it must be, I thought, to be a sailor.

One day clouds piled up in the sky. Birds with black
wings circled the ship, and the choppy sea seemed angry.

"Storm's coming," I heard a sailor say.

We were all sent below as the sailors raced to furl the sails.

Then the storm broke. Wind howled and waves crashed. The ship shuddered as it rose and fell in seas as high as mountains. Some people were crying, others praying. I huddled next to my father, afraid in the dark.

How could a ship so small and helpless ever cross the vast ocean?

The sun came out. We walked on deck and dried our clothes. But just when my shoes felt dry at last, more clouds gathered.

"Storm's coming," I told my father.

So the days passed, each one like the last. There was nothing to do but eat our meals of salt pork, beans, and bread, tidy up our cramped space, sleep when we could, and try to keep dry. When it was not too stormy, we climbed on deck to stretch our legs. But even then we had to keep out of the sailors' way.

How I longed to run and jump and climb!

Once during a storm a man was swept overboard. Reaching out with desperate hands, he caught hold of a rope and clung to it.

Down he went under the raging foaming water.

Then, miraculously, up he came.

Sailors rushed to the side of the ship. Hauling on the rope, they brought him in close and with a boat hook plucked him out of the sea. And his life was saved.

Storm followed storm. The pounding of wind and waves caused one of the main beams to crack, and our ship began to leak.

Worried, the men gathered in the captain's cabin to talk of what to do. Could our ship survive another storm? Or must we turn back?

They talked for two days, but could not agree.

Then someone thought of the iron jack for raising houses that they were taking to the new land. Using it to lift the cracked beam, the sailors set a new post underneath, tight and firm, and patched all the leaks.

And our ship sailed on.

For six weeks we had traveled, and still there was no land in sight. Now we were always cold and wet. Water seeping in from above put out my mother's cooking fire, and there was nothing to eat but hard dry biscuits and cheese. My brother was sick, and many others too.

And some began to ask why we had left our safe homes to go on this endless journey to an unknown land.

Why? I also asked the question of my father that night.

"We are searching for a place to live where we can worship God in our own way," he said quietly. "It is this freedom we seek in a new land. And I have faith that we will find it."

Looking at my father, so calm and sure, suddenly I too had faith that we would find it.

Still the wide dark sea went on and on. Eight weeks. Nine.

Then one day a sailor, sniffing the air, said, "Land's ahead." We dared not believe him. But soon bits of seaweed floated by. Then a tree branch. And a feather from a land bird.

Two days later at dawn I heard the lookout shout, "Land ho!"

Everyone who was well enough to stand crowded on deck. And there through the gray mist we saw it: a low dark outline between sea and sky. Land!

Tears streamed down my mother's face, yet she was smiling. Then everyone fell to their knees while my father said a prayer of thanksgiving.

Our long journey was over.

The ship dropped anchor in a quiet bay, circled by land. Pale yellow sand and dark hunched trees were all we saw. And all we heard was silence.

What lurked among those trees? Wild beasts? Wild men?
Would there be food and water, a place to take shelter?

What waited for us in this new land?

A small party of men in a small boat set off to find out. All day
I watched on deck for their return.

When at last they rowed into sight, they brought armfuls of
firewood and tales of what they had seen: forests of fine trees,
rolling hills of sand, swamps and ponds and rich black earth. But
no houses or wild beasts or wild men.

So all of us went ashore.

My mother washed the clothes we had worn for weeks beside a shallow pond, while my brother and I raced up and down the beach.

We watched whales spouting in the sparkling blue bay and helped search for firewood. And we found clams and mussels, the first fresh food we had tasted in two months. I ate so many I was sick.

Day after day the small party set out from the ship, looking for just the right place to build our settlement.

The days grew cold. Snowflakes danced in the wind. The cold and damp made many sick again. Drawing his coat tightly around him, my father looked worried.

"We must find a place," he said, "before winter comes."

One afternoon the weary men returned with good news. They had found the right spot at last.

When my father saw it, he smiled. It was high on a hill, with a safe harbor and fields cleared for planting and brooks running with sweet water. We named it after the town from which we had sailed, across the sea.

⊛ Think About It ⊛

❶ What problems and questions arose on the journey, and how did the *Mayflower* passengers face them?

❷ How is the author's account of these events different from what you might read in a social studies text?

❸ Do you think the *Mayflower* passengers were courageous or foolish to sail off on such a dangerous journey? Explain your answer.

MEET THE AUTHOR
JEAN VAN LEEUWEN

As a child, Jean Van Leeuwen loved to read. She says, "Anytime, anywhere, I was likely to be found with a book in my hand. I read while riding in the car, even though it made me dizzy. I read late at night under the covers, by flashlight, when I was supposed to be asleep." She would read anything, "just as long as it had a story."

Jean Van Leeuwen has continued her enjoyment of books as an adult. She edited children's books for nearly ten years and has been writing her own books for almost three decades. She says, "I write to rework childhood experiences. And I write in the hope of touching the life of another person." ✦

MEET THE ILLUSTRATOR
THOMAS B. ALLEN

Thomas B. Allen was born in Nashville, Tennessee, and spent much of his childhood playing in woods and creeks. He started art lessons when he was nine and later studied painting at the Art Institute of Chicago. He says, "I spent three summers and three winters living life in a cabin on a pond near Cold Spring, New York. I drew, painted, illustrated, and wrote poetry. I think of those three years as a journey." Thomas B. Allen has since won numerous awards, and his artwork can be found in many magazines and children's books. ✴

ACROSS THE WIDE DARK SKY

COMPARE AND CONTRAST

Imagine taking a trip in a spaceship to explore a distant planet. How would that journey be like the journey of the *Mayflower*? How would it be different? Make two columns on a sheet of paper. In one column, list ways the two journeys would be the same. In the other column, list ways they would be different.

RESPONSE

HISTORY AT HOME

RECORD FAMILY HISTORY

You have learned how and why the *Mayflower* passengers came to what is now the United States. Ask family members to tell you when, how, and why your own family came here. Or read about another family that came to this land. Then write a brief record of how your family or the family you read about came to the United States.

SONGS WE LOVE
CREATE A SONGBOOK PAGE

The new land described in the story would become the United States of America. Many songs have been written about this great and beautiful country. Choose one that you like. Find out who wrote the song and any other related facts. Then use art materials or a computer graphics program to create a page about the song. Add your page to a class book of songs about our country.

ACTIVITIES

A COLONY'S HISTORY
WRITE A REPORT

The *Mayflower* passengers named their new colony after the town in England from which they had sailed. Use a print or on-line encyclopedia to find out about the colony they founded or one of the other early colonies. Write a report about the colony, and tell what it is like today. You might include a map to show where the early colony was located.

Summarize/Paraphrase

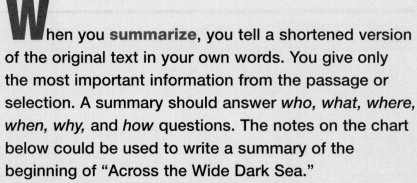

When you **summarize**, you tell a shortened version of the original text in your own words. You give only the most important information from the passage or selection. A summary should answer *who, what, where, when, why,* and *how* questions. The notes on the chart below could be used to write a summary of the beginning of "Across the Wide Dark Sea."

The following chart lists the key ideas from the selection "Across the Wide Dark Sea."

Main Characters

A boy and his father

Setting

On board the Mayflower
The colonial period

Important Events

- After the first calm days, storms begin to pound the ship.
- People stay below deck in cramped spaces. Many are sick.
- A main beam cracks, and the ship begins to leak.
- Using an iron jack, the sailors make repairs.
- People ask why they ever left England.
- Land is sighted. The ship drops anchor.

When you **paraphrase** text, you say the same thing but use your own words. The meaning and often the length stay the same. A paraphrase may use synonyms to replace key words in the original.

A summary should contain the main points of a longer passage or selection. It should not include minor details or examples. Read the following paragraph, and write a summary of it. Then reread the paragraph and paraphrase it. In both, be sure the meaning stays the same.

It took us a long time to settle into the new land we had traveled to. We spent many weeks unpacking our few belongings, clearing land, and collecting lumber. Then my father began building a house. He worked hard to build a sturdy place that would keep us warm during the cold winters. It was a small house, but it was enough to keep us all safe. After the house was built, my mother made a special dinner to celebrate. We were beginning to feel at home.

WHAT HAVE YOU LEARNED?

1 What questions should a summary answer?

2 Why are synonyms helpful when you want to paraphrase something?

TRY THIS • TRY THIS • TRY THIS

Look in an encyclopedia to find more information about the *Mayflower* and its passengers. Write a one-sentence summary of the information you learn.

Visit *The Learning Site!* www.harcourtschool.com

WHAT'S THE

BIG IDEA, BEN FRANKLIN?

What's the Big Idea, Ben Franklin?
by JEAN FRITZ
illustrated by Margot Tomes

ALA Notable Book

Children's Choice

Notable Social Studies
Trade Book

by Jean Fritz

ILLUSTRATED BY MARGOT TOMES

In 1732, when he was 26 years old, Benjamin Franklin had one of his best ideas. He decided to publish an almanac. Every family bought an almanac each year. People read it to find out the holidays, the weather forecasts, the schedule of tides, the time the sun came up and went down, when the moon would be full, when to plant what. It was just the kind of book that Benjamin loved—full of odd pieces of information and bits of advice on this and that. It was, in addition to being a calendar, a grand how-to book and Benjamin figured he knew as many how-to's as anyone else. Besides, he knew a lot of jokes.

He put them all in his almanac, called it *Poor Richard's Almanack*, and published the first edition in 1733. His specialty was short one-line sayings.

Sometimes these one-liners were quick how-to hints for everyday living: "Eat to live, not live to eat"; "A penny saved is a

penny earned"; "Half Wits talk much but say little."

Sometimes his one-liners were humorous comments on life: "Men and melons are hard to know"; "Fish and visitors smell in 3 days."

In a few years Franklin was selling 10,000 copies of his almanac every year. (He kept it up for 25 years.)

This was certainly a good idea, but it was not Benjamin Franklin's Big Idea. He was 40 years old when he first became interested in the idea that would become the Big one. By this time he had 2 children—William Temple, who was 17, and Sarah, who was 2. (A third child, Francis, died in 1736 when he was 4 years old.)

The idea had to do with electricity, which had become a new fad. For some time it had been known that electricity could be generated by rubbing glass tubes with silk. Now a Dutch scientist had found that this electricity could be stored in specially equipped bottles, then drawn from them by applying wires (or conductors) to the 2 sides of the bottle. All over Europe people were meeting in darkened rooms to see these sparks and the tricks that could be performed. Wires twisted into the shape of giant spiders were electrified. Sparks were drawn from a cake of ice and even from the head of a boy suspended from the ceiling by a silk rope. Electrical performers traveled from town to town selling shocks to curious people. Once, before a large audience in Spain, 180 grenadiers were linked together by wire, then given a shock to make them jump into the air at the same time.

Franklin bought electrical equipment and began writing to European scientists. He learned to perform the usual tricks and made up some of his own. Once he gave an electrical picnic. He planned to kill a turkey by an electrical shock, roast it in a container connected to electrical circuits, on a fire lit by an electrical bottle. He was, however, so carried away by his performance in front of his guests that he was careless. He took the whole shock through his own arms and body and was knocked unconscious. When he came to, he was embarrassed. "What I meant to kill was a turkey," he said. "Instead I almost killed a goose."

His Big Idea was that electricity and lightning were the same. Up to that time most people had thought lightning was (and always would be) as mysterious as heaven itself. And here was Franklin saying it was the same stuff that you saw in parlor tricks—only on a grander scale. What was more, Franklin believed he could prove it. Let a sentry box be built on the top of a high tower, he wrote a scientist in Europe. Put a pointed rod in

the tower and let a man stand in the box during a storm. Franklin knew that electricity was attracted to pointed iron rods; if the man in the sentry box could find that lightning was also attracted to a rod, that would prove they were the same. The only reason Franklin didn't make the experiment himself was that Philadelphia didn't have a high enough tower or even a high hill.

In the spring of 1752 three scientists in Europe tried the experiment and all three proved that Franklin's Big Idea was right. (One scientist was killed, but that was because he was careless.) Meanwhile Benjamin thought of a way to prove the Idea himself. One stormy day he raised a kite with a long pointed wire at the tip and felt the electric shock come through a key he had tied to the kite string near his hand. So he already had his own proof when the news reached him about the experiments in Europe. Still, he was surprised to hear how excited people were about his Idea. He was suddenly famous. Indeed, he was becoming the most celebrated man in America. The King of France sent him congratulations; the Royal Society of England presented him with a medal; universities gave him honors and called him Dr. Franklin; newspapers praised him. Benjamin was pleased. He felt secretly as proud, he said, as a girl wearing a new pair of garters.

A Big Idea, however, meant little to Benjamin Franklin unless he could put it to everyday use. So he invented the lightning rod, a pointed iron rod that could be

raised from the roof of a house or barn to attract lightning and lead it harmlessly through a wire and into the ground. For his own lightning rod, he also fixed up a contraption that would ring a bell in the house whenever lightning hit. (Debbie hated that bell.)

Benjamin would have liked to do nothing but experiment with his ideas, but people had discovered that he was more than an inventor. Whatever needed doing, he seemed able and willing to do it. He was made Postmaster General and organized a new system so that it took only 3 weeks instead of 6 weeks for a letter to go from Boston to Philadelphia. (Later he cut the time to 6 days.) He helped organize a fire insurance company, a hospital, and an expedition to seek the

Northwest Passage. And because he was so good at talking people into doing what he wanted them to do, in 1757 he was sent to London. He was to do what he could to further the interests of the people of Pennsylvania.

*I*n London Benjamin began right away to live in style and comfort. He bought new shoes, new wigs, new shirts, a new watch, 2 pairs of silver shoe and knee buckles, new candlesticks, new chinaware, and a new carriage. He had his sword blade repaired and ordered new spectacles because he'd left his best pair at home. He rented 4 large rooms in a house owned by a Mrs. Stevenson, who treated him like a king. When his back itched, she gave him an ivory backscratcher; she warmed his shirts before he put them on;

she even trained her cat not to sit in his favorite chair. Of course she served only the foods he liked best (*never* beef, which upset him), and as if this were not enough, Benjamin received a regular supply of American cornmeal, venison, cranberries, and bacon from his wife, Debbie. (He sent Debbie presents in return, including a crimson satin coat and an apple corer.)

With the exception of 2 years back in America, Benjamin lived in London for 18 years, from the time he was 51 until he was 69. (Debbie, afraid to cross the ocean, died the year before he finally returned.) Benjamin was in London when George the Third was crowned King of England. He was there in 1765 when England began laying down taxes and making trouble for America. He did his best to keep the two countries friendly, but over the years England became more and more stubborn. First one tax. Then another. Sometimes England would repeal a tax, but it would never, never give up its right to tax America. Benjamin discovered that all his rules for arguing which had

worked so well in the past were of no use against such stubbornness. He finally gave up arguing altogether one day in 1774 when he was called before the British government to explain his activities in behalf of America. For 2 hours he stood before the government's Privy Council. He was shouted at, laughed at, insulted, and condemned. Franklin, white with rage, said not one word. He was being treated like an apprentice. Indeed, England was treating America as if it were a country of apprentices instead of a country of free men. And Franklin could stand it no longer. In the spring of 1775 he returned to America, only to find that America and England were already at war. The Battle of Lexington had been fought while he was at sea.

Franklin was so mad that he told Americans if there wasn't enough gunpowder to go around they should use bows and arrows against the English. He was so mad that he would have swum out into the ocean with electric bolts to shoot at the English, if he could have. But America had other uses for him. Right away he was put in the Continental Congress and placed on 10 different committees. When the time came to write the Declaration of Independence, he was one of those asked to do it. As it turned out, Thomas Jefferson did the writing, but Franklin made changes. The "truths" that Jefferson held to be "sacred and undeniable" became "self-evident" truths when Franklin had finished.

But these jobs were small compared to the big one Congress had for him. Benjamin Franklin was still America's best arguer and America's most famous citizen. So, in the fall of

1776, he was sent to France to try to talk the French into entering the war on America's side. George Washington would run the war in America, but Benjamin Franklin would run it in Europe, getting all the help and money from any country he could.

Benjamin was 70 years old now and found the occan trip hard. The seas were rough; the weather was freezing. He had boils on his body, gout in his legs, and a skin disease on his head that bothered him so much that he wore a loose fur hat instead of his usual wig. When he arrived in France he was rumpled, crumpled, and weak— not the stylish, famous-looking figure the French had expected. Of course Benjamin planned to dress up as soon as he felt better, but to his surprise he discovered the French liked him as he was, fur hat and all. Indeed, he was an immediate sensation. A plain man in the most fashionable country in the world! Within a month the French had made him their hero. French ladies found him charming. They fussed over him and called him Papa; they hung his picture over their mantels and wore his picture in their rings. Frenchmen  cleared the way for him when he appeared in the streets. So Benjamin never did dress up. He never wore a wig or carried a sword the whole time he was in France, not even when he went to see the King. If being plain made him popular, Benjamin Franklin had the good sense to stay plain.

Paris suited old Benjamin perfectly. On one side he had the River Seine when he wanted a swim; on the other side he had friends when he wanted company. Altogether, Benjamin had such a good time in Paris that he couldn't always be bothered with his old rules for good behavior. Frequently

he ate too much. But rather than worry, he carried a bottle of oil of wormwood for indigestion and he gained weight. (Sometimes he called himself Dr. Fatsides.) Occasionally he went to extremes. If he became interested in a game of chess, he'd stay up all night playing. And he wasn't neat. His desk was a mess. A Scottish visitor once pointed out the danger of leaving important state papers scattered so carelessly over his desk. There might be spies in the household, the Scotsman said. (And there really were spies.)

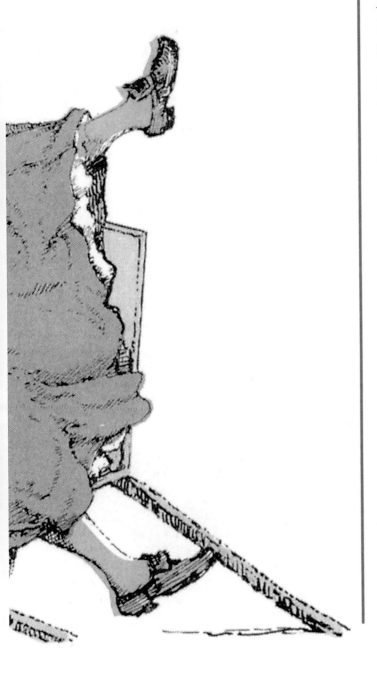

But the important thing was that Benjamin did what he'd set out to do. He talked France into joining America in the war and he took good care of America's business in Europe. And when peace came in 1783, he helped to write the peace treaty.

When Franklin (79 years old now) finally returned to Philadelphia, he was given a wildly enthusiastic welcome. Cannon were fired, bells rung, parades formed, speeches made. His daughter, Sarah, was so excited that she fell into a wheelbarrow. But the people of Pennsylvania put Franklin right back to work. Three years in a row they elected him president of their government, and when Franklin was 82, they asked him to help write the Constitution of the United States. For 4 months he attended meetings of the Constitutional Convention. Sometimes he dozed off during a speech; often he disagreed with what was being done. But in the end he was satisfied with the Constitution. With so many different opinions, he said this was the best they could do.

Now at last Benjamin Franklin was finished with public life. He did not have long to live,

but even when he couldn't get out of bed, he still read and he still wrote. And every afternoon his 9-year-old granddaughter, Deborah, would come to his bedside and he would hear her spelling lesson for the next day. If she did well, he would give her a spoonful of fruit jelly that he kept beside him.

At 11 o'clock on the night of April 17, 1790, Benjamin Franklin died. He was 84 years old—a man who had not only had a Big Idea of his own but had played a large part in one of the Biggest Ideas of his time—the idea of an independent United States.

Think About It

1. What were Ben Franklin's big ideas, and why have they been important?

2. Why do you think the author includes bits of everyday information about Ben Franklin, as well as important historical facts?

3. What do you admire most about Ben Franklin? Why?

Meet the Author
JEAN FRITZ

Why did you begin writing?

I was born in Hankow, China, where I attended an English school until I was twelve. I was an American, but I didn't feel like a real American because I was so far away. When I returned to America, I read many history books and began writing about Americans of the past.

Why do you choose to write about Benjamin Franklin and other historical people?

I think Benjamin Franklin was a very human American hero that students should know about. I want students to know that historical figures were real people and that humorous things happened to them. Most often, historical figures are treated like statues—frozen in one position. I want to show students that these people were once truly alive.

When people ask me how I find ideas, I tell them that I don't. Ideas find me. A character in history will suddenly step right out of the past and demand a book from me. Once I decide to take him or her on, I begin my detective work. I read old books, old letters, and old newspapers. I visit the places where my character lived and worked. I try to figure out as much as I can about the person and the period in which he or she lived. Often I turn up surprises and, of course, I pass these on to my readers.

THE MANY LIVES OF
Benjamin Franklin

BY MARY POPE OSBORNE

Almanacs were a favorite form of reading in colonial America. They were small books that forecast the weather and told about the tides and changes of the moon. They also contained calendars, jokes, poems, and odd facts. In 1732 Ben Franklin began publishing his own almanac which he called *Poor Richard's Almanack*.

Poor Richard, 1733

AN

Almanack

For the Year of Chrift

1 7 3 3,

Being the Firft after LE'AP YEAR;

Wherein is contained
The Lunations, Eclipfes, Judgement of
the Weather, Spring Tides, Planets Motions &
mutual Afpects, Sun and Moon's Rifing and Setting, Length of Days, Time of High Water,
Fairs, Courts, and obfervable Days.
Fitted to the Latitude of Forty Degrees,
and a Meridian of Five Hours Weft from London,
but may without fenfible Error, ferve all the ad-
jacent Places, even from Newfoundland to South-
Carolina.

By RICHARD SAUNDERS, Philom.

PHILADELPHIA
Printed and fold by B. FRANKLIN, at the New
Printing Office near the Market.
The Third Impreffion.

Poor Richard was a gold mine for Ben—after the Bible, it became the most popular reading in the colonies. It came out once a year and was sprinkled with useful information about the weather and stars. The almanac also gave Ben the chance to share his philosophy of self-improvement. He took many of the sayings from ancient writers and rewrote them to make them simple and clear. Today historians believe that the philosophy expressed in *Poor Richard* helped mold the American character, ideas such as:

God helps those who help themselves.

Early to bed and early to rise makes a man healthy, wealthy, and wise.

When you're good to others, you are best to yourself.

There are no gains without pains.

At the working man's house hunger looks in, but dares not enter.

For the next twenty-five years, as "Poor Richard," Ben Franklin preached his ideals to the American people—the value of hard work, common sense, and self-sufficiency. Today people might think that his methods of trying to solve human problems were a bit too simple, but Franklin himself seemed to know that. Though he didn't put it on his list, one of his most outstanding virtues was humor. And he seems to be laughing at himself when he writes in *Poor Richard:*

Who is wise? *He that learns from every one.*

Who is powerful? *He that governs his passions.*

Who is rich? *He that is content.*

Who is that? *Nobody.*

★ ★ ★ ★ ★ ★ ★

Think About It

What needs did Benjamin Franklin's almanacs fill for the people in his day? How do people fill the same kinds of needs today?

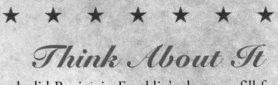

RESPONSE
ACTIVITIES

FROM ACROSS THE SEA

WRITE POSTCARDS — What do you think Ben Franklin experienced while living in London and Paris? Find out what was happening in these cities at the time he visited them. Then write several postcards Ben Franklin might have sent to friends or family back in America. Show how the experiences he had in these cities may have shaped his ideas.

LET'S DANCE

PERFORM A DANCE
With a small group, create a dance based on the electrical performances described in the selection. If you wish, add special effects to make your dance more exciting and dramatic. Practice your dance, and perform it for classmates.

All About Ben

MAKE A LIST — List words and phrases that describe Ben Franklin. Use a thesaurus, or synonym-finder, if you wish. Use a symbol to mark each word or phrase on your list that you could use to describe yourself now. Use another symbol to mark each word or phrase that you hope will describe you as an adult.

Making Connections

GIVE A TALK — Do you agree with historians who say that the ideas expressed in *Poor Richard's Almanack* helped form the American character? In a brief talk, give your opinion and explain why you think as you do. Use examples from both selections about Ben Franklin in your talk.

BLACK FRONTIERS

BY LILLIAN SCHLISSEL

A History of
African American
Heroes in
the Old West

Notable
Social Studies
Trade Book

BLACK HOMESTEADERS

Homesteading was not easy for black or white settlers. Rocks, grass, and trees had to be cleared before crops could be planted. A farmer needed a horse, a mule, and a plow. He needed seed to plant and food for his family until the crops were ready to harvest. Most of all a pioneer needed a home.

Loading sod for a house on the Dismal River, Thomas County, Kansas

Dugout on the South Loup River, near Virge Allen's homestead, Custer County, Nebraska, 1892. A wagon load of sod stands by to repair the roof.

In regions where there were trees, pioneers built log cabins. But in Kansas and Nebraska, there was only tall grass, as high as a man's shoulder. Pioneers learned that tough root systems under the grass held the dirt firmly, and sod could be cut like bricks and piled, layer upon layer, until it took the shape of a house. These homesteaders were called sod busters, and their homes were called soddies.

Sod homes could be warm and comfortable. Some were two stories high, with glass windows and chimneys. But in heavy rain, smaller sod houses leaked, and some families remembered being surprised by a snake slithering through a wall.

In North and South Dakota, where the land was rocky and winter temperatures fell to 30 degrees below zero, early pioneers burrowed into the ground and covered themselves with an earthen roof. They brought their small animals into the house in the winter, while cows and goats huddled on the roof, warming themselves on the house that was under their feet.

During the first seasons in a new settlement, a pioneer woman might have no stove. She dug a hole in the ground and fed the fire with weeds, adding small rocks, like coals, to keep in the fire's heat. Buffalo chips, the droppings of buffalo, provided the fuel. When the great animals migrated across the land, women and children gathered chips for the family's cooking fires.

In the hot and dry climate of the Southwest, pioneers built homes with thick walls made of mud and straw. The mud walls, called adobe, kept the houses cool in the summer and warm in the winter. In desert regions, women learned from the Indians to brew teas out of wild grasses and to make soap and shampoo from the yucca plant.

Even youngsters helped settle the West. These are the children of homesteaders who lived near Brownlee, Cherry County, Nebraska.

In the early days of settlement, there were few black families homesteading. For them, loneliness was part of being a pioneer. But black pioneer families held on, and in sticking it out, they made the way easier for those who came after.

Unidentified child on the Maurice Brown homestead in Nebraska

For black pioneer families, homesteading was a desolate life.

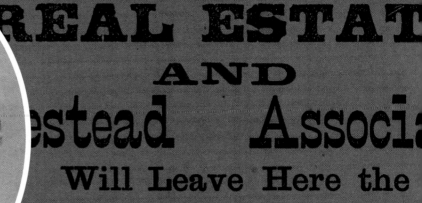

Ho for Kansa

Brethren, Friends, & Fellow C

I feel thankful to inform you t

REAL ESTAT
AND

estead Associa

Will Leave Here the

th of April,

n pursuit of Homes in the Sout
Lands of America, at Transpo
Rates, cheaper than eve
was known before.

For full information inquire of

Benj. Singleton, better known as

NO. 5 NORTH FRONT STR

Beware of Speculators and Adventurers, as it is a d

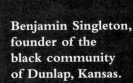

Benjamin Singleton, founder of the black community of Dunlap, Kansas.

THE EXODUSTERS

Men and women who had been slaves read in the Bible about the ancient Israelites who were brought out of bondage and delivered into freedom. Benjamin Singleton, born a slave in Tennessee, was determined that he would bring his people to free soil if it was the last thing he ever did.

After the Civil War, Singleton visited Kansas and over a period of years, he and his friends managed to buy part of a Cherokee reservation. In 1877 they advertised for homesteaders to start an all-black community there. They hoped to attract two hundred families. Fliers promised that settlers who paid one dollar "in installments of 25 cents at a time or otherwise as may be desired" could be part of the new community. By 1879 an exodus of black families out of the Old South began, and before long there were eight hundred homesteaders in the new Kansas communities of Dunlap and Nicodemus. Benjamin Singleton said, "My people that I carried to Kansas came on our own resources. We have tried to make a people of ourselves. . . ." They were known as the Exodusters.

Handbills encouraged black families to move to Kansas. Notice the warning at the bottom of the flier.

Ho for Kansas!

Brethren, Friends, & Fellow Citizens:

I feel thankful to inform you that the

REAL ESTATE

AND

Homestead Association,

Will Leave Here the

15th of April, 1878,

In pursuit of Homes in the Southwestern Lands of America, at Transportation Rates, cheaper than ever was known before.

For full information inquire of

Benj. Singleton, better known as old Pap,

NO. 5 NORTH FRONT STREET.

Beware of Speculators and Adventurers, as it is a dangerous thing to fall in their hands.

Nashville, Tenn., March 18, 1878.

[Beware of Speculators and Adventurers, as it is a dangerous thing to fall in their hands.]

575

Schoolhouse in Dunlap,
Kansas. Pupil in foreground
carries a sign that reads,
"God Bless Our School."

Farmers in Nicodemus
owned only three horses. One man plowed
with a milk cow, and others broke ground
with shovels and spades. White farmers saw
how hard their new neighbors worked and
lent the new settlers a team of oxen and a
plow. Black farmers planted their first crops
and in time they prospered. By the turn of the
century there were about eight thousand black
homesteaders in Nicodemus and Dunlap.

Some black settlers moved farther west to
Nebraska and Oklahoma where they built
three new black communities—Taft, Langston,
and Boley. George Washington Bush went
all the way to Oregon Territory where he
introduced the first mower and reaper into
the area around Puget Sound.

The Shores family in front of their sod house near Westville, Custer County, Nebraska, 1887. The Shores became famous as musicians.

The Moses Speese family — neighbors of the Shores family — outside their sod house near Westville, Custer County, Nebraska

Kansas City Monarchs, 1908 ▶

Satchel Paige, one of baseball's greatest pitchers, playing for the Kansas City Monarchs, 1908

▼

▲ This black baseball team played for the Pullman Club in Tonopah, Nevada, 1907.

Of all the black communities, however, Nicodemus and Dunlap remained the most famous. Each year they celebrated the Fourth of July, and they had their own special holiday, Emancipation Day. On July 31 and August 1, a square mile of land was set aside as a carnival fairground. There were boxing matches and baseball games. In 1907 the town formed one of the nation's first black baseball teams—the Nicodemus Blues. The Blues played black teams as far away as Texas, Nevada, and Louisiana. Satchel Paige, one of the greatest black pitchers in American baseball history, played ball in Nicodemus.

In 1976 Nicodemus was designated a National Historic Landmark. The town's history is being recorded and buildings restored. It marks the proud legacy of black homesteaders in America.

THINK ABOUT IT

1. What do you think it took to be a successful homesteader? Explain your answer.
2. What was the most interesting fact you learned from this selection? Why?
3. Why do you think the author includes the information about Emancipation Day and the Nicodemus Blues?

Lillian Schlissel

Lillian Schlissel remembers that as a schoolgirl, she visited the public library as often as she could. "There was no television," Schlissel says. "So after homework, there were piles of books to read."

Now Schlissel has written a pile of books for others to read. In 1994 she wrote her first children's book — *The Way West: Journal of a Pioneer Woman.* "I wanted to give modern children some idea of what it was like to travel more than a thousand miles in a wagon pulled by oxen, moving only thirteen miles a day, with no motels or restaurants."

Schlissel began collecting photographs for *Black Frontiers* while writing *Women's Diaries of the Westward Journey.* She enjoys reading about the West and uncovering stories that have never been told. She says, "Being a historian and a writer is the best of jobs."

Response Activities

Imagine That!

ROLE-PLAY SETTLERS Work with a small group to think of a funny or dramatic incident that might have happened to a pioneer family like the ones you just read about. Use information from the selection to invent details that are true to life. Role-play the incident for classmates.

Now and Then

WRITE TWO PARAGRAPHS Think about life in your own city or town today. How does it compare with the lives of the homesteaders? Write a paragraph telling one way you think life is better now. Write another paragraph telling one way in which you think life was better then. Explain your reasons in each paragraph.

Dear Diary

WRITE A DIARY ENTRY Imagine that you are an early settler. Think about what you do on a daily basis. Have you met any new settlers? Are you planting crops? Are you working on your home? Write a diary entry describing one day's events.

Home Sweet Home

CONSTRUCT A MODEL Create a model of one of the types of pioneer homes you read about in the selection. You can use any art materials you have available. You may also want to use materials from nature to make your model as realistic as possible. Then help arrange a classroom display of everyone's models.

Main Idea and Supporting Details

In "Black Frontiers," you read about what pioneer life was like. This is the main idea of the selection. The **main idea** of a paragraph or selection is what it is mostly about. The main idea may be stated in a sentence, or it may only be implied or suggested.

Supporting details give more information about the main idea. They answer the questions *who*, *what*, *where*, *when*, *why*, and *how*. This diagram shows the main idea of the first paragraphs in "Black Frontiers."

What
Sod bricks were cut from dirt containing strong root systems.

Where
Some pioneers settled in Kansas and Nebraska.

Why
Homes needed to be warm and comfortable.

MAIN IDEA
Pioneers built their homes out of available materials.

When
Homesteading was not easy in the late 1800s.

How
Sod bricks, piled layer upon layer, took the shape of a house.

Who
Some homesteaders were called sod busters.

When you are asked what a story is about, you can answer in a few words to describe the story's main idea. If you are asked to tell more about the story, you probably offer a few details. The details support the main idea. This is why they are called supporting details.

Being able to identify the main idea and supporting details can help you better understand what you read. Read the following paragraph and identify the main idea. Find supporting details that answer the questions *who, what, when, where, why,* and *how*.

One of the many African American heroes was Satchel Paige. Paige was a baseball player who played for the Kansas City Monarchs during much of his career. Led by Satchel Paige's great pitching skills, the Monarchs won four Negro American League pennants in a row. In 1971 Paige was elected to the National Baseball Hall of Fame, becoming the first player elected from the Negro Leagues.

WHAT HAVE YOU LEARNED?

1 Is the main idea in the paragraph above stated directly, or is it implied?

2 How do details support a main idea and make a passage more interesting?

TRY THIS • TRY THIS • TRY THIS

Read a paragraph or short passage in your science or social studies textbook. Draw a web to show the main idea and details.

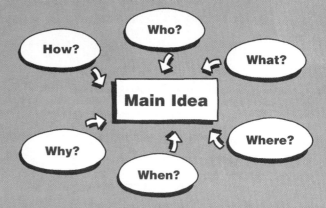

COWBOYS

Cowboys of the
Wild West

RUSSELL FREEDMAN

ALA Notable Book
SLJ Best Book

# of THE WILD WEST

BY RUSSELL FREEDMAN

A CENTURY AGO, in the years following the Civil War, one million mustang ponies and ten million head of longhorn cattle were driven north out of Texas. Bawling and bellowing, the lanky longhorns tramped along dusty trails in herds that numbered a thousand animals or more.

Behind and beside and ahead of each herd rode groups of men on horseback. Often, they sang to the cattle as they drove them on. These old-time cow herders were mostly very young men, and in time they came to be known as cowboys.

Some were boys in fact as well as name. Youngsters still in their teens commonly worked as horse wranglers, caring for the saddle ponies that traveled with every trail outfit. A typical trail-driving cowboy was in his early twenties. Except for some cooks and bosses, there were few thirty-year-old men on the trail.

Cowboys drove great herds across wild prairies from Texas to markets in Kansas and beyond. They swam the cattle across rivers and

I've roamed the Texas prairies.

I've followed the cattle trail;

I've rid a pitchin' pony

Till the hair come off his tail.[C]

stayed with them during stampedes. A man spent eighteen hours a day in the saddle. At night he slept on the ground. Sometimes he lived on the trail for months with no comforts but a campfire and his bedroll.

At the end of the drive, the cattle were sold, the hands were paid off, and the trail outfit split up. Then the cowboys went into town to scrape off the trail dust and celebrate. Usually they stopped at the pineboard photographer's studio found in nearly every western cattle town. Decked out in their best duds and sporting the tools of their trade, they posed proudly for souvenir pictures to send to the folks back home. Some of those old photographs still survive. In them we can glimpse the cowboy as he really was, a hundred years ago.

The cowboy trade goes back more than four hundred years. It began in Mexico during the sixteenth century, when Spanish settlers brought the first domesticated horses and cattle to North America. Back home, the Spanish had kept their cattle penned up in pastures. But in the wide-open spaces of the New World, the cattle were allowed to wander freely, finding their own grass and water.

A Spanish vaquero

The animals flourished. Soon, huge Spanish ranches were scattered across northern Mexico.

Since the cattle roamed far and wide, the ranchers needed skilled horsemen to look after their herds. They began to teach the local Indians to ride horses and handle cattle on the open range. These barefoot Indian cow herders were called *vaqueros*, from the Spanish word *vaca*, for cow. They were the first true cowboys, and they spent their days from sunrise to sunset in the saddle. They became experts at snaring a running steer with a braided rawhide rope, called *la reata* in Spanish. Over the years *la reata*— the lariat— became the cowboy's most important tool, and the Mexican vaquero became a proud and independent ranch hand.

Vaqueros drove the first herds of cattle north into Texas early in the eighteenth century. By the time of the American Civil War (1861–1865), millions of hardy long-horned cattle were roaming the Texas plains. Many of these animals were descended from strays and runaways that had escaped from their owners, and they were as wild as buffalo or deer. They clustered together in small herds, hiding in thickets by day, running by night. If anyone tried to approach them on foot, they would paw the earth and toss their heads in anger.

Like most of the South, Texas was poor when the Civil War ended. Confederate money no longer had any value. The state's economy was in ruins. Yet longhorns were running wild all over the state.

Before the war, cattle had been raised mainly for their hides (for leather) and tallow, or fat (for candles and soap). Now, new methods of meat-packing and refrigeration had created a profitable market for beef in the crowded cities of the North. Texas had plenty of beef on the hoof, but there were no railroads linking Texas with the rest of the country, where the beef was in demand. The only way to get the cattle to market was to walk them hundreds of miles north to the nearest railroad.

As Texas farmers and ranchers came home from the war, they began to organize what they called "cow hunts." By capturing wild longhorns and branding them as his own, a rancher could build up his herds and drive them north to be sold.

An early Texas cowboy

Beef on the hoof—a Texas longhorn

Cow-hunters used the same methods to catch wild cattle that Mexican vaqueros had been using for a long time. They found a herd of longhorns by moonlight and fired a gun to make them stampede. Riding with the herd, they let the longhorns run for hours, until the cattle grew tired and slowed to a trot or walk.

Then the men kept the animals moving for the next day or so, until the longhorns were so hungry and exhausted, they had tamed down and could be handled with ease.

Once the cattle had been caught and branded, they were set loose to graze until they were ready for market. Then they were rounded up and driven in large herds to Kansas railroad towns, where they were loaded aboard freight cars and shipped to meat-packing plants in Kansas City and Chicago.

As the demand for beef grew, the cattle-raising industry spread northward from Texas. New ranches began to spring up all across the northern plains, where only a few years before herds of buffalo had grazed. By the 1870s, most of the buffalo had been slaughtered. They were replaced by longhorn cattle brought up the trails from Texas. Soon, a vast tract of cattle country stretched from Colorado up through Wyoming, Montana, and the Dakotas.

At the heart of this booming cattle industry was the hard-working cowboy. Who was he, where was he from, and what was he like?

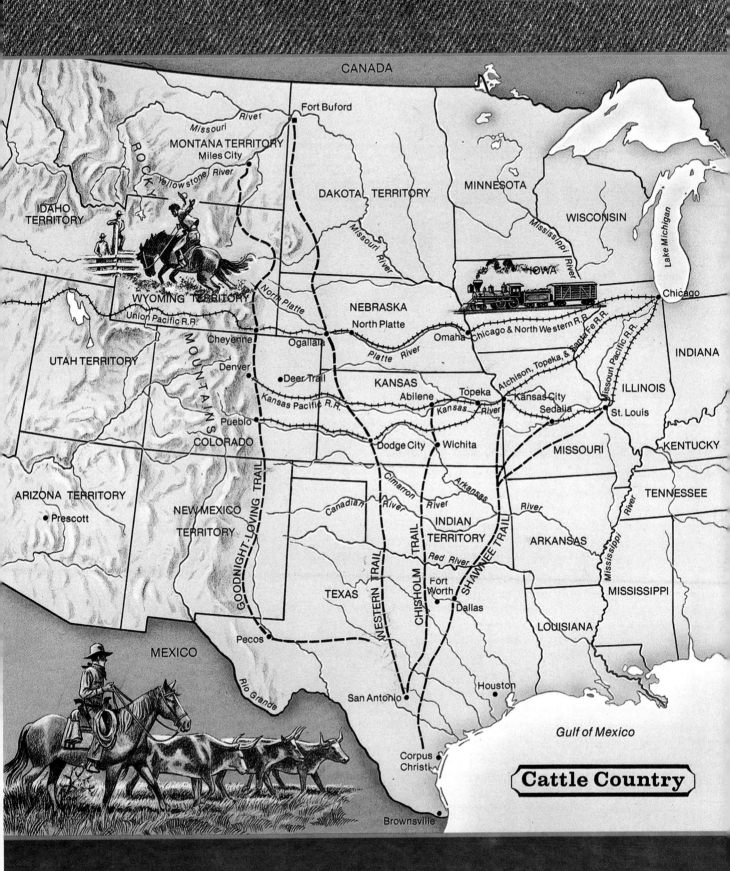

CANADA

Fort Buford

Missouri River

MONTANA TERRITORY
Miles City

Yellowstone River

ROCKY

IDAHO
TERRITORY

WYOMING TERRITORY

DAKOTA TERRITORY

Missouri River

MINNESOTA

WISCONSIN

Lake Michigan

North Platte

Union Pacific R.R.

Cheyenne

Ogallala

NEBRASKA

North Platte

Omaha

IOWA

Chicago & North Western R.R.

Chicago

MOUNTAINS

UTAH TERRITORY

Denver

Deer Trail

Kansas Pacific R.R.

KANSAS

Abilene

Topeka

Kansas City

Kansas River

Atchison, Topeka, & Santa Fe R.R.

Missouri Pacific R.R.

INDIANA

ILLINOIS

Sedalia

St. Louis

Pueblo

COLORADO

Dodge City

Wichita

MISSOURI

KENTUCKY

ARIZONA TERRITORY

Prescott

NEW MEXICO
TERRITORY

Cimarron River

Canadian River

Arkansas River

River

TENNESSEE

GOODNIGHT-LOVING TRAIL

WESTERN TRAIL

CHISHOLM TRAIL

INDIAN
TERRITORY

Red River

SHAWNEE TRAIL

ARKANSAS

Mississippi River

MISSISSIPPI

TEXAS

Fort
Worth

Dallas

LOUISIANA

Pecos

MEXICO

Rio Grande

San Antonio

Houston

Gulf of Mexico

Corpus
Christi

Cattle Country

Brownsville

To begin with, most cowboys were Texans and other southerners, discharged soldiers back from the war. Jobs were scarce in the South, and the prospering cattle ranchers

needed plenty of new hands. Along with the southerners, there were a number of mustered-out Union soldiers. Eventually, men and boys from many backgrounds and all parts of the country began to arrive in Texas, seeking jobs as cowhands. Some had been unlucky at home and were looking for a fresh start. Others were drawn to Texas because they had heard that a cowboy's life was adventurous and exciting.

Today, in movies and TV shows about the Old West, cowboys are usually white. In real life, they were often black or Mexican. Texas had been a slaveholding state before the Civil War. On Texas ranches, slaves broke horses and herded cattle. When the war ended, many freed slaves from Texas and other southern states went to work as professional cowhands. Most Texas trail outfits included black cowboys, and a few outfits were all black.

Mexican cowhands, descendants of the vaqueros, were common in southern Texas, where many ranches were still owned by old Spanish families. Other cowboys were American Indians, or had some Indian blood. In the Indian Territory (now Oklahoma), a number of cattle ranches were operated entirely by Native American cowboys.

In the movies, cowboys seem to spend a good part of their time chasing outlaws, battling Indians, rescuing the rancher's daughter, and hanging out in riotous cow towns like Abilene and Dodge City. They wear huge white hats, skintight shirts, and shiny six-shooters slung low on each hip. That's not quite the way it was in the real Wild West.

A real cowboy was paid to herd cows. He spent most of his time rounding up longhorns, branding calves, and driving the herds to market. He was lucky if he made it into town twice in one year. Out on the range he wore practical

Above: Cowboys at mealtime, photographed in the Texas Panhandle around 1885. Black cowboys, such as the two men in this group, were a part of most Texas trail outfits.

Below: Indian cowboys, photographed in the Cherokee Outlet (now Oklahoma) around 1890. These men are probably Caddo or Kickapoo Indians.

work clothing, rode a horse owned by his employer, and seldom carried a gun. When he did, he wore it high and snug around his waist. He never carried two guns.

"There is one thing I would like to get straight," recalled an old-time cowboy named Teddy Blue Abbott. "I punched cows from '71 on [when he was ten years old], and I never yet saw a cowboy with two guns. I mean two six-shooters. Wild Bill carried two guns and so did some of those other city marshals, like Bat Masterson, but they were professional gunmen themselves, not cowpunchers. . . . A cowboy with two guns is all movie stuff, and so is this business of a gun on each hip."

Most cowboys were not sharpshooters, yet their work demanded exceptional skills. A cowboy had to be an expert roper and rider, an artist at busting broncs and whacking bulls. He had to know how to doctor an ailing cow or find a lost calf, how to calm a restless herd in the middle of the night, how to head off a thousand stampeding longhorns.

On a ranch, he worked ten to fourteen hours a day. On trail drives, he herded cattle from before dawn to after dusk, then spent two more hours on night guard duty. He had a tough, dirty, sweaty job, and often a dangerous one. He might be kicked by a horse, charged by a steer, trampled in a stampede, drowned during a river crossing, or caught on the open prairie in the midst of an electrical storm. Probably more cowboys were killed by lightning than by outlaws or Indians. Riding accidents were the most common cause of cowboy deaths, followed by pneumonia.

Teddy Blue Abbott went up the trail for the first time in 1879, when he was eighteen years old. Sixty years later he recalled the men he had worked with: "In person the cowboys were mostly medium-sized men (as a heavy man was hard on horses), quick and wiry, and as a rule very good natured; in fact, it did not pay to be anything else. In character, their like never was or will be again. They were intensely loyal to the outfit they were working for and would fight to the death for it. I have seen them ride into camp after two days and nights on herd, lay down their saddle blankets in the rain and sleep like dead men, then get up laughing and joking about some good time they had in Ogallala or Dodge City. Living that kind of life, they were bound to be wild and brave."

Think About It

1. What kinds of things might a new cowhand learn on the job?
2. What did you find the most surprising in this selection? Explain.
3. Why does the author mention the way cowboys are shown in movies and on TV?

RUSSELL

How did you become an author of nonfiction books for children?

For many years, I worked as a reporter and editor for newspapers, publishers, and television. I also taught writing in New York City. This kept me involved in the writing world, and I found that I was drawn to children's nonfiction books. I stumbled into the children's book field by chance when I read a newspaper article about a 16-year-old boy who was blind and who invented a Braille typewriter. Then I discovered that the Braille system itself had been invented by another 16-year-old blind boy, Louis Braille. That information gave me an idea for my first book: *Teenagers Who Made History.*

I've found that there is a story to almost everything. The word "history," after all, is mostly made up of the word "story." When I begin a new book, I think of myself mainly as

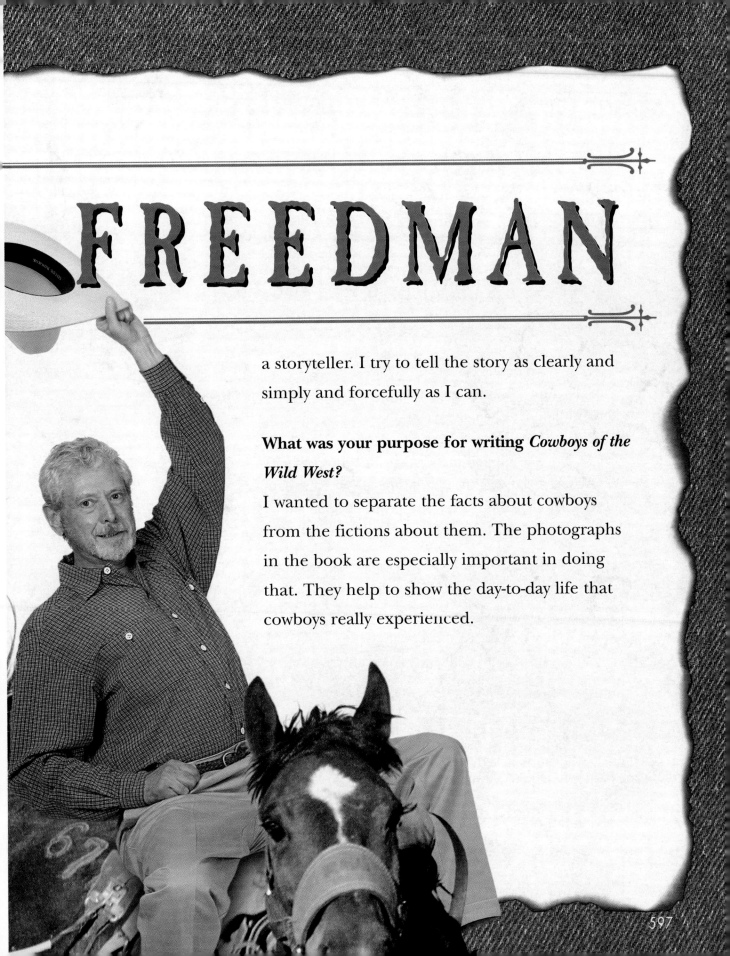

FREEDMAN

a storyteller. I try to tell the story as clearly and simply and forcefully as I can.

What was your purpose for writing *Cowboys of the Wild West?*
I wanted to separate the facts about cowboys from the fictions about them. The photographs in the book are especially important in doing that. They help to show the day-to-day life that cowboys really experienced.

SALLY ANN
THUNDER ANN WHIRLWIND
CROCKETT

A TALL TALE RETOLD AND ILLUSTRATED BY
STEVEN KELLOGG

Sally Ann Thunder Ann Whirlwind astonished folks throughout her childhood. When she was one year old, she beat the fastest runners in the state.

At four she flipped the strongest arm wrestlers.

At seven she was the champion tug-of-war team.

On her eighth birthday Sally Ann decided she was grown-up and ready for new challenges. "I'm off to the frontier!" she announced.

For several years she lived with different animals and learned their habits. She loved life in the wilderness during every season except winter.

Finally, the fierce cold drove her underground to hibernate with the bears. Deep in a cave that bristled with stalactites and stalagmites Sally Ann snuggled close to a large warm grizzly.

Suddenly the bear awakened, and Sally Ann felt a blast of terrible heat from his great ovenlike mouth. It was clear that the bear was more interested in a snack than a roommate.

But before the monster could swallow her, Sally Ann stunned him with a grin as bright as a flash of lightning.

Over backward he went, rolling among razor-sharp stalactites and stalagmites that skinned him from his ears to his toes. Naked and embarrassed, the creature scrambled out of sight. "That was a close shave for both of us!" cried Sally Ann.

She wrapped herself in the bear's fur and set off in search of new adventures.

That bearskin kept Sally Ann cozy for many winters, and she grew tall and strong. But as the years rolled by she became tired of living alone.

One day she came upon an unhappy fellow who had dozed off while leaning against a tree and awakened to find himself stuck.

Two eagles were adding to his misery by yanking out his hair to line their nests.

"You're in a pretty predicament, mister!" exclaimed Sally Ann. "Let me give you a hand."

Sally Ann tried to shoo away the eagles, but they fought her like flapping furies. So she let loose a wild scream that blasted the color off their heads and tails and left them as placid as pigeons.

"Well, star spangle my banner!" cried Sally Ann Thunder Ann Whirlwind. "I've just invented bald eagles!"

Unfortunately, the fellow Sally Ann was trying to rescue had been knocked unconscious by her scream. Quickly she hauled six rattlers out of a nearby snake den, knotted them together, and lassoed a branch. One sharp tug and his head popped free.

He's kind of handsome, thought Sally Ann. I'll freshen up and look my best before I nurse him back to health.

Sally Ann grabbed a hornet's nest for a bonnet and fogged herself with the perfume of a passing skunk.

Then she heaved her patient into the creek.

Just as she expected, the minute he hit that icy water he perked right up. "My heart's pounding like a buffalo stampede," he sputtered.

"So's mine," confessed Sally Ann.

"My name is Davy Crockett. Marry me!" he exclaimed.

Sally Ann was astonished to learn that she had rescued the most famous woodsman in America. Lightning flashed between them, and they fell head over heels in love.

The happy couple celebrated their wedding with a batch of eagle-egg eggnog. Then they settled down in a farmhouse with a fine view of the Mississippi River.

The End
of the Tale

Think About It

What challenges did Sally Ann find on the frontier? What character traits helped her to meet them?

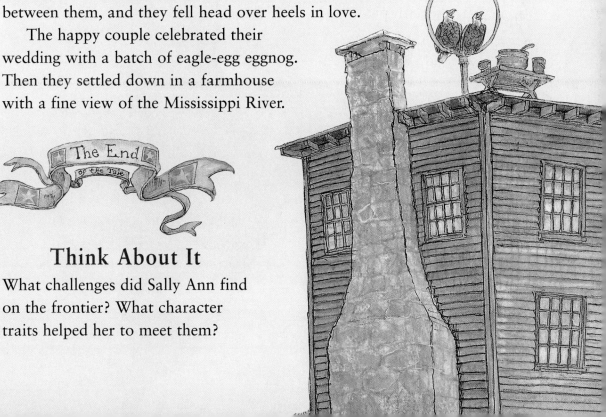

RESPONSE

New Ideas

DRAW PICTURES What new information about cowboys did you learn from the selection? How is that information different from what you thought before? Draw a picture to show how you used to think cowboys looked and what you thought they did. Draw another picture to show what you know about cowboys now. Write captions and labels for both pictures.

ACTIVITIES

Home on the Range

RESEARCH COWBOY SONGS
The selection says that cowboys often sang to the cattle. Research songs the cowboys sang, and learn to sing a real cowboy song. You should be able to find songs in books or on cassettes in the library. If you need help learning to sing a song, ask someone who reads music to help you.

Help Wanted

WRITE AN AD With a small group, discuss the qualities a good cowhand should have. Then write an employment ad a ranch owner might place in a local newspaper. List the duties of a cowhand on that ranch and describe the kind of person the ranch owner is looking for. Display your ad on the class bulletin board.

Making Connections

WRITE A TALL TALE Imagine what might happen if Sally Ann meets a group of cowboys on a trail drive. Write a tall tale in which Sally Ann finds an unusual way to help the cowboys solve a problem. Combine facts from "Cowboys of the Wild West" with the exaggerated style of "Sally Ann Thunder Ann Whirlwind Crockett." Add illustrations if you wish.

Name This American

by Hannah Reinmuth
illustrated by Russ Wilson

Characters

UNCLE SAM
MISS LIBERTY
SIX PANELISTS
WALTER HUNT
GUTZON BORGLUM
MARIA MITCHELL
DOLLEY MADISON
SACAJAWEA
ELIZABETH CADY STANTON
BABE RUTH
LILIUOKALANI

Quiz show keeps panelists guessing.

TIME: *Present.*

SETTING: *The stage of a quiz program.*
Podium is center. Next to it is music stand.
Long table with blindfolds on it and six chairs
are right. Desk and chair are left.

AT RISE: SIX PANELISTS *are seated at long table.*
UNCLE SAM *stands at podium.* MISS LIBERTY
stands behind music stand.

UNCLE SAM: Good afternoon, everyone, and welcome to Name This American! We are honored to have as our guests a number of remarkable Americans. Some you may know, and some you may not know, but I guarantee you'll know them all by the time the show's over. To help us identify these special guests is our panel of distinguished scholars. Let's give them all a hand. (*He and* LIBBY *clap.* PANELISTS *wave and smile.*) Now, my assistant, Miss Liberty, will explain how the game works. (*Gesturing*) Libby?

LIBBY: Thank you, Uncle Sam. The panel will question our guests and the guests will answer yes or no. If a question has a yes answer, the panelist may continue the questioning. If the answer is no, we move on to the next panelist, and the mystery guest receives $50. If our guest stumps all the panelists, he or she wins $500.

SAM: Thank you, Libby. Now, let's begin by bringing in our first guest. (LIBBY *beckons offstage and* WALTER HUNT *enters and sits at desk.*) Welcome to our show.

HUNT: Thank you.

SAM: Panelist number one, please begin the questioning.

1ST PANELIST: Are you famous?

HUNT: No, not really.

SAM: Mystery guest, you've already won $50. (LIBBY *puts $50 sign on stand. Throughout game,* LIBBY *props scores up on stand.*) Let's continue with the next panelist.

2ND PANELIST: Did you discover something?

HUNT: (*Giving* SAM *questioning look*): I suppose you could say so.

SAM: Actually, I'm afraid a yes would be misleading, so we will have to say no and move on to our third panelist.

3RD PANELIST: Let me see. . . . Were you the first to do something?

HUNT: Yes.

3RD PANELIST: Did you, perhaps, invent something?

HUNT: Yes.

SAM: Now we're on the right track.

3RD PANELIST: Is it something you would find around the house?

HUNT: Yes.

3RD PANELIST: Is it electrical?

HUNT: No.

SAM: That's another $50. Panelist four, your turn.

4TH PANELIST: Is it bigger than a bread box?

HUNT: No.

5TH PANELIST: Is it small enough to carry in your pocket?

HUNT: Yes.

5TH PANELIST: Is it a comb?

HUNT: No.

SAM: Panelist six, you're our last chance.

6TH PANELIST (*Pleased*): I think I've got it. Did you invent the pen?

HUNT: No, I did not.

SAM: Mystery guest, congratulations. You stumped our panel of experts. (*All applaud as* LIBBY *puts out the $500 card.*) We are all eager to hear about your invention. Please tell us who you are and what you invented.

HUNT: My name is Walter Hunt. Few people have heard of me, but everyone has used my invention. I am quite proud of my safety pin. (PANELISTS *express surprise.*) I had thought about it for a long time, but it took me only about three hours to make. I had it patented in April, 1849.

SAM: We are certainly honored to meet you, Mr. Hunt. Thank you for playing Name This American.

HUNT: Thank you. (*All applaud as he exits.* GUTZON BORGLUM *enters and sits.*)

SAM: Here's our next challenger, so let's begin.

1ST PANELIST: Are you not very well known?

BORGLUM: Yes, that's true. Few people know my name.

1ST PANELIST: Oh, another hard one! (*Thinks a moment*) Are you involved in the scientific field?

BORGLUM: No.

SAM: That's your first no, panel, and our guest's first $50. Next panelist.

2ND PANELIST: Are you an artist?

BORGLUM: Yes.

2ND PANELIST: Are you a painter?

BORGLUM: I've done some painting, but that's not what I'm known for.

SAM: We'll have to count that as a no and go on to the next panelist.

3RD PANELIST: Are you a musician?

BORGLUM: No.

4TH PANELIST: An entertainer?

BORGLUM: No.

5TH PANELIST (*Thinking, at a loss*): Are you — a sculptor?

BORGLUM: Yes, I am.

5TH PANELIST (*Pleased*): Have I seen your work?

BORGLUM: I'm sure you have.

5TH PANELIST: Have you sculpted any of our presidents?

BORGLUM: Yes.

5TH PANELIST: Do you have any work displayed in Washington, DC?

BORGLUM: Yes.

5TH PANELIST (*Knowingly*): And at Mt. Rushmore?

BORGLUM: Yes.

5TH PANELIST: Then you must be Gutzon Borglum.

OTHER PANELISTS (*Ad lib; surprised, to* 5TH PANELIST): Who? I've never heard of him. (*Etc.*)

SAM: Yes, this is Gutzon Borglum, the artist who designed and carved Mt. Rushmore. Mr. Borglum, please tell us more about yourself.

BORGLUM: My full name is John Gutzon de la Mothe Borglum. I was born in 1867 in Idaho. In 1916, I completed plans to make a Confederate memorial on Stone Mountain near Atlanta, Georgia, but I had a disagreement with my sponsors and by the time it was settled, I had begun the Mt. Rushmore Memorial. I died before it was

finished, so my son completed it.

SAM: We certainly admire your work. Now more of us will remember your name. Thank you for joining us.

BORGLUM: I enjoyed it. (*All applaud as he exits and* MARIA MITCHELL *enters, sits.*)

SAM (*To* MITCHELL): Welcome to Name This American. Are you ready to play?

MITCHELL (*Smiling*): I'm ready.

SAM: Panelist number one, begin.

1ST PANELIST: We've had an inventor and an artist. Could you be in politics?

MITCHELL: No. Politics never interested me.

2ND PANELIST: Were you involved in something related to science?

MITCHELL: Yes, I was.

2ND PANELIST: Are you in the field of medicine?

MITCHELL: No.

3RD PANELIST: Are you involved in the earth sciences?

MITCHELL: No.

4TH PANELIST: Astronomy?

MITCHELL: Yes.

4TH PANELIST: I can't think of any astronomers. (*Thinks a moment, then gets an idea*) Did you, by any chance, grow up on Nantucket Island, Massachusetts?

MITCHELL: Yes.

4TH PANELIST: Are you Maria Mitchell?

609

MITCHELL: Yes, I am. (*All applaud.*)

SAM: Congratulations, panel. Miss Mitchell, please tell us about your interest in astronomy.

MITCHELL: It was unusual for a woman in the mid 1800s to become an astronomer, but I was always interested in the stars — and in the sun, too. I did a lot of research on sun spots. (*Enthusiastically*) In 1847 I discovered a new comet, which was very exciting!

SAM: Thank you, Miss Mitchell. You were way ahead of your time. I'm sorry you didn't win more from our panel.

MITCHELL (*Rising*): I'm sorry, too. (*All applaud. She exits as* DOLLEY MADISON *enters.*)

SAM: Welcome to Name This American.

MADISON: Thank you, Uncle Sam.

SAM: Panelist one, let's start right in.

1ST PANELIST: Your dress makes me think you may have lived about 200 years ago. Is that correct?

MADISON: Yes, that's correct.

1ST PANELIST: Were you involved in the Revolutionary War?

MADISON: I was very young, but yes, I remember it.

SAM: I'm afraid I must count that as a no, since she was only a child at the time.

2ND PANELIST: Were you a seamstress who worked on our first flag?

MADISON: No.

3RD PANELIST: Were you married to one of our presidents?

MADISON (*Smiling*): Yes, I was.

3RD PANELIST: Are you Martha Washington?

MADISON (*Slightly offended*): No, she was much older than I am.

4TH PANELIST: Are you Abigail Adams, the wife of the second president, John Adams?

MADISON: No.

5TH PANELIST: Let's try the next president. Are you Mrs. Jefferson?

MADISON: No.

6TH PANELIST (*Embarrassed*): I can't remember who was the fourth president. Are you Mrs. Monroe?

MADISON: No.

SAM: Too bad, panel. Our fourth president was James Madison. Let me present that famous first lady, Dolley Madison. (*All applaud.*) Tell us about yourself, Mrs. Madison.

MADISON: I was born in North Carolina in 1768 but grew up in Virginia. My first husband, John Todd, was a lawyer. We had two sons, but one of them and my husband died in 1793. I met and married Congressman James Madison a year later and was thrilled to become the first lady in 1809. (*Enthusiastically*) I loved entertaining at the White House. One of my favorite days was when I introduced ice cream to my guests for the first time. What a party! (*More seriously*) I suppose my greatest accomplishment was during the War of 1812. I managed to save a lot of my husband's papers and a portrait of George Washington before the British burned down the White House.

SAM: Mrs. Madison, our country is indebted to you. Thank you for coming today.

MADISON: It was my pleasure. (*All applaud as she exits.*)

SAM: Now, Libby, why don't you explain how the second part of our program works?

LIBBY: I'd be glad to, Uncle Sam. This is the time we ask our panelists to wear blindfolds, as we welcome special celebrities who would be too easy to identify by sight. (PANELISTS *put on blindfolds.*)

SAM: Thank you, Libby. Panel, no peeking, and, audience, no hints. Blindfolds in place? (PANELISTS *nod.*) Then let's bring in our next guest. (LIBBY *motions offstage and* SACAJAWEA *enters.*) Welcome, mystery guest. Are you ready to play?

SACAJAWEA (*Sitting; in deep voice throughout following*): I'm ready.

1ST PANELIST: Are you from the 20th century?

SACAJAWEA: No.

2ND PANELIST: The 19th century?

SACAJAWEA: Yes and no.

SAM: Actually only part of this person's life took place in the 1800s.

2ND PANELIST: Then, I assume, the other part was in the 1700s?

SACAJAWEA: Yes.

2ND PANELIST: And with that voice, I assume you're a man.

SACAJAWEA (*In regular voice*): No, I'm not.

2ND PANELIST (*Surprised*): What? You tricked us.

SACAJAWEA (*Laughing*): I'm sorry. I really am a woman.

3RD PANELIST: If you lived around 1800, did you have anything to do with the westward movement?

SACAJAWEA: Yes.

3RD PANELIST: I can't think of any women of the West except Annie Oakley and Calamity Jane. Are you either of them?

SACAJAWEA: No.

4TH PANELIST: Did you move west with the settlers?

SACAJAWEA: No.

5TH PANELIST (*Thinking*): Were you an explorer?

SACAJAWEA: No.

6TH PANELIST (*Shaking head*): This is a hard one! (*Pause*) Did you help an explorer?

SACAJAWEA: Yes.

6TH PANELIST (*Pleased*): Oh good, now we're getting somewhere! (*Thoughtfully*) Are you an Indian?

SACAJAWEA: Yes.

6TH PANELIST: Are you Sacajawea?

SACAJAWEA: Yes.

SAM: Good work, panel. You may remove your blindfolds (*They do so.*) and take a look at the famous Indian guide for Lewis and Clark, Sacajawea. (*All applaud.*) Please tell us about yourself.

SACAJAWEA: My name, Sacajawea, means Bird Woman in Shoshone. I was captured by enemy Indians and sold to a French-Canadian trader. We joined Lewis and Clark's famous expedition to explore the Louisiana Territory in 1804. I helped as an **interpreter** with the local Indians and was their principal guide.

SAM: And they would not have made it without you. That's why a river, a mountain peak, and a mountain pass have been named after you, not to mention numerous monuments and memorials. (SACAJAWEA *smiles and nods modestly.*) Thank you for joining us today. (*All applaud, as* PANELISTS *put on blindfolds and* SACAJAWEA *exits.* ELIZABETH CADY STANTON *enters and sits.*) Panelist number one, you may begin.

1ST PANELIST: Are you a woman?

STANTON (*Strongly*): Absolutely!

1ST PANELIST (*Taken aback*): Well, that was emphatic! Are you interested in women's rights?

STANTON: Yes, most assuredly I am.

1ST PANELIST: Are you a famous woman suffrage leader?

STANTON: Yes, definitely.

1ST PANELIST: I can think of several women's rights leaders—Lucretia Mott, Susan B. Anthony, and Matilda Gage. Are you any of those?

STANTON: No.

2ND PANELIST: Did you help organize the first women's rights convention held in Seneca Falls, New York, in 1848?

STANTON: Yes, I made the first formal demand for the right to vote to be extended to women.

2ND PANELIST: Were you the first president of the National Woman Suffrage Association?

STANTON: Yes.

2ND PANELIST: In 1868, didn't you even run for Congress?

STANTON (*Angrily*): Yes, and I'd have won if it weren't for the fact that there were only men voting. That was so unfair. Do you realize that women still couldn't vote until the 19th Amendment to the Constitution was passed in 1920!

2ND PANELIST: You're Elizabeth Cady Stanton, aren't you?

STANTON (*Proudly*): Yes, I am! (*Applause. PANELISTS remove blindfolds.*)

SAM: If it weren't for women like you, where would we be today?

STANTON: I was hoping to win $500 for my latest cause, but I suppose I'll be able to get it elsewhere.

SAM: Yes, I'm sure you will.

STANTON: Good day. (*She waves to crowd. Applause as she exits and PANELISTS put on blindfolds. BABE RUTH enters.*)

SAM: Welcome, challenger. (*BABE sits.*) Let's begin.

1ST PANELIST: Are you in politics?

BABE: No, I am not a politician.

2ND PANELIST: Are you involved in sports in any way?

BABE: Yes.

2ND PANELIST: Is that sport football?

BABE: No.

3RD PANELIST: Is it basketball?

BABE: No.

4TH PANELIST: What about baseball?

BABE: That's the one.

4TH PANELIST: Two great players come to mind when I think of baseball, Babe Ruth and Lou Gehrig. Are you one of them?

BABE: Yes.

4TH PANELIST: Well, I have a 50-50 chance. Are you Babe Ruth?

BABE: Yes. (*All applaud.* PANELISTS *remove blindfolds.*)

SAM: Good work, panel. Babe, tell us about some of the highlights of your amazing baseball career.

BABE: I love everything about the game. I set records both from the mound and at the plate. For years I held the record with my total of 714 career homeruns. And in 1936 I was among the first ballplayers elected to the Baseball Hall of Fame.

SAM: Thank you for being part of our show. (*Applause.* PANELISTS *restore blindfolds.* BABE *exits and* LILIUOKALANI *enters.*) It's time for our final contestant. (*To* LILIUOKALANI) Welcome. Are you ready? (*She nods, sits.*) I'm going to help you out, panel, by telling you this is a woman. Now you won't waste any questions on that, and I'm going to give her $50 to start with. (LIBBY *puts up $50 card.*) Panelist number six, let's begin with you.

6TH PANELIST: Thank you. Mystery guest, do we need blindfolds because we would recognize your face or would the clothes you are wearing give you away?

LILIUOKALANI: Which question do you want me to answer?

6TH PANELIST: I'm sorry. Would your clothes give us a clue to your identity?

LILIUOKALANI: Yes, I'm sure they would.

6TH PANELIST: Would a man wear the same outfit?

LILIUOKALANI (*Giggling*): I certainly hope not.

5TH PANELIST: Are you an entertainer?

LILIUOKALANI: No.

4TH PANELIST: Let's get back to the clothes idea. Do they have anything to do with the part of the United States where you live?

LILIUOKALANI: Yes.

4TH PANELIST: Are you from the western part of our country?

LILIUOKALANI: Yes.

4TH PANELIST: The northwest?

615

LILIUOKALANI: No.

3RD PANELIST: Then it must be the southwest, maybe New Mexico, California, or Arizona.

LILIUOKALANI: No — farther southwest.

2ND PANELIST (*Knowingly*): Are you a famous Hawaiian?

LILIUOKALANI: Yes.

2ND PANELIST: Are you Queen Liliuokalani?

LILIUOKALANI: Yes, I am.

SAM: Good work, panel. (*Applause. PANELISTS remove blindfolds.*) Tell us a little about yourself.

LILIUOKALANI: As a child, I loved to write songs. When I got older I wrote the national anthem of Hawaii, but it was never as popular as my song "Aloha Oe." My older sister was supposed to be queen, but she married an American and decided to give

up the throne. Then my brother became King Kalakaua. When he died in 1891, I became Queen Liliuokalani, ruling until 1893, when the United States took over. Hawaii became the 50th state in 1959.

SAM: And a beautiful state it is!

LILIUOKALANI (*Graciously*): It is only one of many.

SAM: Ladies and gentlemen, I'm afraid our time is up, but we are glad you could join us in honoring a few famous Americans. After all, it takes special people to make a great nation like ours. Before we go, we would like to bring out all our contestants. (*Everyone enters.*) Please join us in singing "This Land Is Your Land."

(*All sing. Curtain*)

THE END

Production Notes

NAME THIS AMERICAN

CHARACTERS: *4 male; 6 female; 6 male or female for panelists.*

PLAYING TIME: *25 minutes.*

COSTUMES: *Walter Hunt, Gutzon Borglum, Maria Mitchell, Dolley Madison, and Elizabeth Cady Stanton wear period dress. Sacajawea, Indian outfit. Liliuokalani, colorful Hawaiian outfit and lei. Babe Ruth, baseball uniform. Uncle Sam wears red, white, and blue. Liberty, green dress and crown. Panelists, everyday clothes.*

PROPERTIES: *Large cards marked: $50, $100, $150, $200, $250, and $500; six blindfolds.*

SETTING: *The stage of a quiz program. Podium is center. Next to it is music stand. Long table and six chairs are right. Desk and chair are left.*

LIGHTING AND SOUND: *No special effects.*

Think About It

❶ What do all the mystery guests on the quiz show have in common?

❷ What might have been the author's purpose in writing a play about a quiz show and including these particular characters?

❸ If your class were going to perform this play, which character would you most like to portray? Why?

617

High-Flying Facts

Landmark Moments in the History of the American Flag

by Mary Morton Cowan
illustrated by Rich Harrington

The flag of the United States of America has a story quite different from flags of other nations. The United States was the first country to institute a flag day, a pledge of allegiance, and a flag etiquette code, and the American flag was the first flag for which a national anthem was written. Here are some highlights of our flag's history.

JUNE 14, 1777 The Second Continental Congress adopts the first official American flag, calling for 13 red and white stripes and 13 white stars on a blue background.

MAY 1, 1795 Because there are now 15 states, the official flag has 15 stripes and 15 stars. In 1800, it becomes the first flag to fly over the new U.S. Capitol. Several years later, it is the flag that explorers Meriwether Lewis and William Clark carry across the continent.

SEPTEMBER 13, 1814 The British attack Fort McHenry in Baltimore, Maryland. All night, Francis Scott Key watches the battle. When he sees the U.S. flag still flying at dawn, he writes a poem titled "Defense of Fort McHenry." Soon the poem is set to music and renamed "The Star-Spangled Banner."

APRIL 4, 1818 The Flag Act of 1818 specifies 13 horizontal stripes (to represent the original colonies) and 20 stars (one for each state). It further states that a star be added for every new state on the Fourth of July after its admission.

1861 As southern states drop out of the Union, President Abraham Lincoln refuses to remove their stars from the flag. He maintains that none of the southern states ever legally left the Union. The first local Flag Day is celebrated in Hartford, Connecticut.

JUNE 14, 1877 On the flag's 100th birthday, the federal government requests that it be flown from all public buildings.

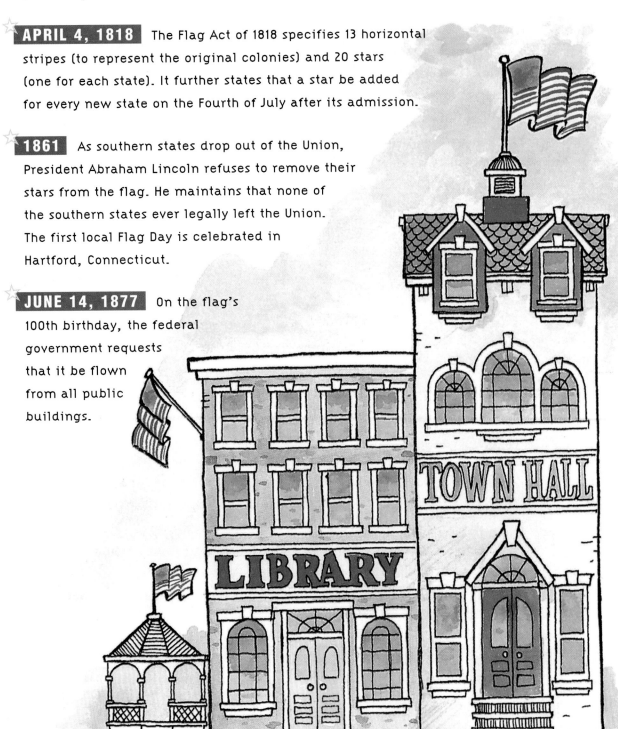

APRIL 6, 1909 The American flag reaches the North Pole! Robert Peary buries a diagonal strip of his flag in the ice.[1]

1916 President Woodrow Wilson proclaims June 14 the first Flag Day, but Congress does not officially recognize it until August 3, 1949, under President Harry S. Truman.

1931 President Herbert Hoover signs a bill designating "The Star-Spangled Banner" as the national anthem, effective March 3.

JUNE 22, 1942 Congress adopts the Flag Code, which tells people how to show respect for the flag and how to display it properly.

FEBRUARY 23, 1945 Near the end of World War II, Americans storm the Japanese island of Iwo Jima. Atop Mount Suribachi, Joe Rosenthal photographs 5 Marines and a Navy corpsman raising the Stars and Stripes. Rosenthal's photo becomes the model for the Marine Corps Memorial in Washington, D.C.

[1] Upon reaching the North Pole, Admiral Peary left a glass jar containing a strip of his flag and two notes as a record of his accomplishment.

AUGUST 3, 1949 President Harry S. Truman officially recognizes June 14 as a national day of observance.

JULY 20, 1969 American astronauts Neil Armstrong and Edwin "Buzz" Aldrin are the first men to land on the moon and to plant an American flag beyond this planet.

JUNE 14, 1983 The world's largest flag is spread out on the Mall in Washington, D.C. Called the "Great American Flag," it weighs 7 tons, and each star is 13 feet across. It measures 411 by 210 feet.

☆ ☆ ☆ ☆ ☆ ☆ ☆ ☆ ☆ ☆ ☆ ☆ ☆

Think About It

What other titles can you think of for the selection "High-Flying Facts"? Explain your answer.

☆ ☆ ☆ ☆ ☆ ☆ ☆ ☆ ☆ ☆ ☆ ☆ ☆

Response Activities

WHO AM I?

ADD A SCENE   With a small group, choose another remarkable American to appear as a guest on the quiz show. You might choose someone you have learned about in social studies. Research facts about this person, using your social studies text or other reference sources. Plan the panelists' questions and your guest's answers. Then perform your scene for classmates.

A REMARKABLE VISIT

WRITE A PARAGRAPH   If you could meet one of the remarkable Americans in this play, who would you choose? Write a paragraph telling why you would like to meet this person and what you think you might learn from him or her.

COMPARE TV SHOWS   Suppose "Name This American" were a real quiz show that you could watch on TV. Would you enjoy watching it? List four TV shows that you have watched, plus the "Name This American" show. Then rank the shows from 1 to 5, with 1 being your favorite and 5 your least favorite. Write a few sentences explaining your reasons for ranking the shows as you did.

★ **MAKING CONNECTIONS**

DRAW A FLAG   Choose a remarkable American from the play, and do research to find out when this person was born. What did the American flag look like when he or she was born? Use what you learned from "High-Flying Facts." Draw the flag as it looked then, and label your drawing with the person's name and the year.

THEME

WRAP-UP

What's the Purpose?

IDENTIFY THE PURPOSE Authors write with a purpose in mind. Think about each selection in the theme "American Adventure." Did the author write the selection to inform, to entertain, to express a point of view about the subject, or to persuade the reader? Make a chart like the one shown here to show the purpose of each selection. Support your responses with examples from the selections.

Selection	Purpose
Across the Wide Dark Sea	
What's the Big Idea, Ben Franklin?	
Black Frontiers...	
Cowboys of the Wild West	
Name This American	

Picture This!

CREATE MENTAL IMAGES
The stories in this theme all have to do with adventure and discovery. Choose one of the selections, and think about why it fits well into the "American Adventure" theme. Write notes and find examples from the selection to support your ideas. Then meet in a small group and explain why your chosen selection belongs in this theme.

What Else Happened?

RESEARCH THE PERIOD
The selections in this theme span many periods of American history. Choose a period that interests you. Then list three questions about that period that you would like answered. You may list questions about a person or an event described in one of the selections in this theme or about other events that happened during that period. Research the answers and report your findings to the class.

Using the Glossary

Like a dictionary, this glossary lists words in alphabetical order. To find a word, look it up by its first letter or letters.

To save time, use the **guide words** at the top of each page. These show you the first and last words on the page. Look at the guide words to see if your word falls between them alphabetically.

Here is an example of a glossary entry:

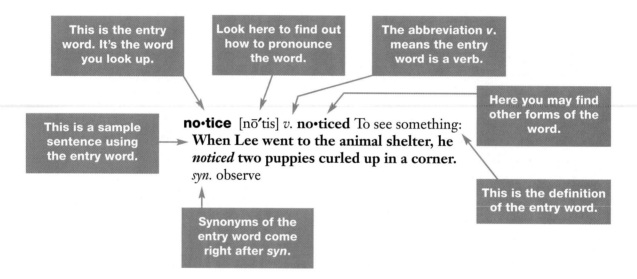

This is the entry word. It's the word you look up.

Look here to find out how to pronounce the word.

The abbreviation *v.* means the entry word is a verb.

Here you may find other forms of the word.

This is a sample sentence using the entry word.

no•tice [nō′tis] *v.* **no•ticed** To see something: **When Lee went to the animal shelter, he** *noticed* **two puppies curled up in a corner.** *syn.* observe

This is the definition of the entry word.

Synonyms of the entry word come right after *syn.*

Word Origins

Throughout the glossary, you will find notes about word origins, or how words got started and changed. Words often have interesting backgrounds that can help you remember what they mean.

Here is an example of a word-origin note:

> **familiar** At first, *familiar* meant "of the family," from the Latin word *familiaris*. Its meaning grew to include friends and to become "known from being around often." *Familiar* began to be used in English in the 1300s.

Pronunciation

The pronunciation in brackets is a respelling that shows how the word is pronounced.

The **pronunciation key** explains what the symbols in a respelling mean. A shortened pronunciation key appears on every other page of the glossary.

PRONUNCIATION KEY*

a	add, map	m	move, seem	u	up, done
ā	ace, rate	n	nice, tin	û(r)	burn, term
â(r)	care, air	ng	ring, song	yo͞o	fuse, few
ä	palm, father	o	odd, hot	v	vain, eve
b	bat, rub	ō	open, so	w	win, away
ch	check, catch	ô	order, jaw	y	yet, yearn
d	dog, rod	oi	oil, boy	z	zest, muse
e	end, pet	ou	pout, now	zh	vision, pleasure
ē	equal, tree	o͝o	took, full	ə	the schwa, an unstressed vowel representing the sound spelled
f	fit, half	o͞o	pool, food		
g	go, log	p	pit, stop		*a* in *above*
h	hope, hate	r	run, poor		*e* in *sicken*
i	it, give	s	see, pass		*i* in *possible*
ī	ice, write	sh	sure, rush		*o* in *melon*
j	joy, ledge	t	talk, sit		*u* in *circus*
k	cool, take	th	thin, both		
l	look, rule	t̶h̶	this, bathe		

Other symbols
- separates words into syllables
- ′ indicates heavier stress on a syllable
- ′ indicates light stress on a syllable

Abbreviations: *adj.* adjective, *adv.* adverb, *conj.* conjunction, *interj.* interjection, *n.* noun, *prep.* preposition, *pron.* pronoun, *syn.* synonym, *v.* verb

* The Pronunciation Key, adapted entries, and the Short Key that appear on the following pages are reprinted from *HBJ School Dictionary*. Copyright © 1990 by Harcourt, Inc. Reprinted by permission of Harcourt, Inc.

ab·a·lo·ne
[ab′ə·lō′nē] *n.* An edible water animal that lives in a shell: **The *abalone* shell has a pearl-like lining.**

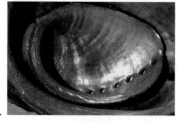

abalone

ab·sorb [əb·zôrb′] *v.* **ab·sorbed** To be so interested in something as not to notice anything else: **Jan was so *absorbed* in her book that she didn't hear the doorbell.** *syn.* preoccupy

ac·com·pa·ni·ment [ə·kum′pə·nē·mənt] *n.* Music that is played along with another's performance: **The dancer needs a piano's *accompaniment*.**

ac·com·pa·nist [ə·kum′pə·nist] *n.* A person who plays music while another person performs: **The *accompanist* waited for the singer's signal.**

ac·cord [ə·kôrd′] *n.* 1. Harmony; agreement. 2. A choice made without being asked: **Cindy cleaned her room on her own *accord*.**

ace [ās] *adj.* Best: **She is the *ace* player on our team.** *syn.* star

aisle [īl] *n.* A passageway, such as between rows of seats: **Don't block the *aisle* when people are leaving the auditorium.** *syn.* walkway

al·tim·e·ter [al·tim′ə·tər] *n.* An instrument that measures height above ground: **The plane's *altimeter* read 5,000 feet when the plane flew over the field.**

an·them [an′thəm] *n.* A song in honor of a country, a school, or some other institution: **"The Star-Spangled Banner" is the national *anthem*.** *syn.* theme song

an·tic·i·pa·tion [an·tis′ə·pā′shən] *n.* The feeling of looking forward to something: **George felt *anticipation* before he started camp.** *syn.* expectation

ap·pren·tice [ə·pren′tis] *n.* A person who is in training in a craft or an art under the supervision of an expert: **The sculptor's *apprentice* polished the finished pieces.**

ar·ti·fi·cial [är′tə·fish′əl] *adj.* Manufactured by humans as a substitute for something natural: **Dentures are *artificial* teeth.** *syn.* synthetic

as·ton·ish [ə·stän′ish] *v.* **as·ton·ished** To amaze or shock: **Paul was *astonished* to learn he had won the contest.** *syn.* surprise

a·toll [a′tôl] *n.* A narrow, ring-shaped island: **The *atoll* was made of coral.**

au·di·tion [ô·dish′ən] *n.* A tryout for a performing role or a job: **We wished Ari luck before his *audition* for the play.** *syn.* test

> **Word Origins**
> **audition** At the root of the word *audition* is the Latin base *aud*, which has to do with hearing. Other related words are *audio*—the sound component of electronics; *auditorium*—a place where you go to hear a performance; and *audience*—the people who hear the performance.

au·thor·i·ty [ô·thär′ə·tē] *n.* A person who knows a lot about a particular subject and is considered to be an expert: **Ray is the class *authority* on baseball.** *syn.* master

bar·ren [bar′ən] *adj.* Without the conditions necessary to support life: **The *barren* desert had received no rain for years.** *syn.* desolate

beam [bēm] 1. *v.* **beam·ing** To smile in a warm way at someone: **Sally was *beaming* at her best friend.** *syn.* glow 2. *n.* A heavy crosspiece of a ship or building: **The main *beam* gave the ship its structure.** *syn.* crossbar

beam

bolt [bōlt] *v.* To move, go, or spring suddenly: **The horse will *bolt* if she is frightened.** *syn.* flee

boom [boom] *v.* **boom·ing** To increase or prosper suddenly: **Business was *booming*, so they opened a second store.** *syn.* expand

break·through [brāk′throo] *n.* An important advance in a field of knowledge: **The medical *breakthrough* saved many lives.** *syn.* discovery

brood [brood] *v.* **brood·ed** To mope and worry for a long time over something: **Lana *brooded* after she had argued with a friend.** *syn.* sulk

bulge [bulj] *n.* A swollen part or place: **The *bulge* in the tire means it needs replacement.** *syn.* protrusion

bulk [bulk] *n.* The largeness of something, including what it weighs or how much room it takes up: **The massive bear threw its *bulk* against the door.** *syn.* mass

bur·row [bər′ō] *v.* **bur·rowed** To dig into the ground for protection: **The mouse *burrowed* into a pile of leaves.** *syn.* tunnel

cam·paign [kam·pān′] *n.* The process of running for elected office: **The candidate made speeches during her *campaign*.**

> **Word Origins**
> **campaign** The word *campaign* traces its origins back to the French word *campagne*, meaning "countryside." The open country was the site of military maneuvers and battles. *Campaign* also means "the military operations involved in winning a battle." The idea of "winning a battle" carries over to politics.

can·o·py [kan′ə·pē] *n.* A rooflike covering: **The forest *canopy* is made up of the uppermost leaves and branches.** *syn.* awning

char·coal [chär′kōl] *n.* A black substance used as a drawing crayon: **Students did their sketches in *charcoal*.**

com·mo·tion [kə·mō′·shən] *n.* A disturbance; confusion: **A *commotion* occurred in the halls on the first day because students didn't know where their classes were meeting.** *syn.* uproar

com·pose [kəm·pōz′] *v.* To calm oneself: **Juan had to *compose* himself before the test.** *syn.* relax

con·coct [kən·käkt′] *v.* **con·coc·ted** To invent or develop something: **Pat *concocted* a delicious shake from five kinds of juice.** *syn.* devise

con·trap·tion [kən·trap′shən] *n.* A mechanical device, sometimes fanciful: **This *contraption* wakes you up and finds your socks in the morning.** *syn.* gadget

con·trol tow·er [kən·trōl′ tou′ər] *n.* The tower at an airport from which planes are guided to take off and land: **The pilot got clearance from the *control tower* to take off.**

cor·re·spon·dence [kôr′ə·spän′dəns] *n.* Communication by means of writing letters or electronic mail: **The pen pals kept up their *correspondence* for three years before they met in person.**

cos·mo·naut [käz′mə·nôt′] *n.* The Russian term for a person trained to make flights in space: **The *cosmonaut*, Yuri Gagarin, was the first human to go into space.** *syn.* astronaut

> **Fact File**
> **cosmonaut** The terms *cosmonaut* and *astronaut* have almost the same meanings. *Cosmonaut* is the Russian term and *astronaut* is the English term. Cosmonaut Yuri Gagarin (1934–1968) was the first person to orbit the Earth. He did so in April 1961, a few weeks before American astronaut Alan Shepard's flight. In 1975 American and Soviet scientists worked together in space as part of the Apollo-Soyuz project. American astronauts worked aboard the Russian space station, *Mir*. Russian cosmonauts and American astronauts will be stationed on the ISS, the International Space Station, now under construction.

coun·sel [koun′səl] *v.* To give advice: **My older brother likes to *counsel* me on how to handle my friends.** *syn.* advise

de·ci·pher [dē·sī′fər] *v.* To make out the meaning of something such as code or illegible handwriting: **My handwriting was hard to *decipher* at first.** *syn.* decode

ded·i·cate [ded′ə·kāt] *v.* **ded·i·cat·ed** To declare—often in writing—that an artwork or a project is in honor of a person: **John *dedicated* his first symphony to his father.** *syn.* inscribe

de·flect [di·flekt′] *v.* **de·flec·ted** To cause something to veer off course; to cause something to bounce off: **The armor *deflected* arrows well.** *syn.* avert

> **Word Origins**
> **deflect** The word *deflect* has in it the root *flect*, meaning "bend," and the prefix *de-*, meaning "off," or "away from." Some other words containing *flect* are *reflect*—"to bend back"—as light waves bend back from a mirror, and *genuflect*—"to bend the knee."

a	add	e	end	o	odd	ōō	pool	oi	oil	th	this	a in *above*
ā	ace	ē	equal	ō	open	u	up	ou	pout	zh	vision	e in *sicken*
â	care	i	it	ô	order	û	burn	ng	ring			i in *possible*
ä	palm	ī	ice	ŏŏ	took	yōō	fuse	th	thin			o in *melon*

ə = { a in *above*, e in *sicken*, i in *possible*, o in *melon*, u in *circus* }

de·ject·ed·ly [di·jek′tid·lē] *adv.* Having a depressed attitude: **The team members walked home** *dejectedly* **after they lost the game.** *syn.* sadly

de·scend [di·send′] *v.* **de·scen·ded** To come down from ancestors or to have a characteristic that comes down from them: **You are** *descended* **from a long line of painters.**

de·sig·nate [dez′ig·nāt] *v.* **de·sig·na·ted** To set something apart for a special honor: **This day has been** *designated* **Best Friends Day.** *syn.* appoint

de·spair [di·spâr′] *n.* A feeling of hopelessness: **Mark felt** *despair* **because he thought he would never understand the work.**

de·spise [di·spīz′] *v.* **de·spised** To dislike intensely: **I** *despise* **television programs that insult my intelligence.** *syns.* loathe, detest

de·vote [di·vōt′] *v.* To dedicate oneself to a person, a career, and so on: **Lana knew that she would** *devote* **herself to achieving her dream.** *syn.* commit

dig·ni·ty [dig′nə·tē] *n.* The state of having pride and self-worth: **Aunt Flo always carried herself with** *dignity***.**

dis·charge [dis·chärj′] **dis·charged** *v.* To relieve of duty; to dismiss from a job: **Irene was** *discharged* **from being class president after the term ended.** *syn.* dismiss

dis·en·gage [dis·ən·gāj′] *v.* To unfasten or release: **The spacecraft can** *disengage* **itself from the space station.** *syn.* detach

disengage

dis·may [dis·mā′] *n.* Worry; discouragement; a feeling of alarm, uneasiness: **Gwen sighed in** *dismay* **when so few came to the meeting.**

dis·re·gard [dis·ri·gärd′] *v.* **dis·re·gard·ed** To pay no attention: **The loud student** *disregarded* **the whisper policy in the library.** *syn.* ignore

dis·tin·guished [dis·tin′gwisht] *adj.* Having high position and honor: **The mayor was one of the** *distinguished* **guests.** *syn.* famous

dis·tress [dis·tres′] **dis·tressed** *v.* To feel discomfort or sorrow: **Paul was** *distressed* **that he had missed the bus.** *syn.* upset

dis·trib·u·tor [dis·trib′yə·tər] *n.* A person or thing that provides a product or a service throughout a certain area: **Stripes Company is the** *distributor* **of school software in our county.** *syn.* dealer

do·mes·ti·cat·ed [də·mes′tə·kāt·əd] *adj.* Accustomed to people or trained to work with people: *Domesticated* **elephants can do heavy work, such as carrying large logs.** *syn.* tame

du·pli·cate [doo′plə·kit] *n.* An exact copy: **This ring is a** *duplicate* **of one we saw in the museum.** *syn.* reproduction

dwin·dle [dwin′dəl] *v.* **dwin·dled** To shrink in size, value, or quantity: **Joseph's savings** *dwindled* **because he often bought snacks from vending machines.** *syn.* decrease

e·di·tion [i·dish′ən] *n.* A number of copies of something, such as a book, all printed in the same way and at about the same time: **The first** *edition* **of her book came out in May.**

ember

em·ber [em′bər] *n.* **em·bers** In a fire, a glowing piece of wood or coal: **We toasted marshmallows over the** *embers***.** *syn.* coal

en·cour·age [in·kər′ij] *v.* **en·cour·aged** To give confidence, praise, or emotional support to another person: **The teacher** *encouraged* **her students to succeed.** *syn.* inspire

en·dorse [in·dôrs′] *v.* To give support to something or someone, such as a product or a candidate for office: **The company asked famous sports stars to** *endorse* **its products.** *syn.* recommend

en·er·gy [en′ər·jē] *n.* Power that is used to do work: **Food gives your body** *energy* **to move and grow.**

en·gross [in·grōs′] *v.* **en·grossed** To be occupied completely: **Rita was so *engrossed* in her book that she did not notice the time.** *syn.* absorb

> ### Word Origin
>
> **engross** This word traces its origins to the Old French word *engrosser*, "to acquire in large quantity." One might buy up all of something, creating a monopoly (controlling all sales and prices). The word *engross* came to mean "to take all of something" or "to require all of something." The connection between the word's original meaning and its current meaning lies in the idea of taking up all of something, whether an object or one's attention.

en·roll [in·rōl′] *v.* **en·rolls** To sign up for a club, membership, or a school: **Kayla *enrolls* in college next year.** *syn.* register

er·rand [er′ənd] *n.* **er·rands** A short trip on which someone does something, often a trip for someone else: **Sally's job was to run *errands* for her father's grocery store.**

er·ror [er′ər] *n.* A mistake in thinking or in judgment; in baseball, a mistake in fielding the ball: **Noel was charged with an *error* when he dropped the ball and the runner made it to second base.** *syn.* blunder

e·vap·o·rate [i·vap′ə·rāt′] *v.* **e·vap·o·rat·ing** To vanish, in the same way water turns to vapor: **She spent her allowance so fast it seemed to *evaporate*.** *syn.* disappear

ex·ag·ger·ate [ig·zaj′ə·rāt′] *v.* To add to the facts in a way that distorts the meaning: **If you *exaggerate* the facts of the news story, then it is no longer good journalism.** *syn.* overstate

ex·haust [ig·zôst′] *v.* **ex·haust·ed** To make tired: **The mule was *exhausted* from carrying the heavy packs.** *syn.* fatigue

ex·o·dus [ek′sə·dəs] *n.* A large group of people going out from a place: **At first only a few refugees left, but soon an *exodus* began.** *syn.* migration

ex·quis·ite [eks·kwi′zit] *adj.* Beautiful and elegant: **The art lover filled his home with *exquisite* paintings and sculptures.** *syn.* charming

field [fēld] *v.* **field·ed** In baseball or softball, to catch a ball that is in play and throw it if necessary: **Emily *fielded* a ground ball and tossed it to home plate.** *syn.* retrieve

flex·i·bil·i·ty [flek′sə·bil′i·tē] *n.* The quality of being able to bend without breaking: **Some types of plastic have *flexibility*, but wood does not.** *syn.* malleability

for·lorn [fər·lôrn′] *adj.* Feeling miserable, lost, or abandoned: **Sarah wore a *forlorn* expression when no one played with her.** *syn.* sad

for·mu·la [fôr′myə·lə] *n.* **for·mu·las** In math, a set of symbols that stands for a fact or an exercise: **Luis memorized many *formulas* so he could easily use them.** *syn.* method

furl [fûrl] *v.* To wrap up tightly and then tie, such as a sail: **Dori had to *furl* the sail after tying the small sailboat to the dock.** *syn.* roll

gen·er·ate [jen′ə·rāt] *v.* **gen·er·at·ed** To cause something to happen because of a physical or a chemical change: **The light *generated* a lot of heat.** *syn.* produce

gey·ser [gī′zər] *n.* A spring of water heated by an underground source so that it boils at regular intervals, shooting water and steam into the air: **The tourists were misted with warm water when the geyser shot upward through the ground.**

> ### Fact File
>
> **geyser** The word *geyser* is the only Icelandic word commonly used in the English language. *Geysir* is the name of a certain geyser in southern Iceland. The word means "gusher." Geysir has quieted in the past 60 years, but other Icelandic geysers are quite active.

geyser

a	add	e	end	o	odd	o͞o	pool	oi	oil	<u>th</u>	this
ā	ace	ē	equal	ō	open	u	up	ou	pout	zh	vision
â	care	i	it	ô	order	û	burn	ng	ring		
ä	palm	ī	ice	o͝o	took	yo͞o	fuse	th	thin		

ə = { *a* in *above*; *e* in *sicken*; *i* in *possible*; *o* in *melon*; *u* in *circus* }

gorge [gôrj] *v.* **gorged** To overeat; to gobble food like an animal: **The hungry lions *gorged* themselves on their prey.** *syn.* stuff

grade [grād] *n.* The steepness of the land; the steepness of an angle: **The road's *grade* grew steeper as it approached the mountain.**

graf·fi·ti [grə·fē'tē] *n.* A kind of vandalism in which people write their names or draw pictures on others' property: **The students who wrote the *graffiti* had to stay after school and scrub it off.** *syn.* scrawl

grav·el·ly [grav'əl·lē] *adj.* Having a rough sound: **Her bad cold made her voice sound *gravelly*.** *syn.* raspy

grav·i·ta·tion·al [grav'ə·tā'shən·əl] *adj.* Having to do with the law in physics that states that two objects exert a pull on each other: **The Earth's *gravitational* pull is one reason objects have weight; the other is the mass of the objects themselves.**

gri·mace [grim'əs] *v.* **gri·maced** To twist one's face, as if in pain: **Cal *grimaced* as he heard the off-key music.**

guar·an·tee [gar'ən·tē'] *v.* To pledge that something will be done as promised: **We *guarantee* that you will like our product, or we will give you back your money.** *syn.* affirm

han·dler [han'dlər] *n.* **han·dlers** A person who trains or manages an animal in a race, a show, or a contest: **The show dogs looked to their *handlers* for instructions.** *syn.* manager

har·ness [här'nis] *n.* Leather straps or bands used to hitch an animal to something it will pull: **The *harness* fastened the horse to the carriage.**

head·quar·ters [hed'kwôr'tərz] *n.* The central office for controlling an operation, campaign, or business: **Lila sent a letter of complaint to company *headquarters* and got a reply.**

Word Origins

headquarters The head, because it houses the brain and contains four major sense organs, is the center of control for all of the body's functions. Some words in our language that expand on this idea are *headline*—the most important part of a news story; *headmaster*—the principal of a school; and *headspring*—the source of a spring of water.

---

heave [hēv] *v.* **heaved** To use much effort to lift and toss something: **The passenger *heaved* her knapsack onto the luggage rack.** *syn.* pitch

home·stead [hōm'sted] *v.* To develop a substantial piece of land, including building on it and farming it: **The Smith family decided to *homestead* rather than stay in the crowded city.**

hon·or [än'ər] *n.* Recognition of or respect for someone's achievement: **She received a certificate of *honor* for her high grades.** *syns.* tribute, award

hud·dle [hud'əl] *v.* **hud·dled** To nestle close together, as for protection: **The pigeons *huddled* together under the awning.** *syn.* crowd

il·lus·trate [il'ə·strāt'] *v.* **il·lus·trat·ing** To make pictures that go along with written material, such as books: **Emily enjoys writing and *illustrating* her own books.** *syn.* draw

---

Word Origins

illustrate The word *illustrate* is derived from the Latin word *illustratus*, "to light up." One meaning of *illustrate* is "to make clear or explain" by using examples and comparisons. Illustrations "shed light on" the words of a book.

---

im·mo·bil·i·ty [i·mō·bil'ə·tē] *n.* The condition of not being able to move: **An engine problem caused the car's *immobility*.** *syn.* motionlessness

im·pact [im'pakt] *n.* The effect of an idea or an action on someone's feelings or behavior: **The movie about fire safety had an *impact* on the audience.** *syn.* influence

im·pul·sive·ly [im·pəl'siv·lē] *adv.* With suddenness; without hesitation: **Josh makes decisions *impulsively* and pays the consequences later.**

in·cred·i·ble [in·kred'ə·bəl] *adj.* Too unusual to be believed: **Eighty years ago, space travel seemed an *incredible* idea.** *syn.* unbelievable

in·cred·u·lous·ly [in·krej'ə·ləs·lē] *adv.* With disbelief: **The team listened *incredulously* as the coach explained why the soccer tournament had been canceled.** *syn.* skeptically

in·debt·ed [in·det'id] *adj.* Feeling that one owes something in return for a favor: **We are *indebted* to you for your help after the earthquake.** *syn.* obligated

in·ef·fi·cient [in′ə·fish′ənt] *adj.* Not able to do the job in the best way: **The old engine made *inefficient* use of its fuel.** *syn.* ineffective

in·let [in′let] *n.* A narrow strip of water; a small bay or creek: **We traveled the *inlet* in a small canoe.** *syn.* passageway

in·spire [in·spīr′] *v.* To motivate someone to accomplish or feel something: **A good teacher seeks to *inspire* the class.** *syn.* encourage

in·stall·ment [in·stôl′mənt] *n.* **in·stall·ments** One part of a total amount of money that is owed: **Jennie paid her mother back for the broken vase in three *installments*.** *syn.* payment

in·su·late [in′sə·lāt′] *v.* **in·su·lat·ed** To cover, as with a material that does not conduct electricity or a material that does not allow heat or cold to pass through: **The wires were not *insulated* well and so posed a fire hazard.** *syn.* wrap

in·ter·na·tion·al [in′tər·na′shə·nəl] *adj.* Having to do with many nations: **Antarctica is the site of *international* scientific research.** *syn.* global

in·ter·pret·er [in·tür′prə·tər′] *n.* A person who translates spoken words from one language into another: **Kim acted as *interpreter* between her sister and the salesclerk.** *syn.* translator

jaun·ty [jôn′tē] *adj.* Stylish; lively in appearance: **Jessica looked confident and *jaunty* as she walked to the podium to deliver her speech.**

la·goon [lə·gōon′] *n.* An area of water that is surrounded by a circular thin strip of land called an atoll: **The water in the *lagoon* was very calm.**

lagoon

lair [lâr] *n.* The home of some kinds of animals: **The bear hibernated all winter in her *lair*.** *syn.* den

line·up [līn′up′] *n.* In baseball or softball, the batting order for a team: **Ken batted third in the *lineup*.** *syn.* order

lurk [lûrk] *v.* **lurked** To be ready to attack while hiding from view: **The leopard *lurked* in the jungle, quietly searching for food.** *syn.* skulk

me·an·der [mē·an′dər] *v.* To move back and forth in a snakelike fashion: **The cat likes to *meander* through the garden.** *syn.* wind

men·tor [men′tər] *n.* An advisor and tutor who works one-on-one with a young person: **With a *mentor's* help, Cyd became a music protégé.** *syn.* teacher

> **Fact File**
>
> **mentor** In Greek mythology, Mentor was a friend of Odysseus, the hero of Homer's epic poem *The Odyssey*. Mentor became the helper and teacher of Odysseus' son, Telemachus. Odysseus had been called away to battle, and he encountered many adventures and difficulties during his return journey. Throughout Odysseus' absence, Mentor often helped Telemachus choose the right course of action.

mi·grant [mī′grənt] *adj.* Moving regularly from place to place: ***Migrant* farmers must often move from place to place.** *syn.* nomadic

mi·grate [mī′grāt] *v.* **mi·grat·ed** To move with others of the same group to a place that is far away: **The birds *migrated* south in winter in search of food and warmth.** *syn.* relocate

mis·lead [mis·lēd′] *v.* **mis·lead·ing** To give a false idea to others: **The robber tried *misleading* the police when he was questioned.** *syn.* deceive

moss [môs] *n.* A class of small plants that grow in moist, shaded areas: ***Moss* grows on the north side of trees in the Northern Hemisphere.**

muf·fle [muf′əl] *v.* To lower the volume by covering or enclosing the source of the noise: **Dina used a pillow to *muffle* the ringing of the alarm clock.** *syn.* deaden

a add	e end	o odd	ōō pool	oi oil	th this	
ā ace	ē equal	ō open	u up	ou pout	zh vision	*a* in *above*
â care	i it	ô order	û burn	ng ring		*e* in *sicken*
ä palm	ī ice	ŏŏ took	yōō fuse	th thin	ə =	*i* in *possible*
						o in *melon*
						u in *circus*

mur·mur [mûr′mər] *n.* A soft, constant, unclear sound: **The audience began to *murmur* when the movie ended.** *syn.* mumble

ne·go·ti·ate [ni·gō′shē·āt] *v.* **ne·go·ti·at·ing** To hold a discussion with the goal of making an agreement: **The student government is *negotiating* with the principal for the right to run a radio station.** *syn.* arbitrate

nu·mer·ous [nōō′mər·əs] *adj.* Consisting of a large group of things or events: **He tried *numerous* times to grow plants from seeds in his backyard.** *syn.* many

oath [ōth] *n.* An oral or written promise about a serious matter, such as honesty or faithfulness to an ideal: **At his inauguration, President Washington took the first *oath* of office.** *syn.* vow

oath

ob·nox·ious [əb·näk′shəs] *adj.* Extremely unpleasant or offensive: **The landfill gave off an *obnoxious* smell.** *syn.* intolerable

> **Word Origins**
> **obnoxious** The word *obnoxious* is from the Latin word *obnoxiosus*, meaning "exposed to danger." It is made up of the word parts *ob*, which means "to" or "toward," and *noxa*, which means "harm." The word is used today with a meaning that is closer to "annoying," such as "an obnoxious attitude." However, the original meaning was more danger-oriented. (See *ominous*.)

om·i·nous [äm′ə·nəs] *adj.* Threatening, dangerous: ***Ominous* storm clouds darkened the sky.** *syn.* menacing

over·come [ō′vər·kum′] *v.* To feel weak or helpless: **Elizabeth was *overcome* with fear because she had to compete.** *syn.* overwhelm

pace [pās] *n.* A rate of walking, running, or doing other activities: **The scouts hiked at a fast *pace*.** *syn.* tempo

par·ti·tion [pär·tish′ən] *n.* A divider; a wall: **A *partition* usually divides the big gym into two smaller ones.** *syn.* separation

pas·tel [pas·tel′] *n.* **pas·tels** A chalklike colored crayon, used for art: **The technique for using *pastels* often involves blending colors.**

pawn·shop [pôn′shäp′] *n.* A business in which a person is licensed to lend money in exchange for goods, which may be redeemed if the loan is repaid: **In the *pawnshop* were cases of watches and jewelry.**

perch [pûrch] *n.* A place to sit or stand, especially at a height: **Our parakeet thinks my shoulder is her *perch*.** *syn.* roost

per·spec·tive [pər·spek′tiv] *n.* A point of view that puts things in correct relation to each other: **Greg put the lost watch in *perspective* when he heard about the car accident.**

pitch [pich] *v.* **pitched** For a ship to plunge down and rise up again repeatedly: **The ship *pitched* violently on the rough waves.** *syn.* dip

po·di·um [pō′dē·əm] *n.* A small platform on a stage where a conductor or a speaker may stand: **The lecturer stepped up to the *podium* and began to speak.**

point·ed·ly [poin′tid·lē] *adv.* Clearly showing one's sharp feelings: **Katie *pointedly* asked Mona why she hadn't been invited.** *syn.* bitingly

pol·i·cy [päl′ə·sē] *n.* A set of rules of an organization that are in keeping with its philosophical point of view: **The restaurant has a good *policy* toward refunding money to unsatisfied customers.** *syn.* practice

po·li·o [pō′lē·ō] *n.* Short form of *poliomyelitis*, a virus that causes paralysis and deformity, especially in children: **Dr. Jonas Salk developed a vaccine that conquered** *polio*. *syn.* infantile paralysis

> **Fact File**
>
> **polio** Polio was a terrifying killer and a crippler of both children and adults. Franklin D. Roosevelt was paralyzed by polio in 1921. After he returned to public life, he was elected governor of New York State and President of the United States, the office he held from 1932 until his death in 1945. Dr. Jonas Salk's vaccine was introduced in 1955, followed by the Sabin vaccine. These vaccines have practically eradicated polio.

po·si·tion [pə·zish′ən] *n.* **po·si·tions** The places occupied by people or things: **The runners took their** *positions* **in their lanes before the race began.** *syn.* post

po·ten·tial [pō·ten′shəl] *n.* An ability that has not yet been used: **Zoe has the** *potential* **to be a great violinist.** *syn.* capacity

pro·duce [prō′dōōs] *n.* Something that has been grown, such as fruits and vegetables: **You'll find fresh corn in the** *produce* **department of the supermarket.** *syn.* harvest

pros·per [präs′pər] *v.* **pros·per·ing** To have success and wealth: **Todd's dog grooming business is** *prospering***, and now he needs to hire an assistant.** *syn.* flourish

prowl [proul] *v.* **prowls** To search around like an animal hunting prey: **Our cat** *prowls* **around the backyard searching for mice.** *syn.* stalk

qui·ver [kwiv′ər] *n.* A container for arrows: **Sean drew an arrow from the** *quiver* **and pulled back the bowstring.** *syn.* sheath

quiver

ra·tion [rash′ən] *n.* **ra·tions** A system of distributing goods that would be scarce if they were not controlled: *Rations* **were a way for both soldiers and civilians to get enough supplies during World War II.** *syn.* quota

> **Fact File**
>
> **ration** During World War II many countries, including the United States, practiced rationing. Basic supplies, like meat, eggs, footwear, gasoline, rubber tires, and butter, were rationed rather than freely available. Each family received a coupon book and then gave stores ration coupons along with money to buy items.

re·ac·tion [rē·ak′shən] *n.* A feeling one has or response one makes as a result of a situation: **His immediate** *reaction* **to the cry for help was to run toward it.** *syn.* response

reef [rēf] *n.* A ridge of rock or coral lying near or just above the surface of the water: **Anna and James used snorkels as they explored the coral** *reef*. *syn.* shoal

re·fin·er·y [ri·fīn′ə·rē] *n.* A place where a raw material is processed into a finished product, such as sugar or oil: **All impurities from the sugarcane were filtered out at the** *refinery*. *syn.* plant

re·peal [ri·pēl′] *v.* To cancel or withdraw something, such as a penalty: **The judge will** *repeal* **the parking fine.** *syn.* annul

rep·u·ta·tion [rep′yə·tā′shən] *n.* The opinion most people have about the character of someone or something: **Our school has a** *reputation* **for graduating many honor students.**

re·sem·ble [ri·zem′bəl] *v.* **re·sem·bled** To be similar in appearance or character to someone or something else: **This case** *resembled* **an earlier case the police had solved.** *syn.* parallel

res·i·dence [rez′i·dəns] *n.* The place where one lives: **Our** *residence* **was an apartment on the top floor of a three-story house.** *syn.* dwelling

re·tire [ri·tīr′] *v.* **re·tired** To take something out of use because of advancing age: **Andrew** *retired* **his baseball glove when it became too small for his hand.**

a	add	e	end	o	odd	ōō	pool	oi	oil	th	this
ā	ace	ē	equal	ō	open	u	up	ou	pout	zh	vision
â	care	i	it	ô	order	û	burn	ng	ring		
ä	palm	ī	ice	ōō	took	yōō	fuse	th	thin		

ə = {
a in *above*
e in *sicken*
i in *possible*
o in *melon*
u in *circus*
}

rid·i·cule [rid′ə•kyool] *v.* **rid·i·culed** To criticize or make fun of someone in a way that embarrasses him or her: **The boys *ridiculed* the new student for the way she dressed.** *syns.* mock, belittle

rig·ging [rig′ing] *n.* The lines and chains used with sails and masts on a sailing vessel: **Julian found that the hardest part of making a model ship was setting up the *rigging* correctly.**

rook·ie [rook′kē] *n.* A beginner in a given profession: **The basketball player was a *rookie*, but she surprised the crowd by racking up 20 points in her first game.** *syns.* apprentice, novice

sat·el·lite [sat′əl•īt′] *n.* A human-made object that has been sent into space to orbit Earth: **A *satellite* was launched that will send weather information back to Earth.**

schol·ar·ship [skäl′ər•ship] *n.* Money that is awarded to pay for a student's tuition: **Charles was admitted to college with a full *scholarship*.** *syns.* stipend, grant

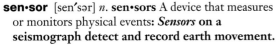

satellite

sen·sor [sen′sər] *n.* **sen·sors** A device that measures or monitors physical events: **Sensors on a seismograph detect and record earth movement.**

se·ries [sir′ēz] *n.* A number of things coming one after another in time or place: **A *series* of concerts will be held at Town Hall this winter.** *syn.* sequence

set·tle·ment [set′əl•mənt] *n.* A place people develop so they can live there: **These ruins show that there was once a large *settlement* here.** *syn.* colony

shal·low [shal′ō] *adj.* Something, such as water, that is not deep: **Shallow puddles were all over the parking lot after the rainstorm.**

side·track [sīd′trak] *v.* To make something go off the proper course: **The rodeo clown's most important job is to *sidetrack* a charging bull.** *syn.* distract

> ### Fact File
> **sidetrack** The word *sidetrack* has a more literal meaning than the one we commonly use. It means to switch a train from its main track to a siding—a short piece of track where the train can wait while it is being loaded or while another train passes.

si·mul·ta·ne·ous·ly [sī′mul•tā′nē•əs•lē] *adv.* At the same time: **The children explained the story simultaneously.** *syn.* concurrently

snort [snôrt] *v.* To make a noise by quickly forcing air through the nostrils: **Horses only breathe through their noses, so when they run, they *snort*.**

so·na·ta [sə•nät′ə] *n.* A musical piece written for one or two instruments, consisting of one or more movements, or sections: **Beethoven's "Moonlight Sonata" is a piano piece.**

sou·ve·nir [soo′və•nir′] *n.* **sou·ve·nirs** An item that is a reminder of a person, place, or event: **The tourist bought a *souvenir* postcard in the gift shop.** *syn.* remembrance

> ### Word Origins
> **souvenir** The word *souvenir* is the French verb meaning "to remember." It contains the root word *venir*, "to come." On Quebec's license plates, the motto "*Je me souviens*" ("I remember") is imprinted.

spon·sor [spän′sər] *v.* **spon·sor·ing** To promote and pay for an event: **The PTA is *sponsoring* this year's bike safety campaign.** *syn.* support

sta·di·um [stā′dē•əm] *n.* A large structure where sports events are played on a field before an audience: **Tickets for the playoffs went on sale at Lions *Stadium* today.** *syn.* arena

> ### Fact File
> **stadium** In ancient Greece and Rome, a stadium was a unit of measurement equal to about 607 feet. Some foot races were a stadium long. These races were held on a track, and alongside the track were tiers of seats for the cheering spectators.

stam·pede [stam•pēd′] *n.* **stam·pedes** An occurrence in which a herd of animals suddenly runs at top speed, usually in fear: **The roar of hooves was deafening during the cattle *stampede*.**

stampede

stern·ly [stûrn′lē] *adv.* In a severe, strict, or scolding manner: **The teacher talked to him *sternly* about listening in class.** *syn.* sharply

sto·lid·ly [stä′lid·lē] *adv.* With little or no emotion: **While the rest of her class was excited when the teacher announced they would be taking a field trip, Kim met the news *stolidly*.** *syn.* impassively

stump [stump] *v.* **stumps** To puzzle or baffle someone, as during a quiz: **The spelling word "xyster" *stumps* even our best contestants.** *syn.* confuse

sub·mit [sub·mit′] *v.* **sub·mit·ted** To display or show something so that others can judge it or comment upon it in some way: **Jan *submitted* her poem to the school magazine, and it was printed.** *syn.* present

suf·frage [suf′rij] *n.* The right to vote for candidates for political office: **Women's *suffrage* became a reality after World War I in the United States.**

sus·cep·ti·ble [sə·sep′tə·bəl] *adj.* Able to be affected by something: **In the winter people seem more *susceptible* to catching colds.** *syn.* vulnerable

sus·pend [sə·spend′] *v.* **sus·pen·ded** To hang up and leave dangling: **The fish was *suspended* from Libby's line.** *syn.* dangle

tan·gle [tang′əl] *n.* Something that is snarled or muddled: **There was a *tangle* in Melissa's hair that was so stubborn it had to be cut out.** *syn.* knot

thrive [thrīv] *v.* **thrived** To prosper under the effect of something: **The plant *thrived* when it got enough sun and water.** *syns.* flourish, succeed

tim·id [tim′id] *adj.* Lacking self-confidence; fearful; shy: **The *timid* child found it hard to make new friends.** *syn.* bashful

tin·der [tin′dər] *n.* Material that catches fire easily because it is very dry, brittle, and thin: **The camper added dry twigs as *tinder* to get the campfire started.** *syn.* kindling

tread [tred] *n.* Soft, careful steps: **My brother's quiet *tread* allowed him to surprise people all the time.** *syn.* footfall

treaty [trē′tē] *n.* An official agreement between peoples or countries, stating what each side will do about a certain issue: **The peace *treaty* ended the long war.** *syns.* arrangement, compact

un·de·ni·a·ble [un′di·nī′ə·bəl] *adj.* Something that one is sure of beyond question: **It is *undeniable* that Lewis is the best student in class.** *syn.* indisputable

un·du·late [un′dyə·lāt] *v.* **un·du·lat·ing** To move in waves or like a wave: **The snake was *undulating* its way across the desert road.**

vain [vān] *adj.* **vain·er** Being excessively proud of one's appearance and honor: **The actor had become *vainer* and demanded the largest dressing room.** *syn.* conceited

vast [vast] *adj.* Of very large size; enormous; huge: **The Atlantic Ocean is *vast* in size.** *syn.* great

veer [vēr] *v.* **veered** To turn sharply from one direction to another: **The driver *veered* sharply to the right.** *syn.* swerve

vow [vou] *n.* A promise about a serious matter: **Ted made a *vow* to help the new classmate in any way that he could.** *syn.* pledge

wrang·ler [rang′lər] *n.* **wrang·lers** A cowboy whose job it is to herd livestock, especially horses: **The *wranglers* are herding the horses into the corral.**

a	add	e	end	o	odd	o͞o	pool	oi	oil	th	this		*a* in *above*
ā	ace	ē	equal	ō	open	u	up	ou	pout	zh	vision		*e* in *sicken*
â	care	i	it	ô	order	û	burn	ng	ring			ə =	*i* in *possible*
ä	palm	ī	ice	o͝o	took	yo͞o	fuse	th	thin				*o* in *melon*
													u in *circus*

Index *of* Titles

Page numbers in color refer to biographical information.

and Authors

Printed in the United States of America

Acknowledgments

For permission to reprint copyrighted material, grateful acknowledgment is made to the following sources:

Atheneum Books for Young Readers, an imprint of Simon & Schuster Children's Publishing Division: Cover illustration by Kimberly Bulcken Root from *Birdie's Lighthouse* by Deborah Hopkinson. Illustration copyright © 1997 by Kimberly Bulcken Root. Cover illustration by Deborah Lanino from *Maria's Comet* by Deborah Hopkinson. Illustration copyright © 1999 by Deborah Lanino.

Molly Bang: Illustration by Molly Bang for Haiku by Kyoshi from *Red Dragonfly on My Shoulder*, translated by Sylvia Cassedy and Kunihiro Suetake. Illustration copyright © 1992 by Molly Bang.

Brandt & Brandt Literary Agents, Inc.: From *The Many Lives of Benjamin Franklin* by Mary Pope Osborne. Text copyright © 1990 by Mary Pope Osborne. Published by Dial Books for Young Readers, a division of Penguin Putnam Inc.

Caroline House, Boyds Mills Press, Inc.: Cover illustration by Michael Garland from *The Violin Man* by Maureen Brett Hooper. Illustration © 1991 by Michael Garland.

Maria Carvainis Agency, Inc.: "Hattie's Birthday Box" by Pam Conrad from *Birthday Surprises: Ten Great Stories to Unwrap*, edited by Johanna Hurwitz. Text copyright © 1994 by Pam Conrad. Published by William Morrow & Company, Inc.

Ellen Cassedy: Haiku by Kyoshi from *Red Dragonfly on My Shoulder*, translated by Sylvia Cassedy and Kunihiro Suetake. Text copyright © 1967 by the Estate of Sylvia Cassedy and Kunihiro Suetake.

Childrens Press, Inc.: *Evelyn Cisneros: Prima Ballerina* by Charnan Simon. Text copyright © 1990 by Childrens Press®, Inc.

Clarion Books/Houghton Mifflin Company: From *Cowboys of the Wild West* by Russell Freedman, map by George Buctel. Text and map copyright © 1985 by Russell Freedman.

Cobblehill Books, an affiliate of Dutton Children's Books, a division of Penguin Putnam Inc.: From *Earthquake Terror* by Peg Kehret. Text copyright © 1996 by Peg Kehret.

Cobblestone Publishing Company, 30 Grove Street, Suite C, Peterborough, NH 03458: From "High-Flying Facts" by Mary Morton Cowan, illustrated by Rich Harrington in *Cobblestone: Our Grand Old Flag*, January 1997. © 1997 by Cobblestone Publishing Company.

Coward-McCann, a division of Penguin Putnam Inc.: From *What's the Big Idea, Ben Franklin?* by Jean Fritz, illustrated by Margot Tomes. Text copyright © 1976 by Jean Fritz; illustrations copyright © 1976 by Margot Tomes.

Dial Books for Young Readers, a division of Penguin Putnam Inc.: Cover illustration from *The Young Artist* by Thomas Locker. Copyright © 1989 by Thomas Locker. From *Across the Wide Dark Sea* by Jean Van Leeuwen, illustrated by Thomas B. Allen. Text copyright © 1995 by Jean Van Leeuwen; illustrations copyright © 1995 by Thomas B. Allen.

Doubleday, a division of Random House, Inc.: "Celebration" and "Eagle Flight" by Alonzo Lopez from *Whispering Wind*, edited by Terry Allen. Text copyright © 1972 by the Institute of American Indian Arts.

Katherine Froman: "When Birds Remember" from *Seeing Things: A Book of Poems* by Robert Froman, lettering by Ray Barber. Copyright © 1974 by Robert Froman.

Greenwillow Books, a division of William Morrow & Company, Inc.: From *The Hot & Cold Summer* by Johanna Hurwitz, cover illustration by Gail Owens. Text copyright © 1984 by Johanna Hurwitz; cover illustration copyright © 1984 by Gail Owens. "Pandora's Box" from *The Robber Baby: Stories from the Greek Myths* by Anne Rockwell. Text and cover illustration copyright © 1994 by Anne Rockwell.

Harcourt, Inc.: From *The Hundred Dresses* by Eleanor Estes, cover illustration by Louis Slobodkin. Text copyright 1944 by Harcourt, Inc., renewed 1971 by Eleanor Estes; cover illustration copyright 1944 by Harcourt, Inc., renewed 1971 by Louis Slobodkin. Cover photograph from *Baseball in the Barrios* by Henry Horenstein. Copyright © 1997 by Henry Horenstein. Cover illustration by Brian Pinkney from *Dear Benjamin Banneker* by Andrea Davis Pinkney. Illustration copyright © 1994 by Brian Pinkney. From "Arithmetic" in *The Complete Poems of Carl Sandburg* by Carl Sandburg. Text copyright © 1970, 1969 by Lilian Steichen Sandburg, Trustee.

HarperCollins Publishers: Cover illustration by Richard Cowdrey from *The Tarantula in My Purse and 172 Other Wild Pets* by Jean Craighead George. Cover illustration © 1996 by Richard Cowdrey. From *The World of William Joyce Scrapbook* by William Joyce, photographs by Philip Gould. Text and illustrations copyright © 1997 by William Joyce; photographs copyright © 1997 by Philip Gould. "About Notebooks" from *Hey World, Here I Am!* by Jean Little, cover illustration by Sue Truesdell. Text copyright © 1986 by Jean Little; cover illustration copyright © 1989 by Susan G. Truesdell.

Holiday House, Inc.: Illustrations by Leonard Everett Fisher from *Earth Songs* by Myra Cohn Livingston. Illustrations copyright © 1986 by Leonard Everett Fisher.

Houghton Mifflin Company: From *Island of the Blue Dolphins* by Scott O'Dell, cover illustration by Ted Lewin. Text copyright © 1960, renewed 1988 by Scott O'Dell; cover illustration copyright © 1990 by Ted Lewin.

Hyperion Books for Children: From *Sees Behind Trees* by Michael Dorris, cover illustration by Linda Benson. Text copyright © 1996 by the estate of Michael Dorris; cover illustration © 1996 by Linda Benson. Cover illustration by Mark Buehner from *The Million Dollar Shot* by Dan Gutman. Illustration © 1997 by Mark Buehner.

Alfred A. Knopf, Inc.: From *Mick Harte Was Here* by Barbara Park, cover illustration by John Nickle. Text copyright © 1995 by Barbara Park; cover illustration copyright © 1995 by John Nickle.

Lee & Low Books Inc., 95 Madison Ave., New York, NY 10016: Cover illustration by Cornelius Van Wright and Ying-Hwa Hu from *Zora Hurston and the Chinaberry Tree* by William Miller. Illustration copyright © 1994 by Cornelius Van Wright and Ying-Hwa Hu. From *Dear Mrs. Parks: A Dialogue with Today's Youth* by Rosa Parks with Gregory J. Reed, cover photograph by Mark T. Kerrin. Text copyright © 1996 by Rosa L. Parks; cover photograph copyright © 1996 by Mark T. Kerrin.

Little, Brown and Company (Inc.): Cover illustration by Glenn Harrington from *Baseball Flyhawk* by Matt Christopher. Cover illustration by Kevin Hawkes from *The Librarian Who Measured the Earth* by Kathryn Laksy. Illustration copyright © 1994 by Kevin Hawkes. Limerick from "Write Me a Verse" in *Take Sky* by David McCord. Text copyright © 1961, 1962 by David McCord. From *Yang the Third and Her Impossible Family* by Lensey Namioka, illustrated by Kees de Kiefte. Text copyright © 1995 by Lensey Namioka; illustrations copyright © 1995 by Kees de Kiefte. Cover illustration by Kees de Kiefte from *Yang the Youngest and His Terrible Ear* by Lensey Namioka. Illustration copyright © 1992 by Kees de Kiefte.

Stephen Marchesi: Cover illustration by Stephen Marchesi from *Earthquake Terror* by Peg Kehret. Cover illustration © 1996 by Stephen Marchesi.

William Morrow & Company, Inc.: From *Dear Mr. Henshaw* by Beverly Cleary, cover illustration by Paul O. Zelinsky. Text and cover illustration copyright © 1983 by Beverly Cleary. Cover illustration by Paul O. Zelinsky from *Strider* by Beverly Cleary. Illustration © 1991 by William Morrow & Company, Inc. Cover illustration from *Live Writing: Breathing Life into Your Words* by Ralph Fletcher. Copyright © 1999 by Ralph Fletcher. "The Empty Box" by Johanna Hurwitz from *Birthday Surprises: Ten Great Stories to Unwrap*, edited by Johanna Hurwitz, cover illustration by Michael Garland. Text copyright © 1995 by Johanna Hurwitz; cover illustration copyright © 1997 by Michael Garland. From *Sally Ann Thunder Ann Whirlwind Crockett*, retold by Steven Kellogg. Copyright © 1995 by Steven Kellogg. "The Case of the Shining Blue Planet" from *Einstein Anderson, Science Detective: The On-Line Spaceman and Other Cases* by Seymour Simon, cover illustration by S. D. Schindler. Text copyright © 1997 by Seymour Simon; cover illustration copyright © 1997 by S. D. Schindler. From *Oceans* by Seymour Simon, illustrated by Frank Schwartz. Copyright © 1990 by Seymour Simon.

John Muir Publications, Santa Fe, NM: Cover illustration by Tony D'Agostino from *Kids Explore the Gifts of Children with Special Needs* by Westridge Young Writers Workshop. © 1994 by Jefferson County School District No. R-1.

National Geographic Society: "Mountains of Fire: Earth's Amazing Volcanoes" by Renee Skelton from *National Geographic WORLD* Magazine, March 1998. Text copyright © 1998 by National Geographic Society.

Harold Ober Associates Incorporated: From "Children and Poetry" in *The Langston Hughes Reader* by Langston Hughes. Text copyright © 1958 Langston Hughes; text copyright renewed 1986 by George Houston Bass.

Orchard Books, New York: From *Seeing Earth from Space* by Patricia Lauber. Text copyright © 1990 by Patricia Lauber. From *Summer of Fire: Yellowstone 1988* by Patricia Lauber. Text copyright © 1991 by Patricia Lauber.

Richard C. Owen Publishers, Inc., Katonah, NY 10536: Cover photograph by Andrea Fritz Pfleger from *Surprising Myself* by Jean Fritz. Photograph copyright © 1992 by Andrea Fritz Pfleger.

Oxford University Press: From "Musical Instruments" (Retitled: "Brass Instruments") in *Oxford Children's Encyclopedia*, Volume 4. Text and illustrations © 1991 by Oxford University Press.

Penguin Books Canada Limited: From *Little By Little: A Writer's Education* by Jean Little. Text copyright © 1987 by Jean Little.

Plays, Inc.: *Name This American* by Hannah Reinmuth from *Plays: The Drama Magazine for Young People*, May 1995. Text copyright © 1995 by Plays, Inc. This play is for reading purposes only; for permission to produce, write to Plays, Inc., 120 Boylston St., Boston, MA 02116.

G. P. Putnam's Sons, a division of Penguin Putnam Inc.: Illustrations from *Tomie dePaola's Book of Poems* by Tomie dePaola. Illustrations copyright © 1988 by Tomie dePaola. Cover illustration by Margot Tomes from *And Then What Happened, Paul Revere?* by Jean Fritz. Illustration copyright © 1973 by Margot Tomes.

Random House Children's Books, a division of Random House, Inc., New York, NY: Cover illustration by Tony Meers from *The Black Stallion* by Walter Farley. Cover illustration copyright © 1998 by Tony Meers. From *Satchmo's Blues* by Alan Schroeder, illustrated by Floyd Cooper. Text copyright © 1996 by Alan Schroeder; illustrations copyright © 1996 by Floyd Cooper. From *Off and Running* by Gary Soto, cover illustration by Eric Velasquez. Text copyright © 1996 by Gary Soto; cover illustration copyright © 1996 by Eric Velasquez.

Marian Reiner: *Earth Songs* by Myra Cohn Livingston. Text copyright © 1986 by Myra Cohn Livingston. Published by Holiday House, Inc. "Souvenir" from *The Singing Green* by Eve Merriam. Text copyright © 1992 by Estate of Eve Merriam. Published by William Morrow & Company, Inc.

Scholastic Inc.: From *We'll Never Forget You, Roberto Clemente* by Trudie Engel. Copyright © 1996 by Trudie Engel. Cover illustration by Kim Howard from *A Cloak for the Dreamer* by Aileen Friedman. Copyright © 1994 by Marilyn Burns Education Associates. From *Aesop's Fables*, retold by Ann McGovern. Text and cover illustration copyright © 1963 by Scholastic Inc. Published by Apple Classics, an imprint of Scholastic Inc.

Simon & Schuster Books for Young Readers, an imprint of Simon & Schuster Children's Publishing Division: Cover illustration by Salvatore Murdocca from *The Landry News* by Andrew Clements. Illustration copyright © 1999 by Salvatore Murdocca. From *Frindle* by Andrew Clements, cover illustration by Brian Selznick. Text copyright © 1996 by Andrew Clements; cover illustration copyright © 1996 by Brian Selznick. Cover illustration by Ronald Himler from *The Cat Who Escaped from Steerage* by Evelyn Wilde Mayerson. Illustration copyright © 1990 by Ronald Himler. Cover illustration by Marjorie Priceman from *Zin! Zin! Zin! a Violin* by Lloyd Moss. Illustration copyright © 1995 by Marjorie Priceman. From *Woodsong* by Gary Paulsen, cover photograph by Ruth Wright Paulsen. Text copyright © 1990 by Gary Paulsen; cover photograph copyright © 1990 by Ruth Wright Paulsen. From *Black Frontiers* by Lillian Schlissel. Text copyright © 1995 by Lillian Schlissel.

Sports Illustrated for Kids: "Honorable Mention—Mark McGuire and Sammy Sosa" from *Sports Illustrated for Kids, 1998 Sports Yearbook*. Text copyright © 1999 by Time Inc.

Viking Penguin, a division of Penguin Putnam Inc.: From *The Boonsville Bombers* by Alison Cragin Herzig, cover illustration by Dan Andreasen. Text copyright © 1991 by Alison Cragin Herzig; cover illustration copyright © 1991 by Daniel Andreasen. Cover illustration by Lane Smith from *Math Curse* by Jon Scieszka. Illustration copyright © 1995 by Lane Smith.

Walker and Company, 435 Hudson Street, New York, NY 10014: From *Iditarod Dream* by Ted Wood. Copyright © 1996 by Ted Wood.

YouthLine USA (www.youthline-usa.com): "Educating About the Internet: Gore Announces New Plan" from *YouthLine USA*, Vol. 1, Issue 22, December 13, 1997.

Photo Credits

(t), top; (b), bottom; (c), center; (l), left; (r), right

Page 59, Parallel Productions; 84, AP/Wide World Photos; 85(l), AP/Wide World Photos; 85(r), AP/Wide World Photos; 97, AP/Wide World Photos; 111, courtesy, Barbara Park; 131, UPI/Bettmann; 139(l), UPI/Bettmann; 162-172, Ted Wood; 168(inset), Ted Levin/Animals Animals; 173, David Swift; 174 (l), Ted Wood; 174 (tr), Ted Levin/Animals Animals; 174 (br), Ted Wood; 175(all), Ted Wood; 234-235, Erwin & Peggy Bauer; 236-237, Yellowstone National Park; 238-239, 240-241, 242, Jim Peaco/National Park Service; 243, Jeff Henry/National Park Service; 244(t), Jim Peaco/National Park Service; 244(b), Ted Wood; 248, Alberto Garcia/Saba; 248 (inset), Alberto Garcia/Saba; 249, Douglas Peebles; 249 (inset), G. Brad Lewis; 251(t), Alain Buu/Liaison Agency; 251(b), Lee Stone/Sygma; 254-255, Chuck Place; 256, NASA, 258(both), Tourism Nova Scotia, 259 (all), NOAA; 260-261, Terraphotographics/BPS; 261, John Broda/Woods Hole Oceanographic Institute; 262-263, US Coast Guard; 264-265(both), Chuck Place; 266, BPS; 267, Chuck Place; 269, US Coast Guard; 284, Presslink; 288- 305, NASA; 310-311(all), NASA; 329, Steve Gravano; 357(all), William Joyce; 385(r), Tom Sobolik/Black Star; 390-391, 392, Marty Sohl; 393. 394-395; Lloyd Englert/San Francisco Ballet; 395, courtesy, Evelyn Cisneros; 396, Marty Sohl/San Franciso Ballet; 397, 398, 399, 400, Marty Sohl; 401, Bonnie Kamin/San Francisco Ballet; 402, courtesy, Evelyn Cisneros; 403, Marty Sohl; 404(t), Marty Sohl; 404(b), courtesy, Evelyn Cisneros; 431, Dale Higgins/Harcourt; 539, Ron Kunzman/Harcourt; 568-569, Library of Congress, 571, 572, Solomon D. Butcher Collection, Nebraska State Historical Society; 573(both), Nebraska State Historical Society; 574(both), 575, 576, Kansas State Historical Society; 577 (both), Solomon D. Butcher Collection, Nebraska State Historical Society; 578(l), (c) National Baseball Hall of Fame; 578(r) Nevada Historical Society; 584-585, Montana Historical Society; 586, Kansas State Historical Society; 587, 588, Denver Public Library, Western History Collection; 589, 590, Library of Congress; 592, Denver Public Library, Western History Collection; 593(both), Western History Collections, University of Oklahoma; 595, Library of Congress, Everett E. Smith Collection; 597(t), Lisa Quinones/Black Star; 630(l), NASA; 636(l), NASA.

Illustration Credits

Murray Kimber, Cover Art; Anne Smith, 4-5, 18-19, 20-21, 120-121; David Groff, 6-7, 122-125, 208-209; Dave LaFleur, 8-9, 210-213, 312-313; Marc Mongeau, 10-11, 314-317, 410-411; Will Terry, 12-13, 412-415, 516-517; Kris Wiltse, 14-15, 518-521, 624-625; Ethan Long, 16-17, 67, 70, 72, 77, 78-79, 142-143, 178, 189, 190-191, 334, 346-347, 416-417, 430-433, 582-583; Greg Couch, 22-43; Laura Coyle, 44-45, 234-235, 368-369; Rocco Baviera, 46-61, 64-65; Laura Greer, 63; Kelly Kennedy, 82-83, 270-271, 332-333; Lori McElrith Eslick, 84-97, 102-103; David Scott Meir, 98-101; Mark Mohr, 104-119; Gil Adams, 126-141; Bob Commander, 144-157; 160-161; Klaus Heesch, 144, 478-479, 568, 579, 580; Stephen Schudlich, 176-177, 476-477; Lee Christiansen, 178-191; Rich Nelson, 192-203, 206-207; Kurt Nagahori, 204-205; Mike Steirnagle, 214-233; Leo Espinosa, 272-283, 286-287; Charles Glaubitz, 284-285; Tim Ladwig, 318-331; Mark Bender, 334-347, 352-353; Rafael Lopez, 348-351; Jerry Tiritilli, 416-433; Mary Lynn Blasutta, 434-435, 542-543; Allen Garns, 436-449, 452-453; Jean Oppenheimer, 450-451; David Goldin, 454-475; Si Huynh, 478-497, 500-501; Kitty Meek, 498-499; Sheila Bailey, 502-511, 514-515; Eric Westbrook, 512-513; Janet Hamlin, 564-565; Russ Wilson, 604-617, 622-623.